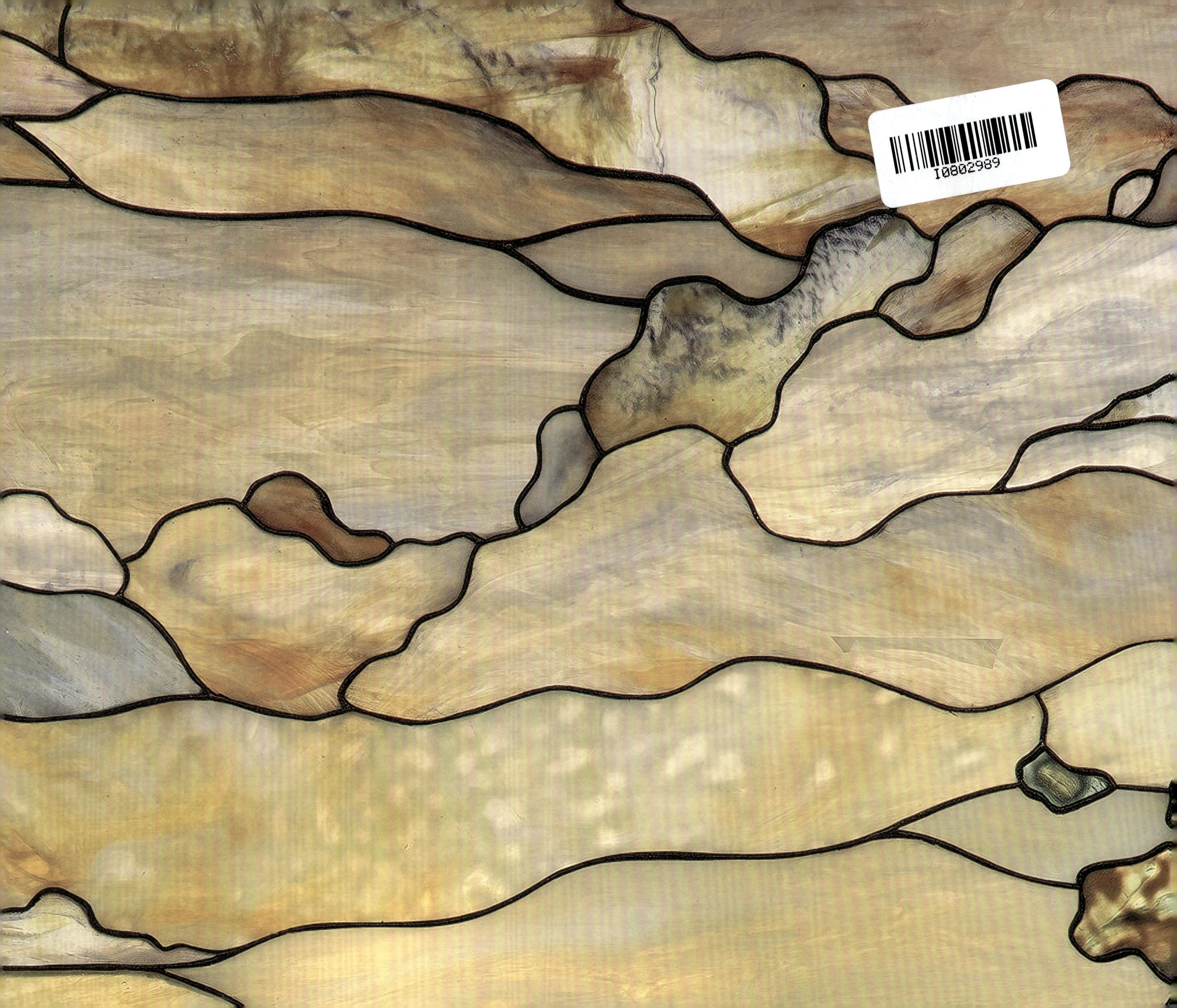

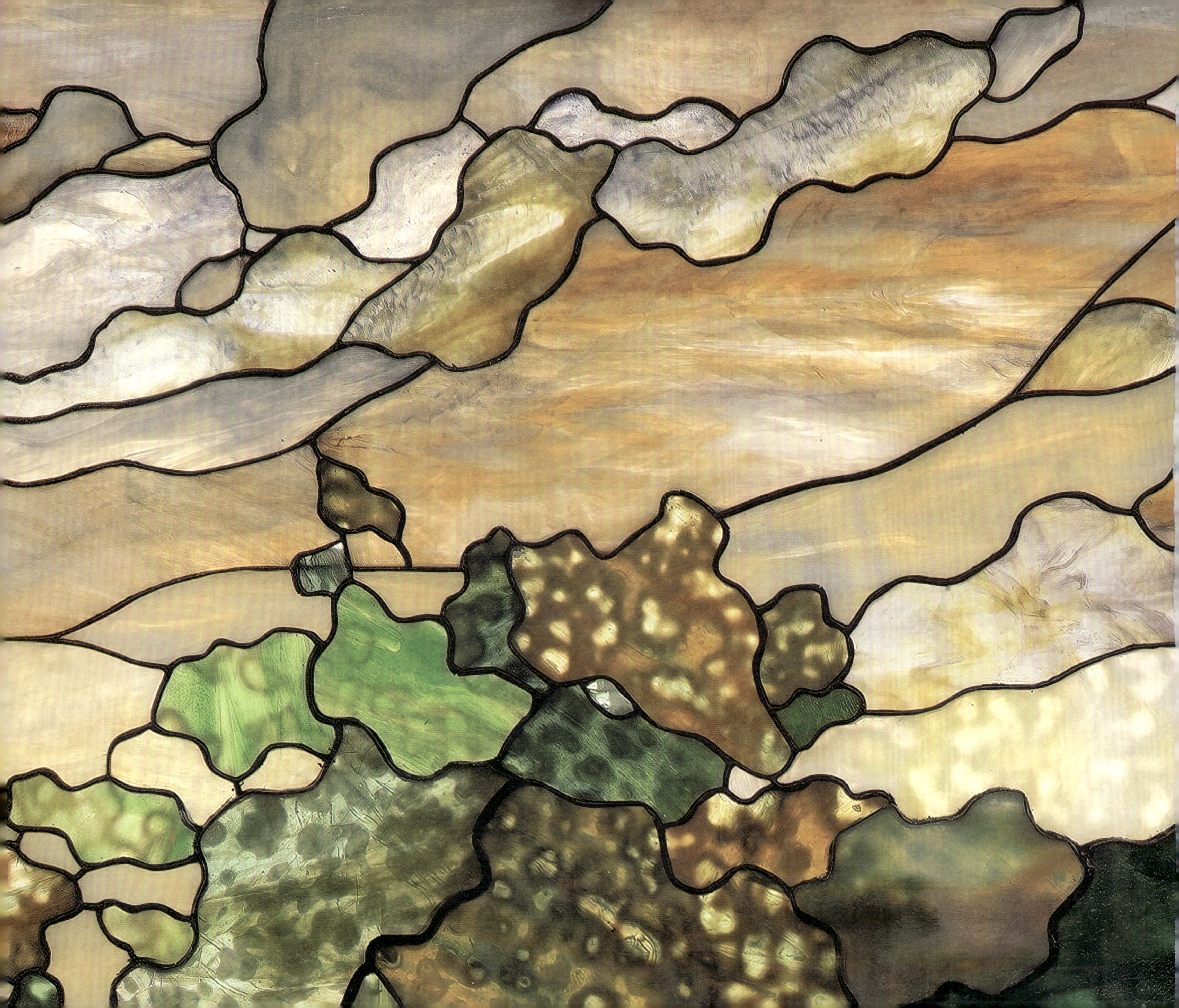

Believe

in

Him

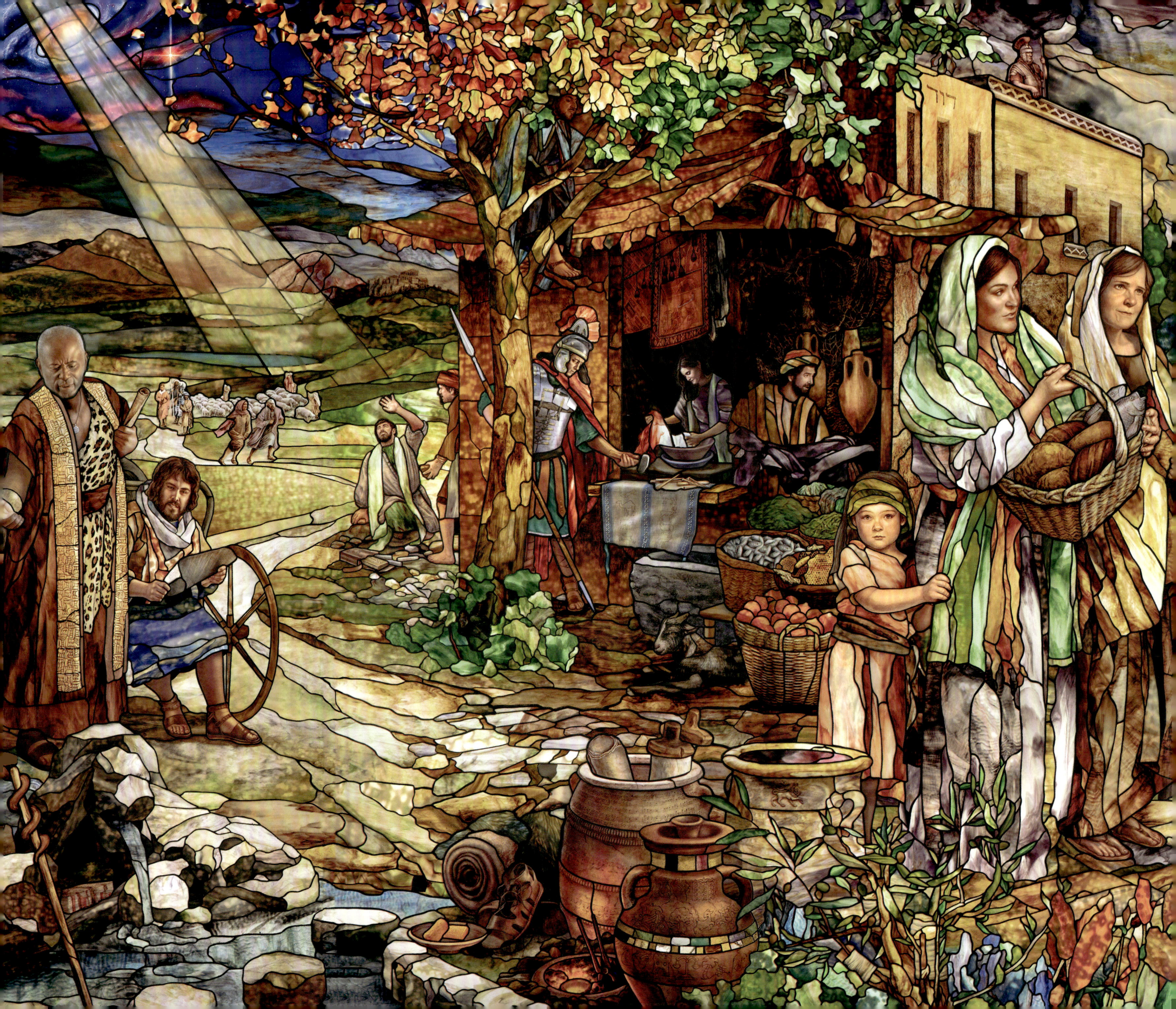

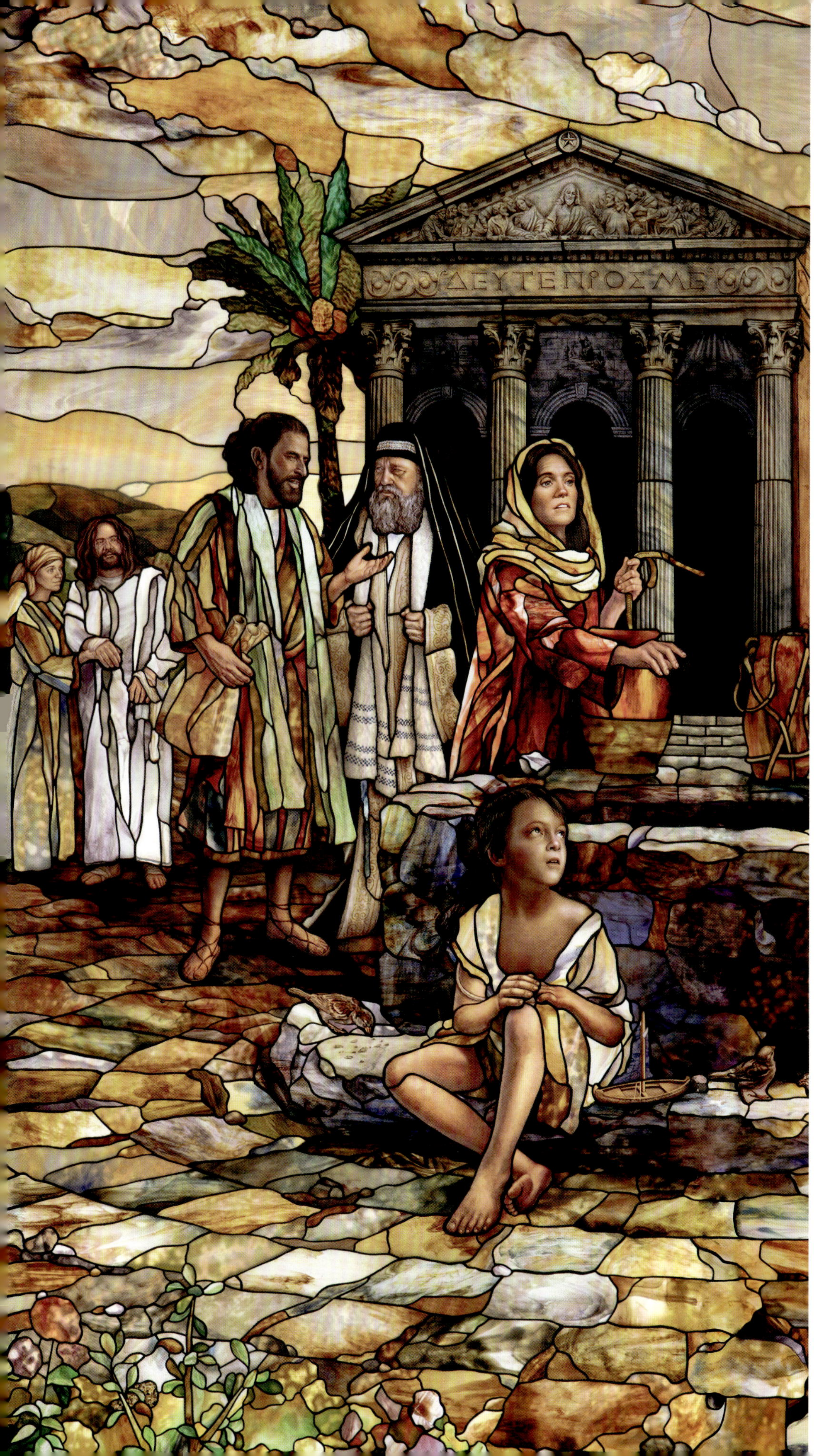

Believe *in* Him

Illuminating the **SAVIOR'S LIFE AND MISSION** Through Stained Glass

A Traveling World Art Exhibit by
Tom *and* Gayle Holdman
and Holdman Studios

Commentary by
Tyler Griffin, Gayle Holdman,
Anthony Sweat, and Brad R. Wilcox

Foreword by Rev. Dr. Andrew Teal

SHADOW MOUNTAIN PUBLISHING

Dedicated to King and Diane Husein

Visit us at shadowmountain.com

Library of Congress Cataloging-in-Publication Data

(CIP data on file)
ISBN 978-1-63993-389-1

Printed in China
RR Donnelley, Dongguan, China

10 9 8 7 6 5 4 3 2 1

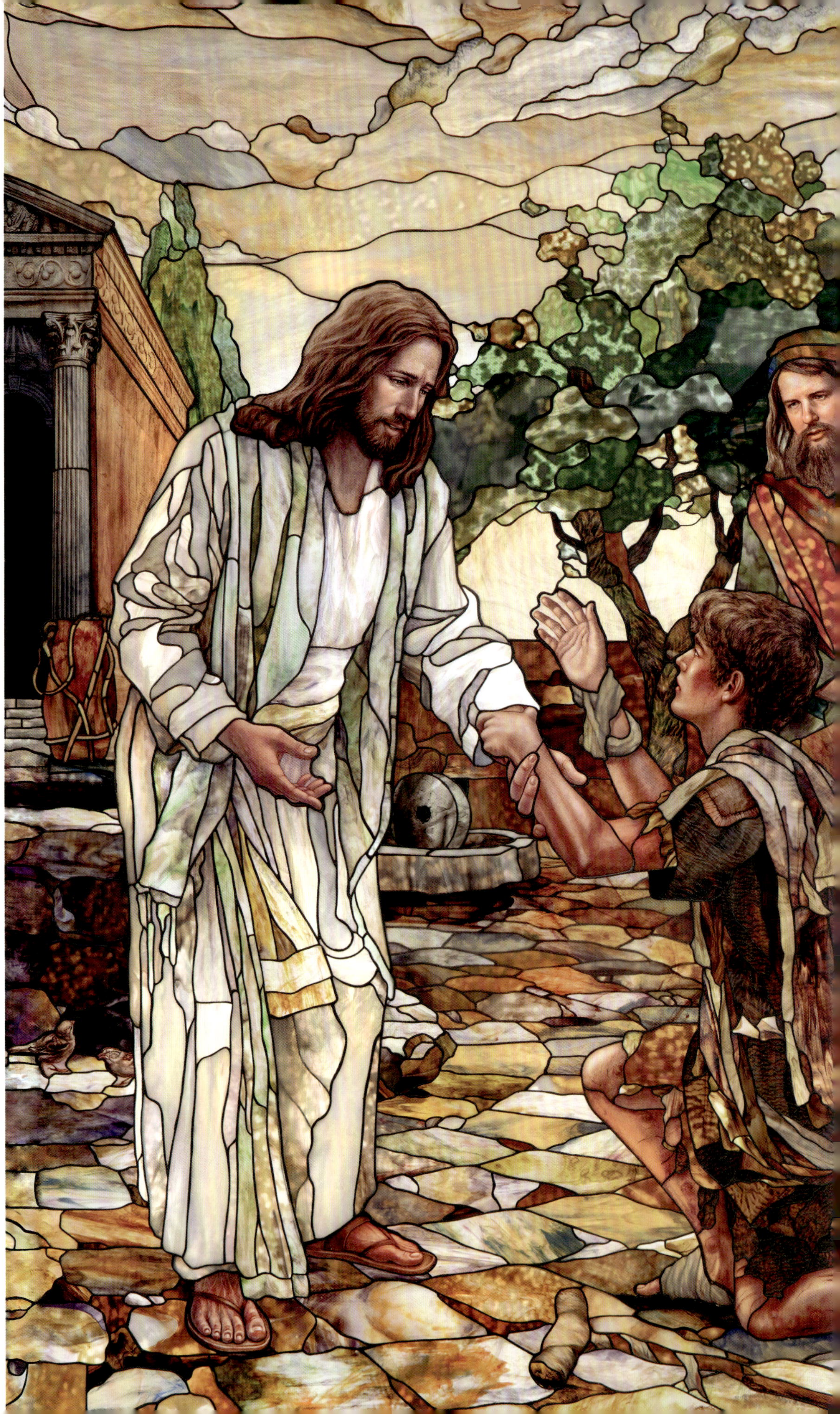

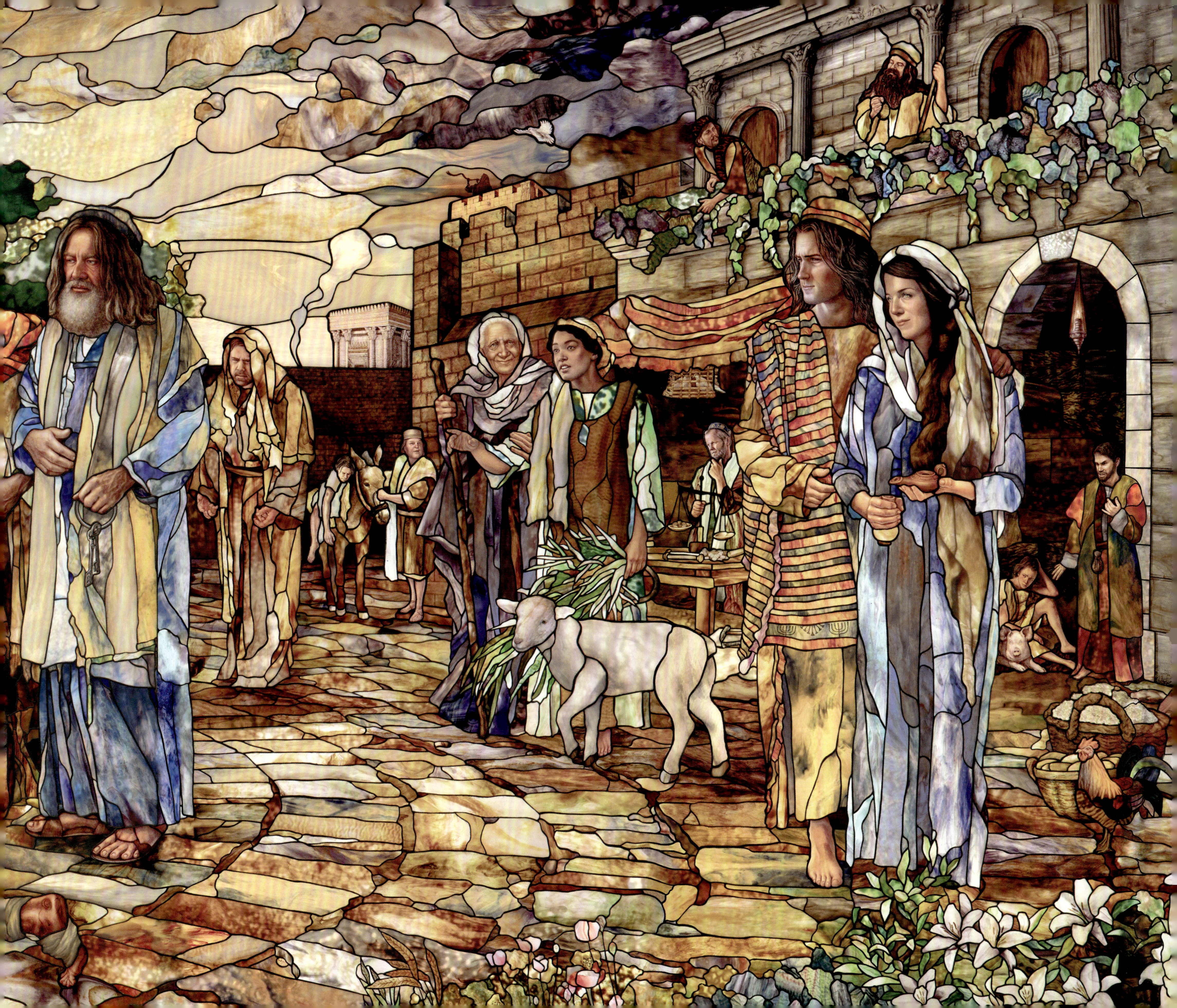

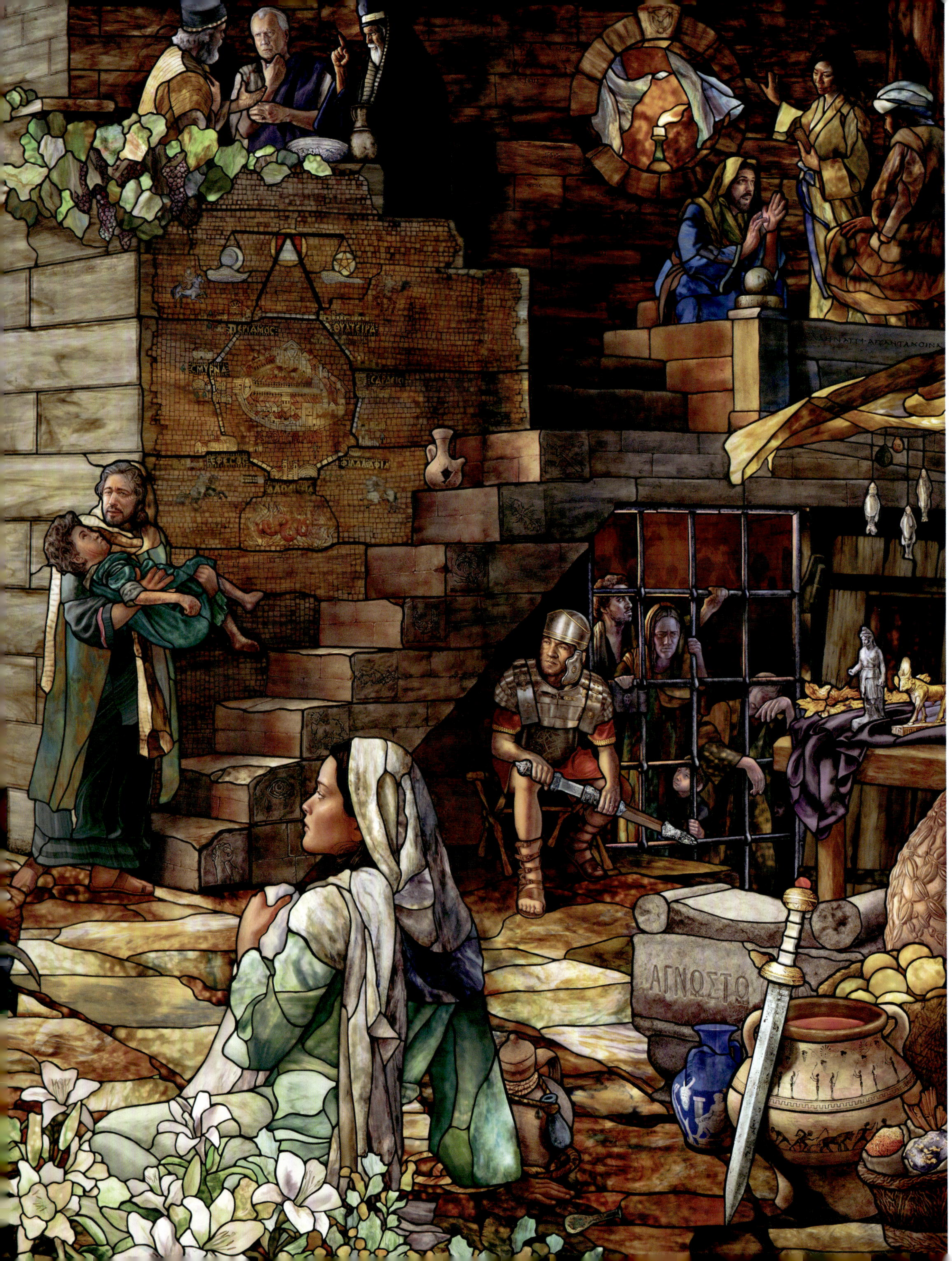
ΘΥΑΤΕΙΡΑ
CMYPNA
CAPΔΙC
ΦΙΛΑΔΕΛΦΙΑ
ΑΓΝΩΣΤΩ

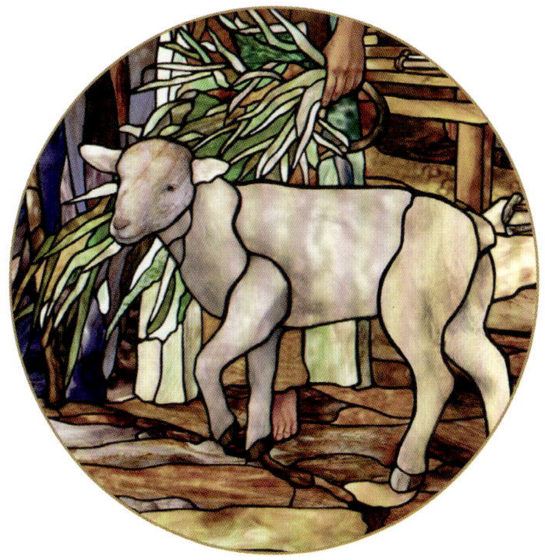

Contents

Acknowledgments IX

Foreword by Rev. Dr. Andrew Teal X

Preface XII

PANELS

Panel A: Featuring the Ethiopian and Philip 1

Panel B: Featuring Cornelius and Lydia 11

Panel C: Featuring Mary and Martha 27

Panel D: Featuring the Woman at the Well 39

Panel E: Featuring Christ and the Beggar 53

Panel F: Featuring the Widow 63

Panel G: Featuring John and Mary 73

Panel H: Featuring Mary Magdalene 89

Panel I: Featuring the Flame in the Window 99

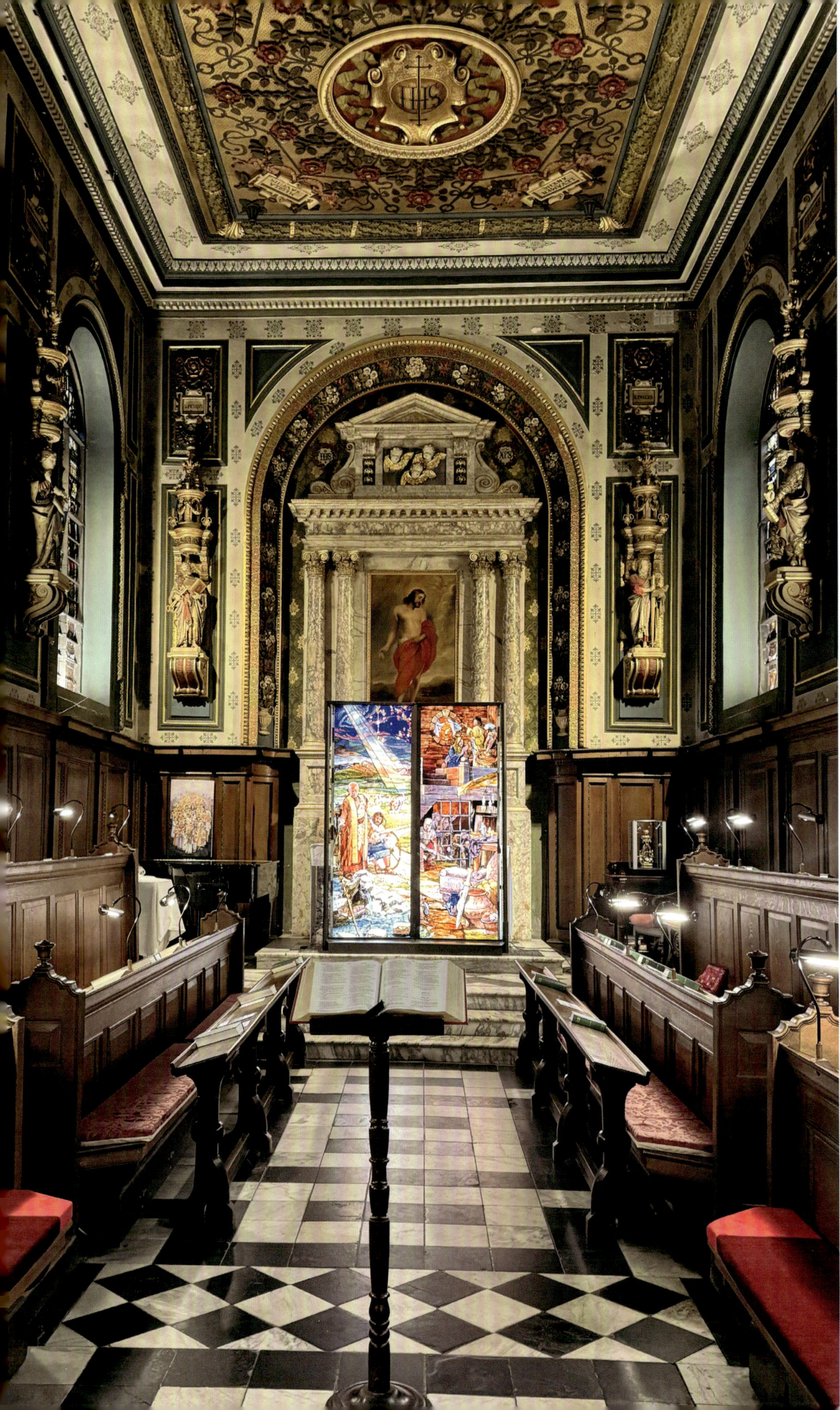

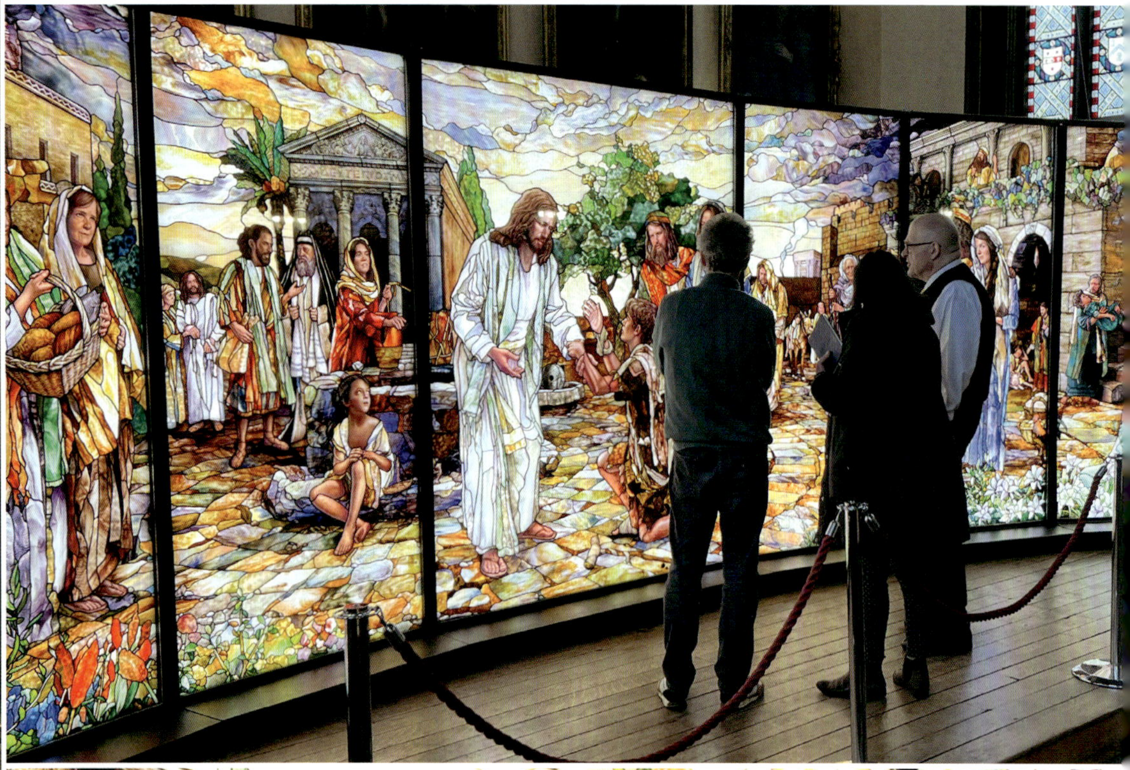

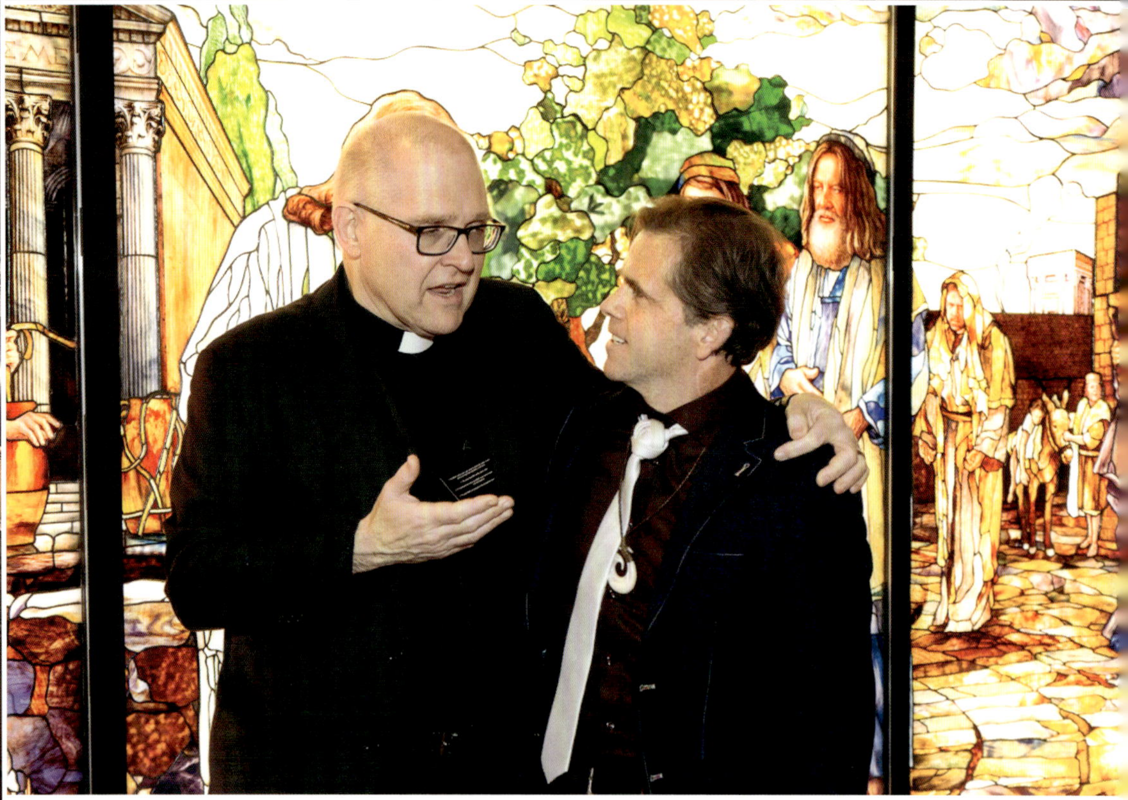

Left: Damon Wells Chapel, Pembroke College Oxford
Top: Reverend Andrew Teal sharing the window's message with visitors, Pembroke College Dining Hall
Bottom: Reverend Andrew Teal speaking with Tom Holdman, Parliament, London
Right: Hyde Park Chapel Visitor's Center, London

Acknowledgments

The purpose of *Believe in Him* was to share the good news of Jesus Christ and His gospel throughout the world. The creation of the window and the book was a Herculean task and would not have been possible without the selfless support and talents of the following remarkable people: Marilyn Terry Allen, Ann Holdman, TJ Holdman, Vandon Holdman, Tori and Bryson Webb, Don and Tammy Webb, Kiplin Griffin, Cynthia Sweat, Debi Wilcox, Jason and Amy Zander, and the teams at Holdman Studios (north and south) and Shadow Mountain (especially Chris Schoebinger, Heidi Taylor Gordon, Derk Koldewyn, Heather Ward, and Rachael Ward).

In addition, our heartfelt gratitude goes to (in alphabetical order) Karen and Alan Ashton; Matthieu and Natacha Bennasar; Adrian Bettridge; Sharon Black; Brigham Young University Department of Geological Sciences; Michel and Edneia Cadin; Dominique and Françoise Calmels; James, Andrea, and Jack Clarke; Debora and Claudio Correa; Blake and Chelsea Davis; Mike Dufur; Patrick, Leslie, and Eva Mae Evans; Ryan and Lisa Freeman; Ryland Freeman; James Graham; Michael and Jeanne Hansen; Irina Harding; Jose Luis Herrera Aguilar and Erika Lizeth Vazquez Sanchez; Robert and Cheryl Horne; King and Diane Husein; Mark and LuAnn Jenkins; Jonathan and Hélène Judas; Kahlert Family Foundation; Toby Khung-Roylance; Ho Yun Ki; Alan and Diane Knight; Greg and Rebecca Lambright; Nick and Britney Lawyer; Larry, Lisa, and Landon Laycock; Louis-Marie Liebard; Corey and Janis Lindley; Geoff Long; Drew and Mary Major; Eric Malandain; Jim and Kris Maxwell; Kim Wilson and Gail Miller; James Morris; Jim and Linda Moss; Brendan O'Hara; Dallin and Sophie Orr; Cameron and Amber Oscarson; Amanda and Ho Park; Trevor Petersen; Carsten Phillip; Brad and Jan Porter; Franck and Véronique Poznanski; Jani Radebaugh; Sissel Kyrkjebø and Ernst Ravnaas; Jim and Krista Sorenson; Don and Kathy Stapley; Orville and Heidi Thompson; Kyle and Laura Tresner; Aaron and Susie Yorgason; and Chad and Amy Jo Young.

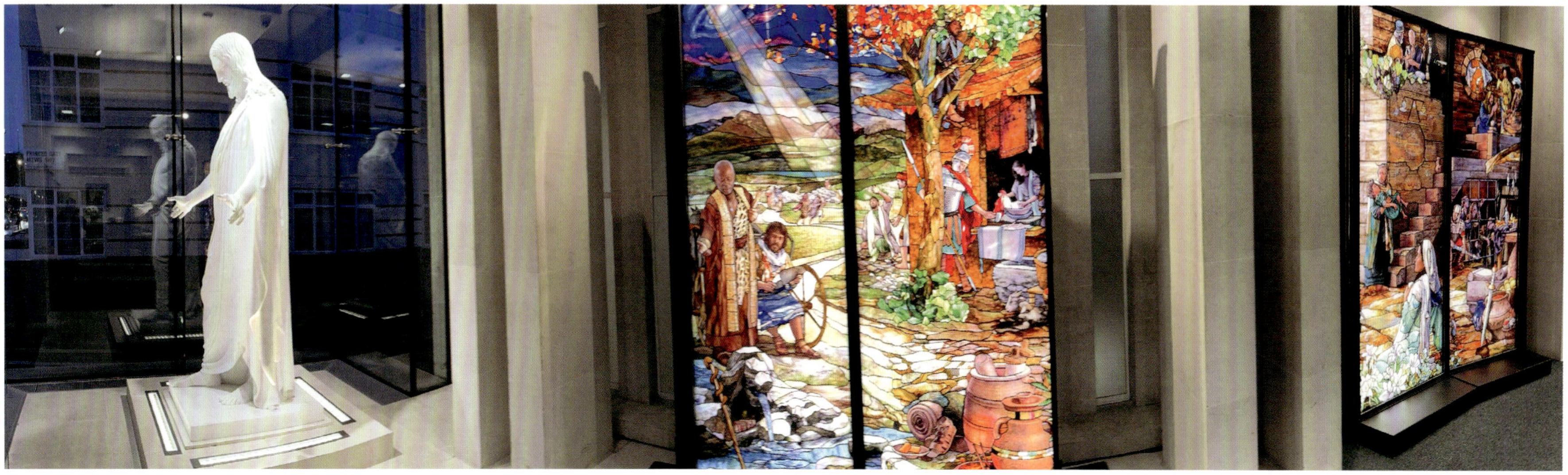

Foreword

by Reverend Dr. Andrew Teal

In April 2024, Pembroke College Oxford, England, was blessed to have displayed in our hall an extraordinary art glass window created by Tom and Gayle Holdman and the many talented and creative hands at their studio. It is an extensive and comprehensive work that references almost every episode and character from the Savior's life and throughout the New Testament. It is called *Believe in Him*.

Almost by miraculous chance, the coordinators of an international conference hosted in the college by Professor Spencer Fluhman and me, had visited the Hyde Park Visitors' Center in London when Tom and Gayle Holdman and their team were setting up the window there. Everyone was impressed by the piece and immediately saw how the luminous portrayals could complement the theme of our upcoming conference: "Seek This Jesus." The Holdmans were kind enough to offer to deliver and set up the window at Pembroke College right on our 400th birthday.

Scholars and people of faith from many Christian traditions (Roman Catholic, Anglican, Methodist, and The Church of Jesus Christ of Latter-day Saints) joined together for an unforgettable conference. In lectures and papers, we explored together—in a tender and trusting honesty—the nature and work of Jesus Christ. And in the middle of it all was this glorious window.

The panels caused extraordinary excitement. People who confessed various faiths, and those whose faith is known to God alone, met, talked, and ate amid this incredible backdrop. One member of the staff said with amazement, "It is stunning, and what a privilege to be able to eat our lunch together surrounded by this story." This art fulfilled a profound mission. It built friendships and opened channels of communication and grace.

Now this book offers the same experience to readers everywhere. What a wonderful pastoral and evangelistic mission Gayle Holdman, Tyler Griffin, Anthony Sweat, and Brad Wilcox have accomplished. The moments readers spend in this volume are sure to combine with many other spiritual moments to create powerful momentum. Like a rough stone rolling, we will not be the same again and together we will watch how the Lord's kingdom grows, and heaven's banner unfurls.

After Pembroke, the panels were moved to the Houses of Parliament in Westminster, the seat of British government and democracy. There, members of the Houses of both Lords and Commons came and marveled. The vibrant depictions reached all those who looked, both those well-accustomed to the corridors of power and the serving staff. The artwork witnessing to the words and works of Christ through the medium of glass was a great equalizer. In a world that mitigates division, this window evoked an awe-inspiring hope for unity.

"Who do you say that I am?" Jesus seems to be asking the characters portrayed in the panels and each of us who viewed them. Whatever our answers in words, the response of the Lord to every soul that has ever lived, everyone who is now alive in mortality, and all who will ever live, is the same: "Come unto me" just as you are, as incomplete and sinful as you may be. As we "Believe in Him," we will not stay stuck where we are but can grow into the full stature of Christ.

When Gayle Holdman spoke in the Houses of Parliament, she explained that stained glass takes all the creative energy and care an artistic team can offer but is incomplete without God's light. "It is the light that He gives—both physically and spiritually—that makes the work truly beautiful," she said. I am convinced that this was an occasion of enlightenment for all who were there. Her words reminded me of the words spoken by Thomas Browne (1605–1682) when Pembroke College was opened officially in 1624: "Life is a pure flame, and we live by an invisible sun within us." That invisible sun is the Light of Jesus Christ, the Light of the World, who beckons all humanity to "Believe in Him."

Tom Holdman also spoke in the Houses of Parliament and listeners realized quickly that he stutters. He joked about being able to sing his words more easily than speak them. Then, humbly and bravely, he shared some of the real pain and frustration he has known—especially in his youth. He reminded me of a student who once came to Pembroke named Charles Kempe (1837–1907). Influenced by the Anglo-Catholic revival, he offered himself for priesthood. But Kempe had a very significant stammer which, in that era, meant he could not be considered able to be a public minister. Kempe reflected in his diary, "If I was not permitted to minister in the sanctuary, then I would use my talents to adorn it." Similarly, Tom Holdman has become amazingly articulate in the medium of glass, an eloquent expositor of scripture and—most especially—of the Savior's kindness, mercy, and grace. His window demonstrates much skill and creativity, but it drips grace. Tom's life reminds us that if we lack abilities that others may have, we—like Kempe and him—still have an obligation to use our talents to reach out, heal, forgive, and love in the service of Jesus Christ. In our deficiencies, we can become His "ambassadors in chains."

This amazing window and book encourage all to believe in the Savior's power to save and heal. Each panel and page encourage us to trust His will and patience to help us understand that we are truly destined to be recipients of His mercy and infinite Atonement.

I, like many thousands of people—of all faiths and none—have been blessed by this window and book. I am confident that they will bless all who are willing to engage with them. I am also confident in the power of Jesus Christ to bless all who engage with Him.

Reverend Dr. Andrew Teal
Pembroke College Oxford

Preface

Considering the struggles and difficulties facing mankind, including the challenges of living in today's complex world, what message would you share to offer God's children peace, hope, and happiness? For Tom and Gayle Holdman and the artists in their studio, the answer is found in this scripture from the Bible: "For God so loved the world that he gave his one and only Son, that whosoever believes in him shall not perish but have eternal life" (NIV, John 3:16). They have chosen to portray the eternally significant invitation to believe in Christ artistically in a breathtaking stained-glass window.

Tom and Gayle, with their associates at Holdman Studios, are known worldwide for their beautiful art glass. This majestic window brings light and inspiration to the life and mission of Jesus Christ. Its stunning nine panels portray Christ's actions, miracles, and parables, along with the many people forever changed by His touch. Those early disciples demonstrated their deep conversion by living what He taught and traveling far and wide to spread the good news of God's loving gift throughout the world. Similarly, this window was created to travel far distances, inviting viewers to feel the perfect love of God and His Son Jesus Christ.

THE ART AND ITS DEVELOPMENT

Art can represent life through a variety of mediums and techniques. Perhaps one of the most difficult and gloriously captivating is stained glass. Working with glass is labor intensive and requires patience and skill. The small fragile pieces by themselves might seem insignificant, but when brought together each becomes a vital part of a masterpiece.

A stained-glass window is not just one work of art, but many. Because the light shining through it continually changes, viewers are treated to fascinating displays of dazzling colors and rich textures that vary from day to day—even from moment to moment.

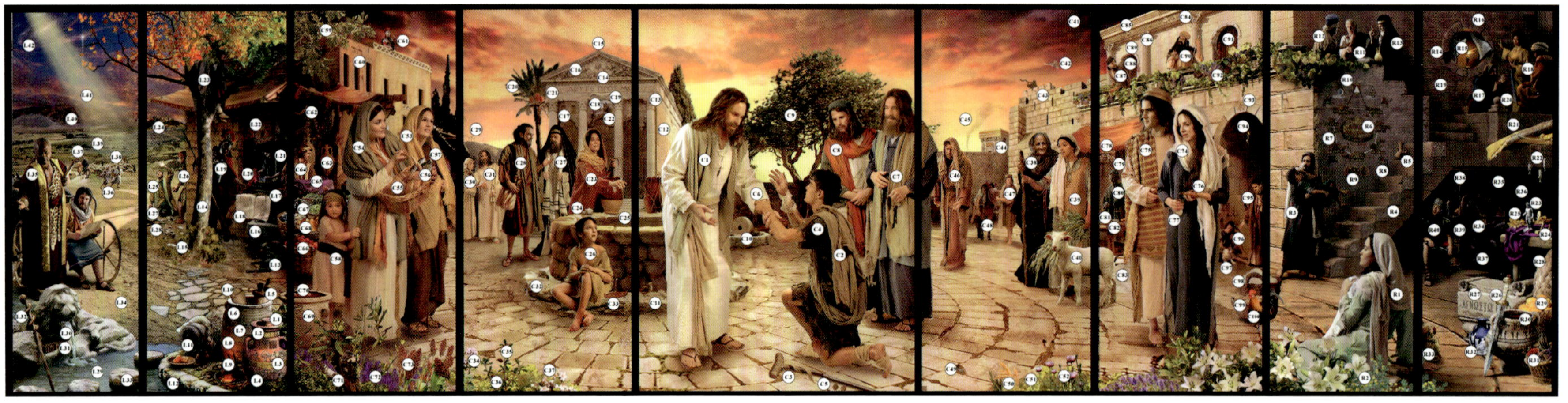

In 2019 Tom and Gayle Holdman and the artists who work with them completed a 20-by-7-foot window housed in Rome. They created an intricate five-panel window depicting important aspects of Christ's life and ministry as well as all of His parables and miracles. Viewers have engaged with the prodigal son, the good Samaritan, and the woman reaching out to touch the Savior's robe. Children have delighted in finding an actual widow's mite embedded in the window, and adolescents have been fascinated to find real gemstones representing the twelve tribes of Israel.

A NEW DISPLAY TO TRAVEL

Concerned about the number of people who might never be able to go to Rome, the artists were inspired to replicate and expand the window in a portable exhibition that would travel to people throughout the world. The original five panels have been extended with two additional panels on each side depicting the New Testament beyond the four gospels. It was first unveiled in Paris, France, in 2023 and then traveled to London, England, in 2024. The response was astounding. Thousands viewed the glorious window and have been touched by its message.

CHARACTERS AND PHOTOGRAPHS

The new panels were designed, and models for the required characters were chosen. Prospective choices, dressed in time-period costumes, were prepared by professional makeup artists and hairstylists to be photographed in a variety of poses and with multiple facial expressions.

Artists then examined hundreds of photographs to find the ones they needed. They carefully considered the importance of maintaining balance, symmetry, and perspective in the overall piece, with the Savior as the focal point.

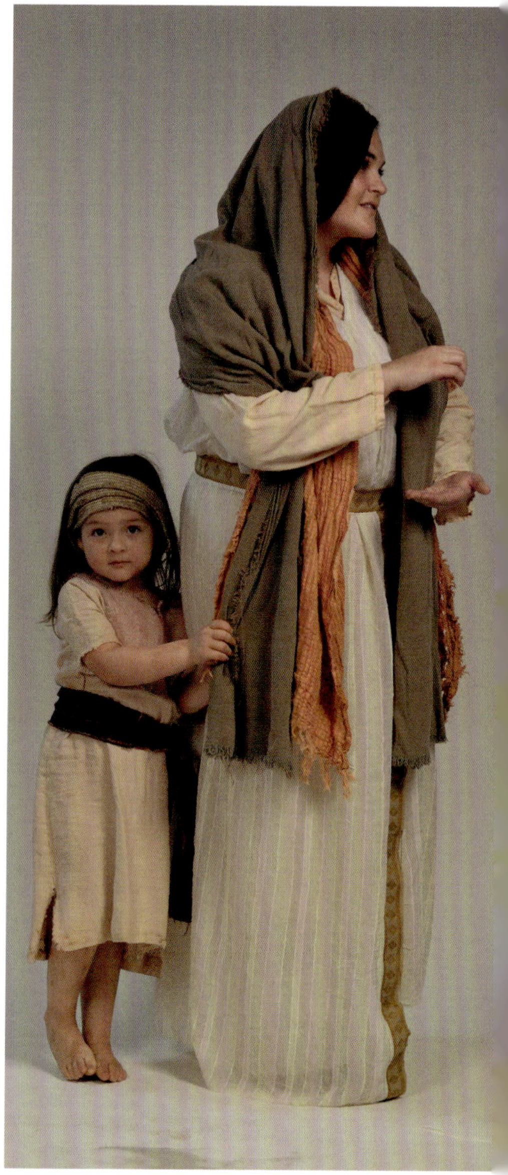

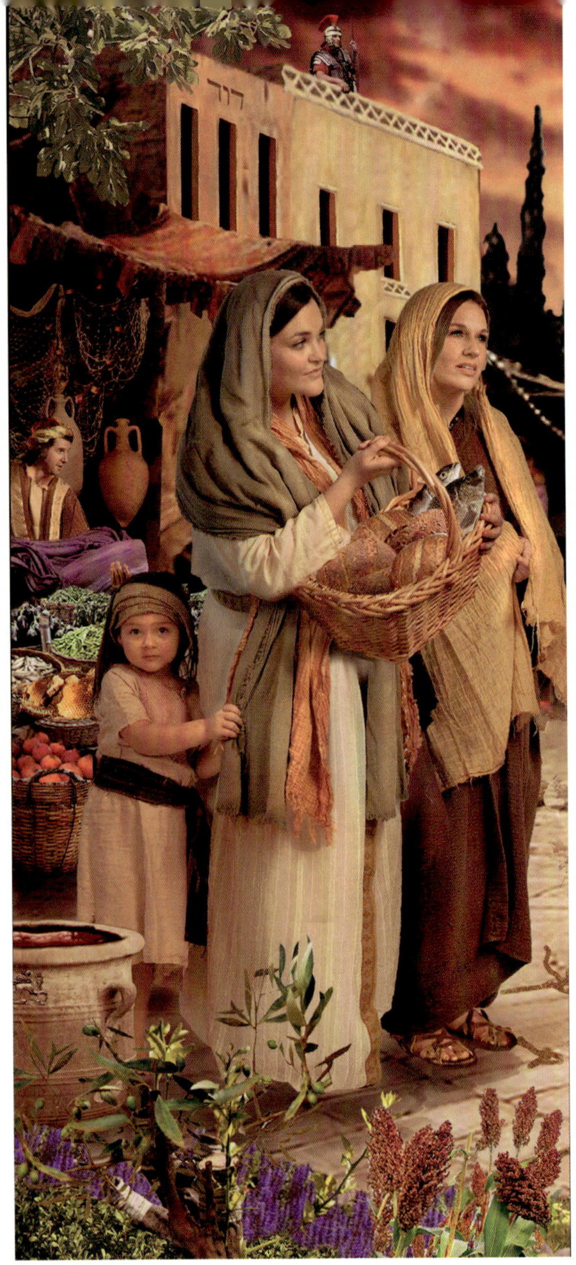

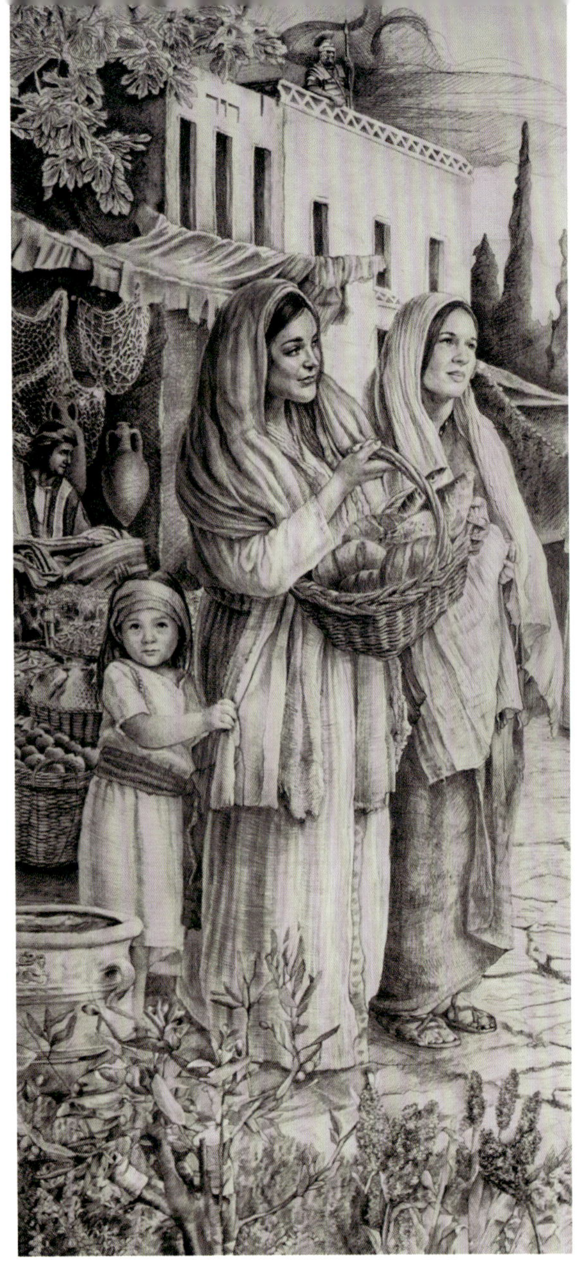

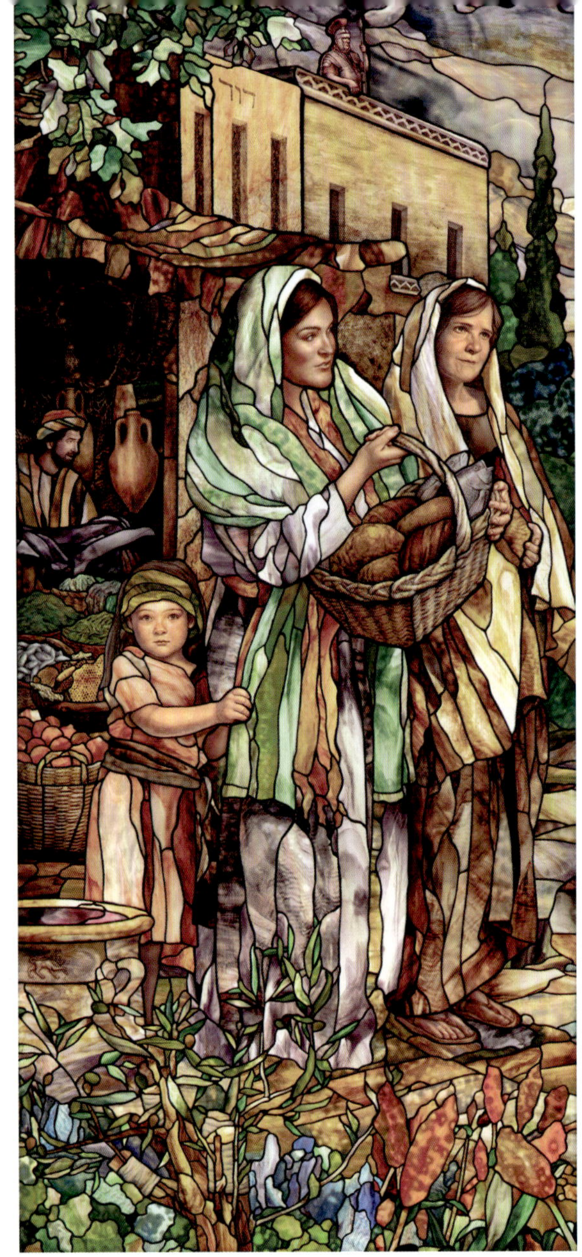

DIGITAL AND HAND-DRAWN DESIGNS

Many painters and sculptors often follow the same steps in the early stages. But creating a stained-glass window requires its own processes and resources. In art glass, thousands of individual pieces are bound together with lead that must become part of the design. The artists used a computer to add dark lines indicating lead placement. They revised this work many times to ensure that the lines enhanced the original design.

After this painstaking digital creation, sketches were drawn to fine-tune the details, ensure consistency of the light source, and determine the black and white values for the pieces of glass that would need to be painted. Then the artists created a pattern based on both the digital design and the drawings to show the exact dimensions for each piece of glass that they would cut by hand or with a water-jet machine and ultimately fit together.

FINAL GLASS CRAFTING

Artists next selected the glass they needed. Even with modern technology, the bulk of glass fabrication is still done by hand, so each large sheet is unique.

Artists searched not only for the perfect colors, but also for the exact location on each sheet with the correct texture. In some places they had to layer glass to achieve the effect they sought. Viewers of this window will see this layered effect in the basket holding the bread, in some of the stones beneath people's feet, and in the pillar of light descending in the panel on the far left.

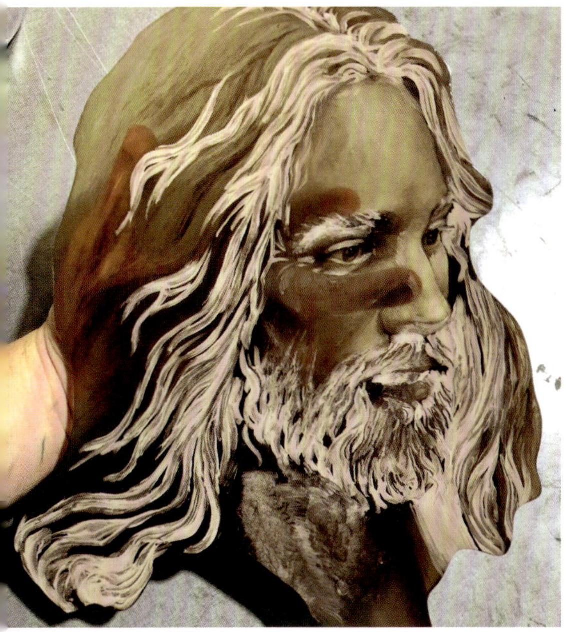

Stained glass of Jesus Christ being painted with powdered glass

Some pieces of glass—such as heads, hands, and feet—must be painted. Regular paints would fade over time, so the artists used paints combining finely powdered glass and liquid (primarily clove oil with the addition of other oils, water, and vinegar).

First, they brushed the paints over an entire piece of glass. Next, they used paintbrushes—some so tiny that they had only a few bristles—to gently remove paint from the areas they had chosen for light to shine through.

HEAT AND DELICATE ARTISTRY

At this point the pieces of glass looked like photo negatives and were placed carefully in a kiln, where the intense heat melted the paint permanently into the glass. The slightest smudge or mistake becomes apparent in the firing process, and at times the artists had to start over again with some pieces. Firing also makes glass more fragile, and broken pieces have also had to be re-created.

Painted pieces and non-painted pieces were then leaded together. This required that each piece be fitted into grooved channels of lead strips and then held firmly in place as the next pieces are fitted around it. Precision required that small or oddly shaped pieces be wrapped in copper foil to which melted lead could adhere.

When all the pieces were finally in place, artists used a soldering iron to seal the joints between lead lines and copper foils. They shaped additional metal bars and placed them along the main lead lines on the back of the piece to provide the window with structural support. They also coated every lead line in a liquid patina that ensured they were all the same shade. Finally, the windows were carefully cleaned of the residue from the soldering process and protected with a sheet of strong, clear glass covering everything.

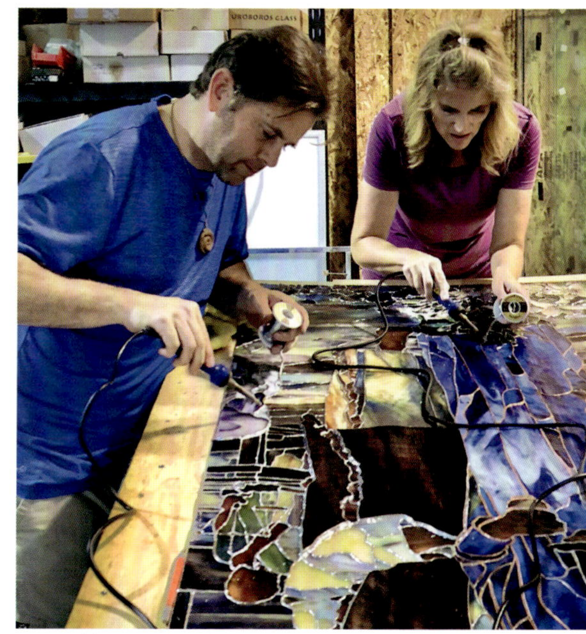

Tom Holdman and Gayle Holdman soldering windows

Only the window's creators truly know how much work the entire process required, but they rarely speak of it. The artists want to be sure that the window's individual components never overshadow its main message. The window was created to focus viewers on the reality of God's love, which can be best understood and internalized as we consider the life, acts, and teachings of Jesus Christ and those who spread His word throughout the world.

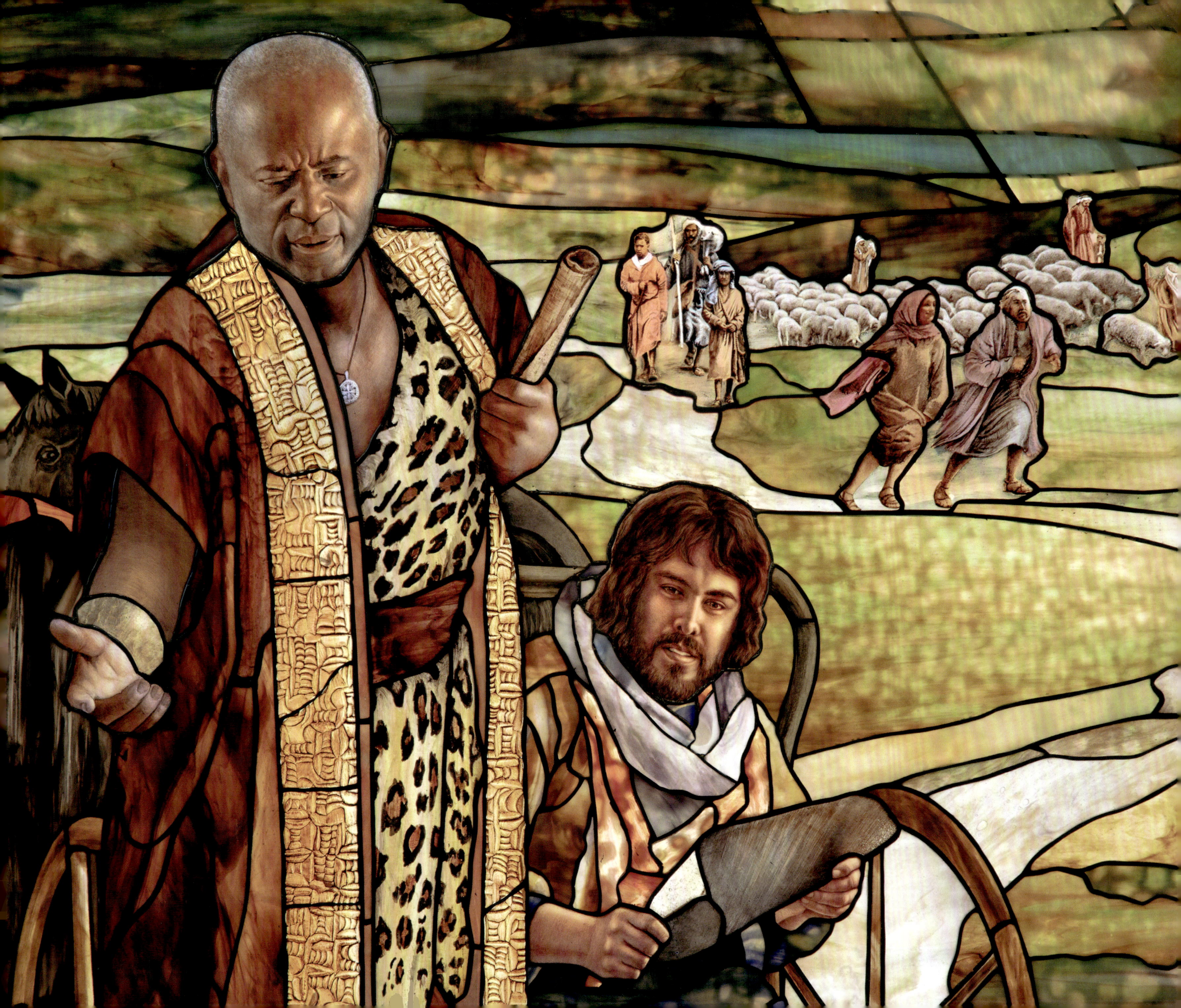

Panel A

Featuring the Ethiopian and Philip

LIGHTS AND LANDMARKS | 2

1. Creation of all things by the Word
2. Pillar of light seen by Saul on the road to Damascus
3. Mount of Temptation
4. Lake called the Sea of Galilee

CONVERSATIONS AND CHRIST'S MISSION | 4

5. Simon of Cyrene with his two sons, Alexander and Rufus
6. Shepherds and flock of sheep as described in Psalm 23 and in Luke 2
7. Ethiopian eunuch and Philip the evangelist
8. Two disciples on the road to Emmaus

CLEANSING AND HEALING | 6

9. Serpent on staff of Moses
10. Path of discipleship
11. Living water from rock—a metaphor for Christ, the Lion of Judah
12. Lamb of God
13. Cleansing waters
14. Stones in the water as principles of the gospel

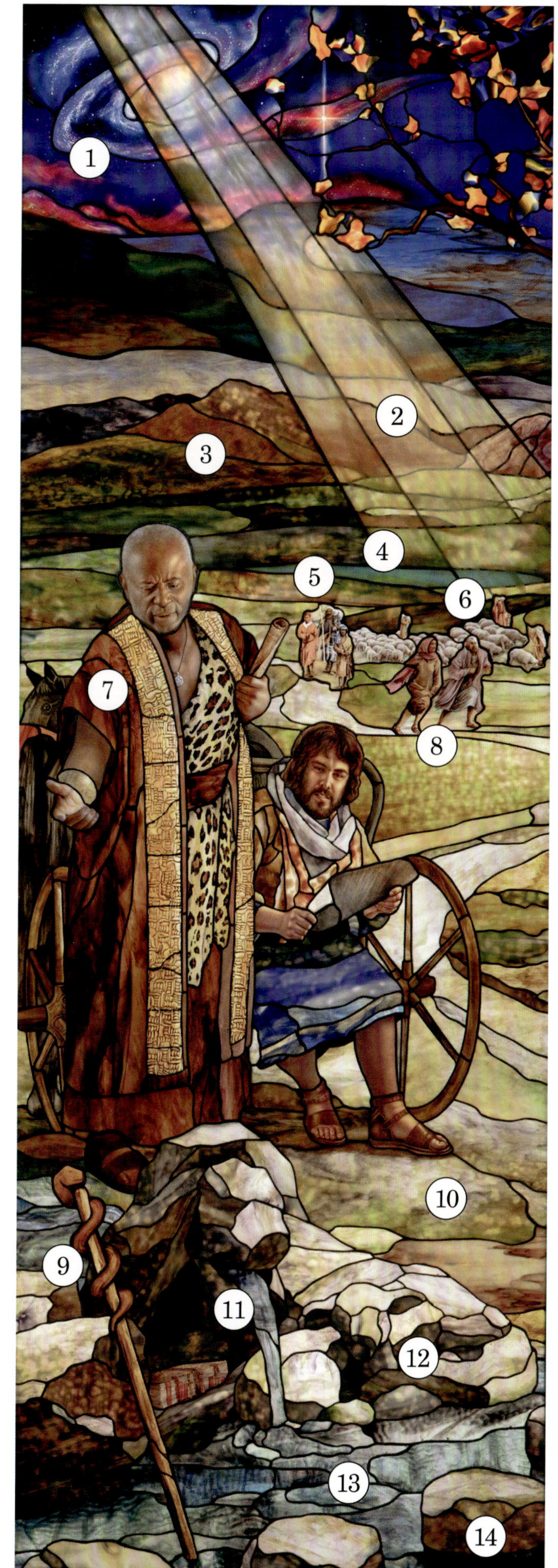

To help viewers as they engage with the window, each panel is labeled from left to right by a letter. The far-left panel is A, and the far-right panel is I. The center panel featuring Christ is letter E. The images within each panel are numbered so viewers can easily connect each detail with its description. All scriptures are from the New International Version (NIV) of the Bible unless otherwise indicated.

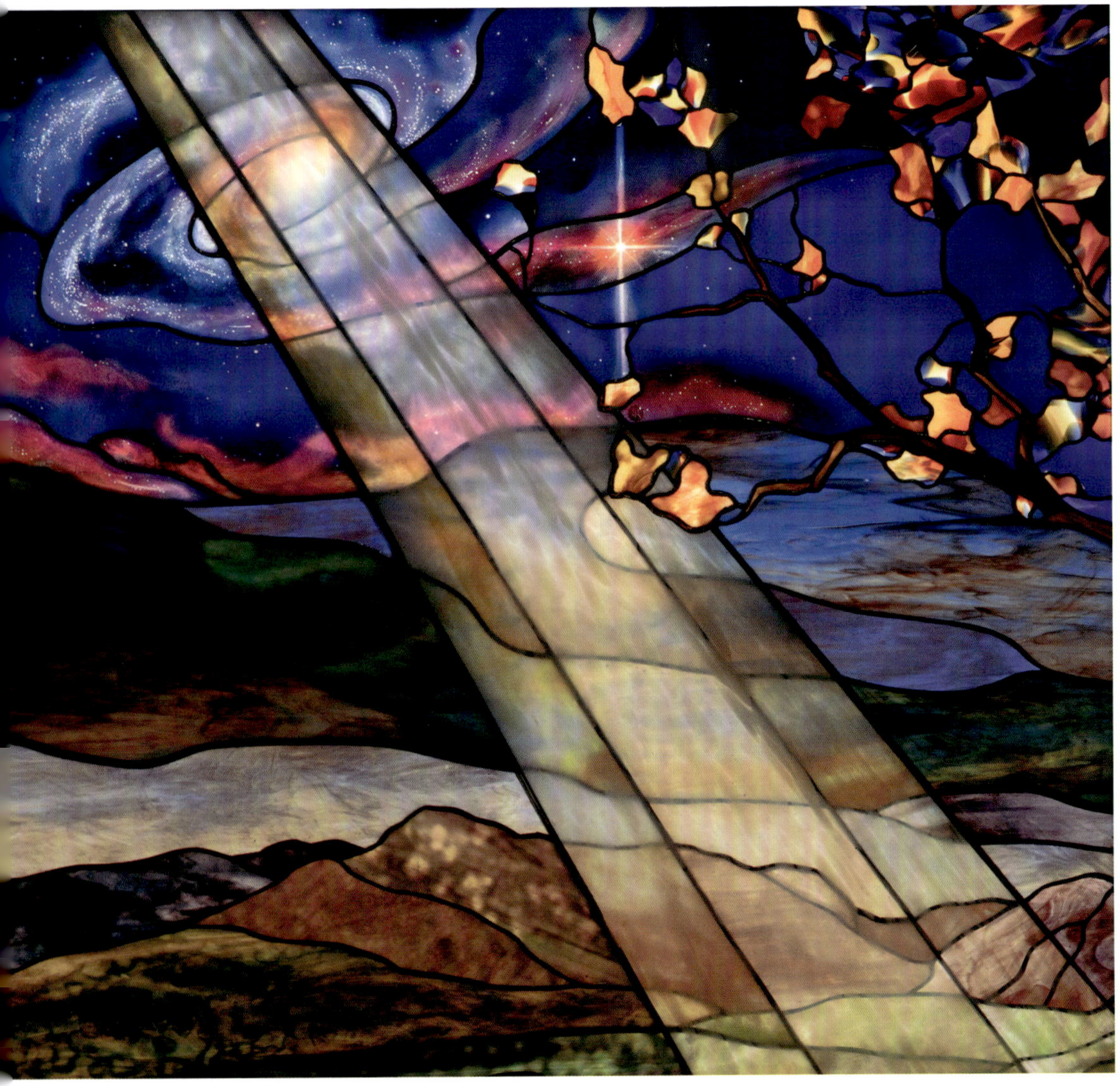

LIGHTS AND LANDMARKS

1. CREATION OF ALL THINGS BY THE WORD

"In the beginning was the Word, and the Word was with God, and the Word was God. . . . Through him all things were made. . . . In him was life, and that life was the light of all mankind" (John 1:1, 3–4). The window follows the same pattern as the Bible and the Gospel of John—it begins in the upper-left corner with a depiction of the cosmos, the light of creation, and an acknowledgment of the great Creator, Jesus Christ. The prominent position reminds us that Jesus is the "light of the world" and any who look to Him and walk in the light He offers "will never walk in darkness, but will have the light of life" (John 8:12). For those who have eyes to see, the light of Christ is illuminated in every aspect of this window as well as in every aspect of our own lives. This is especially true when we find ourselves in dark places surrounded by disorder. Contrast the many places in the window where the light is not shining as brightly and consider what those people could have done to seek, find, and reflect the light of Jesus. After all, in the morn of creation, it was in the darkness and chaos of space where the piercing voice of God commanded, "Let there be light" (Genesis 1:3). That same command can still be heard in our lives today as we choose to turn away from spiritual darkness and hear the assurance that "the light shines in the darkness, and the darkness has not overcome it" (John 1:5).

2. PILLAR OF LIGHT SEEN BY SAUL ON THE ROAD TO DAMASCUS

One of the greatest conversion stories of all time was initiated by a pillar of "light from heaven [that] flashed around" (Acts 9:3) a zealous student of the Pharisees named Saul. He was on his way to arrest followers of Christ living in Damascus. After falling to the ground, Saul heard a voice, and asked, "Who are you, Lord?" (Acts 9:5). Saul knew many things *about* the Lord, but he didn't *know* the Lord. In contrast,

Ananias was a disciple in Damascus who may not have known as many details about the Hebrew Bible as Saul, but he recognized the Lord's voice when he was asked to heal Saul. Ananias obeyed the command even though it is possible that his name was included on Saul's arrest warrants. Placing his hands on Saul, he said, "Brother Saul, the Lord—Jesus, who appeared to you on the road as you were coming here—has sent me so that you may see again" (Acts 9:17). This is a powerful story of redemption and change—from Saul to Paul, from blindness to sight, from persecutor to evangelist. The artists portrayed this experience in the window as a visual reminder that "if anyone is in Christ, the new creation has come: The old has gone, the new is here!" (2 Corinthians 5:17).

3. MOUNT OF TEMPTATION

After being baptized by John, "Jesus was led by the Spirit into the wilderness to be tempted by the devil" (Matthew 4:1). The root of the word *wilderness* is "wild." This is not a tame place where one can rely on his or her own abilities or past successes. The Mount of Temptation is portrayed in the window as a desolate and dreary place, far removed from the people. It reminds us that it is often in the wildernesses of our lives, much more than in places of comfort and ease, that we come to know God better and trust Him more. It is where we also learn more about ourselves. The artists have beautifully portrayed that the only thing to pierce through the darkness of the wilderness is the light emanating from the Lord: "The people living in darkness have seen a great light; on those living in the land of the shadow of death a light has dawned" (Matthew 4:16).

4. LAKE CALLED THE SEA OF GALILEE

Shortly after beginning His public ministry, Jesus moved from Nazareth to Capernaum, a Jewish town on the northern coast of the Sea of Galilee. Most of the New Testament events shared in the gospels took place in or around the region of this sea. The artists portrayed the pear shape of Galilee just under the ray of light in the window. This inland lake measures 13 miles from north to south and 7 miles from east to west and is the lowest freshwater lake in the world at roughly 700 feet below sea level. All the water flowing into this sea eventually empties out through the Jordan River to the Dead Sea. The Sea of Galilee is filled with life in the form of fish, and is surrounded by birds, and plants of many varieties. The Dead Sea, by contrast, is perfectly named because there is very little life that can survive in or around water that is ten times saltier than the ocean and has no rivers flowing out because it lies at the lowest point on Earth (1400+ feet below sea level). These bodies of water can teach us gospel lessons. People who follow Christ's example of turning outward and sharing what they have with others will be filled with an abundance of life. Those who only take can become stale and bitter. Many people portrayed in the window reflect one or the other of these two seas in the way they lived their lives.

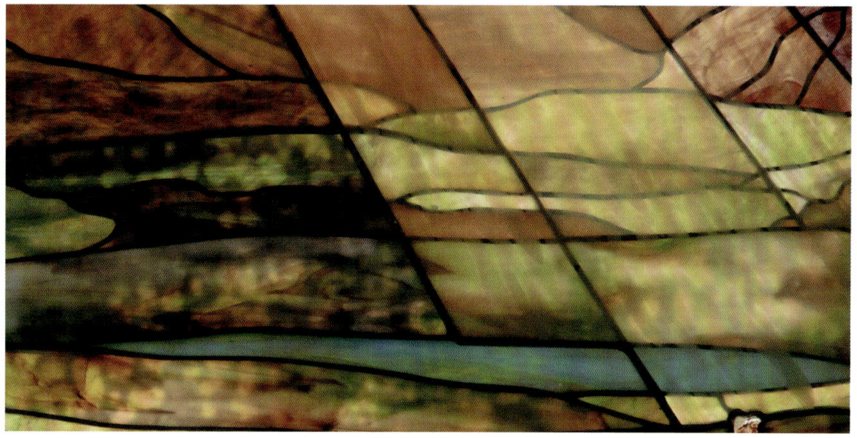

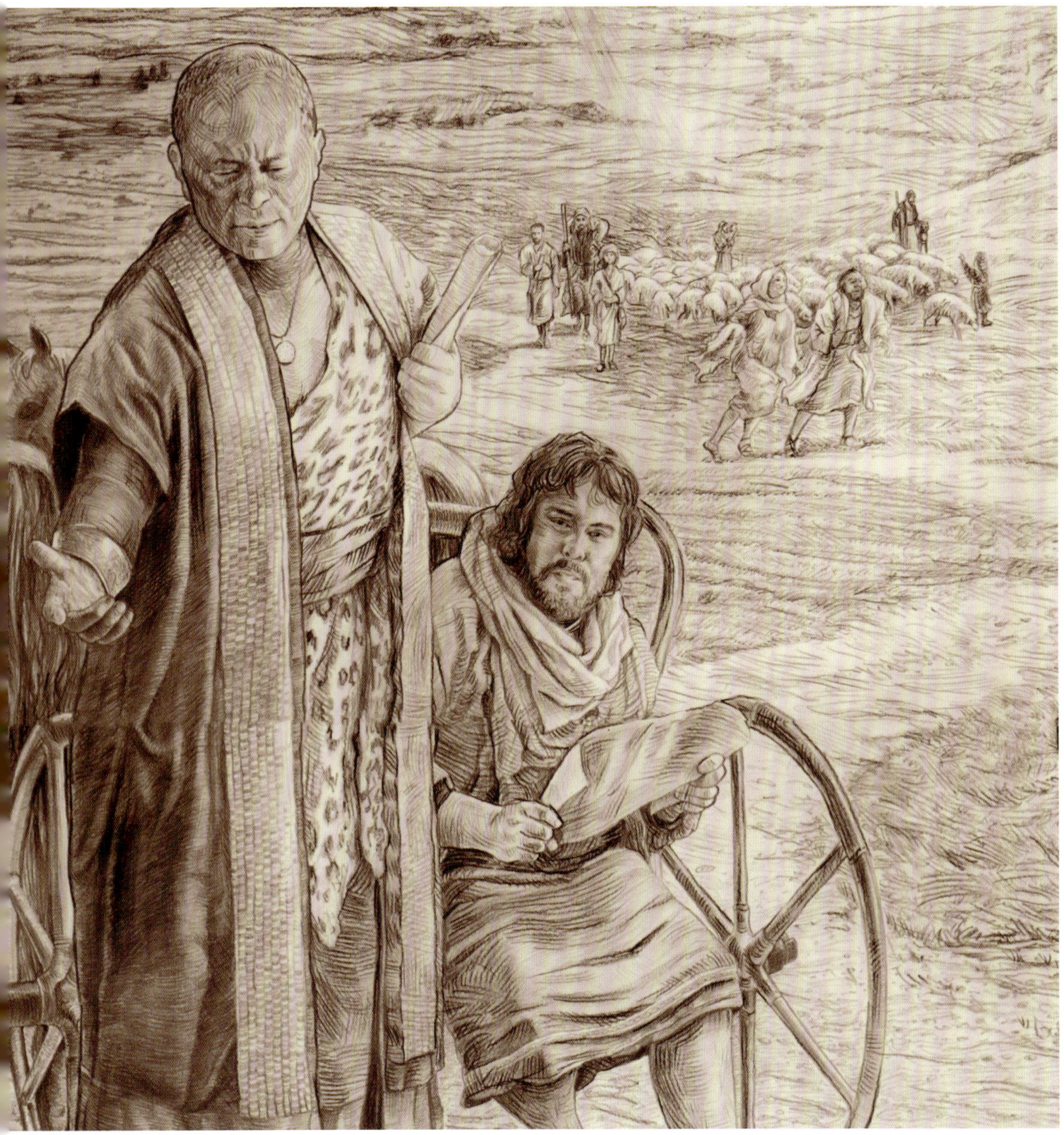

CONVERSATIONS AND CHRIST'S MISSION

5. SIMON OF CYRENE WITH HIS TWO SONS, ALEXANDER AND RUFUS

It is hard to find examples of people in the New Testament who were forced to do something for Jesus. Simon of Cyrene has the distinction of being on that very short list. Simon had brought his two sons, Alexander and Rufus (see Mark 15:21), on a long journey to Jerusalem from their home in Cyrene, known today as Libya in north Africa. Simon was pulled out of the crowd by the Roman soldiers and forced to carry the cross of Jesus to the place of crucifixion. What lessons might Alexander and Rufus have learned from their father in this situation? What lessons might they have learned from watching Jesus throughout this process? The artists have portrayed Simon carrying a sheep on his shoulders, an innocent lamb without blemish that would be offered up as a Passover sacrifice. Little did he know that this symbolic lamb would soon be replaced on his shoulders with a cross that would be used for the ultimate sacrifice of the Lamb of God.

6. SHEPHERDS AND FLOCK OF SHEEP AS DESCRIBED IN PSALM 23 AND IN LUKE 2

"The Lord is my shepherd; I shall not want. He maketh me to lie down in green pastures: he leadeth me beside the still waters. He restoreth my soul: he leadeth me in the paths of righteousness for his name's sake" (KJV, Psalm 23:1–3). The artists have portrayed a flock of sheep under the watchful care of good shepherds. One of the shepherd boys is looking heavenward, noticing a new star that appeared. The heavenly light also represents the angelic visitation on the night of Jesus's birth, which sent the shepherds to the stable to worship the newborn Lamb of God (see Luke 2). Near the end of His life, Jesus deepened this pastoral theme by teaching, "I am the good shepherd; I know my sheep and my sheep know me . . . and I lay down my life for the sheep" (John 10:14–15). He was willing to do all this for His sheep.

The question that remains is how much do we as sheep trust the shepherd? He taught that "his sheep follow him because they know his voice" (John 10:4). Even though we might not be walking the streets of Jerusalem and Galilee with *Him*, our good shepherd is walking with *us* today! As we come to know His voice, we can all say, "Even though I walk through the darkest valley, I will fear no evil, for you are with me; your rod and your staff, they comfort me" (Psalm 23:4).

7. ETHIOPIAN EUNUCH AND PHILIP THE EVANGELIST

In Acts 8, Philip was called to go in a different direction even though he was experiencing great success. He was teaching and baptizing among the Samaritans when an angel of the Lord instructed him to leave and go to a desert road "that goes down from Jerusalem to Gaza" (Acts 8:26). There are hundreds of reasons why Philip should have stayed in Samaria and continued to teach there, but there was one reason why he should leave and go down to the desert road—because the Lord asked him to. As an instrument in the hands of God, he obeyed and, in the process, "he met an Ethiopian eunuch, an important official in charge of all the treasury [of the queen of Ethiopia]" (Acts 8:27). The elegantly dressed eunuch is portrayed in the window wearing a Coptic cross around his neck and a leopard skin representing Africa. The eunuch was sitting in his chariot reading aloud from Isaiah 53. Philip was directed by the Spirit to approach the chariot and ask the eunuch if he understood the words. "Then Philip began with that very passage of Scripture and told him the good news about Jesus" (Acts 8:35). As they continued down the road, they soon came to some water and the eunuch said, "Look, here is water. What can stand in the way of my being baptized?" (Acts 8:36). After his baptism, logic would dictate that Philip should travel with the eunuch to Ethiopia and then preach the gospel in that part of the world. Once again, the Lord had a different direction: "When they came up out of the water, the Spirit of the Lord suddenly took Philip away, and the eunuch did not see him again, but went on his way rejoicing" (Acts 8:39). What will we do the next time the Spirit of the Lord prompts us with an unanticipated command?

8. TWO DISCIPLES ON THE ROAD TO EMMAUS

On the very day that Jesus rose from the grave, two of His disciples were going to Emmaus, a village about seven miles from Jerusalem. As they walked and talked about the events they had witnessed over the past few days, a stranger approached and began walking with them. Cleopas informed the man about Christ's crucifixion and how they had "hoped that he was the one who was going to redeem Israel" (Luke 24:21). The excitement must have mounted as they then recounted how some of the women had been to the tomb early that very morning and found it empty and had seen angels who told them Jesus was alive again. The stranger then explained how all the Old Testament prophets testified of the Messiah. As the threesome approached Emmaus, the two disciples invited their fellow traveler to join them for the night. It was in the breaking of bread that their eyes were finally opened, and they recognized the stranger was Jesus just before He "disappeared from their sight" (Luke 24:31). "They got up and returned at once to Jerusalem" (Luke 24:33) to let the apostles know what they had seen. The artists have portrayed Cleopas and his wife as the two disciples who are hurrying toward the city to share the glorious news: "Were not our hearts burning within us while he talked with us on the road and opened the Scriptures to us?" (Luke 24:32).

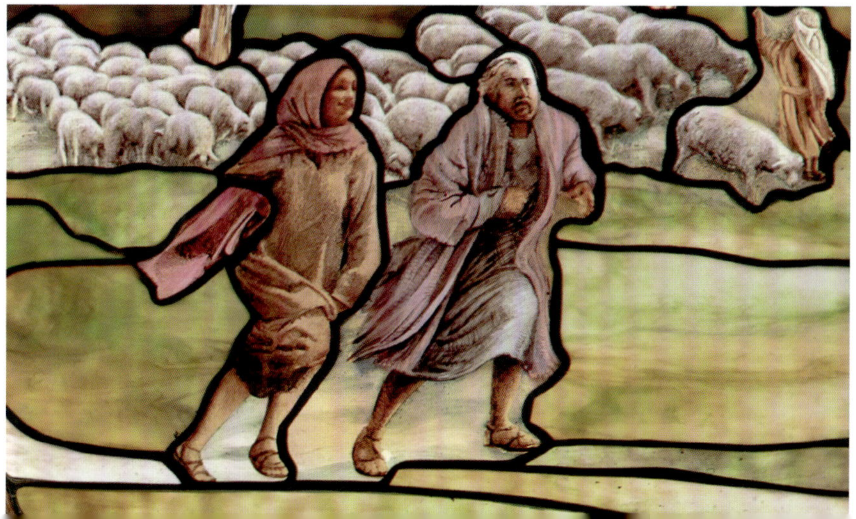

CLEANSING AND HEALING

9. SERPENT ON STAFF OF MOSES

On the journey from Egypt toward the Promised Land, the Israelites "grew impatient on the way" (Numbers 21:4) and began to speak against God and Moses. Shortly thereafter, venomous snakes began biting the people, causing many deaths. Moses prayed on behalf of the people, and the Lord instructed him to make a bronze snake and mount it on a pole. "Then when anyone was bitten by a snake and looked at the bronze snake, they lived" (Number 21:9). This was a powerful symbol of Jesus Christ and the healing He offers. A snake sheds its skin, signifying a new life. In the window, the rod with the snake is in a mirror-image location to the sword at the bottom of panel I, emphasizing the choice we all have between healing and destruction. The Ethiopian eunuch is portrayed as looking at the bronze snake and thus finding new life.

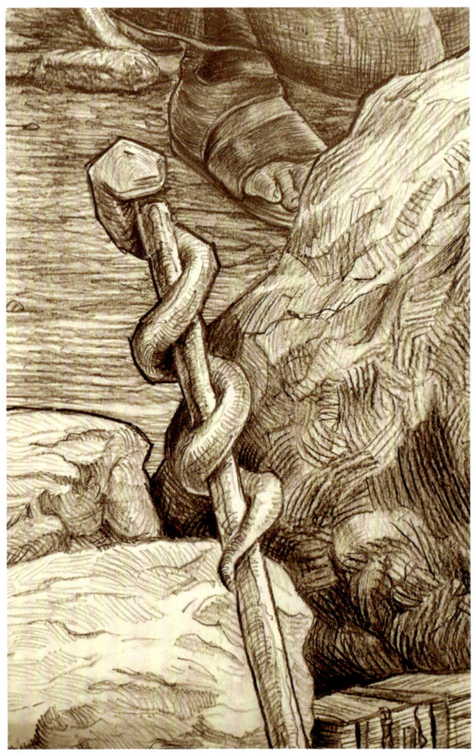

10. PATH OF DISCIPLESHIP

In His Sermon on the Mount, Jesus invited followers to enter His small gate and walk the narrow road that leads to life (see Matthew 7:14). What is that path and how can we be sure we are not part of the crowds on the broad road that "leads to destruction" (Matthew 7:13)? On His final night in mortality, Jesus answered that question when His apostle Thomas asked, "'Lord, we don't know where you are going, so how can we know the way?' Jesus answered, 'I am the way and the truth and the life. No one comes to the Father except through me'" (John 14:5–6). He laid out and marked the path we should follow and then reminded His disciples, "If you love me, keep my commands" (John 14:15). The artists have portrayed a long and winding path that leads to the Savior in the center of the window. Christ's amazing grace can be experienced as we begin the disciple's journey on the path, at every step and misstep along the way, and especially at the end when we enter His glorious presence. There are many unknowns along the path of discipleship, but there is one constant—Jesus Christ is the way, He is our traveling companion, and He is our target destination! He never intended for us to walk that path alone. As we continue forward, He is with us, because He *is* the way!

11. LIVING WATER FROM ROCK—A METAPHOR FOR CHRIST, THE LION OF JUDAH

Many scriptures speak of life-giving water. Flowing—or living—water is a powerful symbol for Christ and the life He offers us. In Numbers 20, we read how Moses struck a rock with a staff and water gushed out. In John 4, Jesus invited the woman of Samaria to drink of His living water, so she need not thirst spiritually anymore. In John 7, on the last day of the Feast of Tabernacles, when the priests were dumping water gathered from the Pool of Siloam on the altar of the Temple, Jesus boldly declared to the crowd, "Let anyone who is thirsty come to me and drink. Whoever believes in me, as Scripture has said, rivers of living water will flow from within them" (vv. 37–38). The window portrays the water flowing out of a lion, another symbol of Christ as seen by John in Revelation 5: "'Who is worthy to break the seals and open the scroll?' [The elder answers,] 'The Lion of the tribe of Judah'" (vv. 2, 5). Christ was able to triumph in opening the scroll, allowing all of us to experience life. Perhaps the greatest scriptural manifestation of life-giving water is found on the cross when the soldier pierced the side of Jesus with a spear, "bringing a sudden flow of blood and water" (John 19:34). The life blood and living water that flowed out of Christ can be for us "a spring of water welling up to eternal life" (John 4:14).

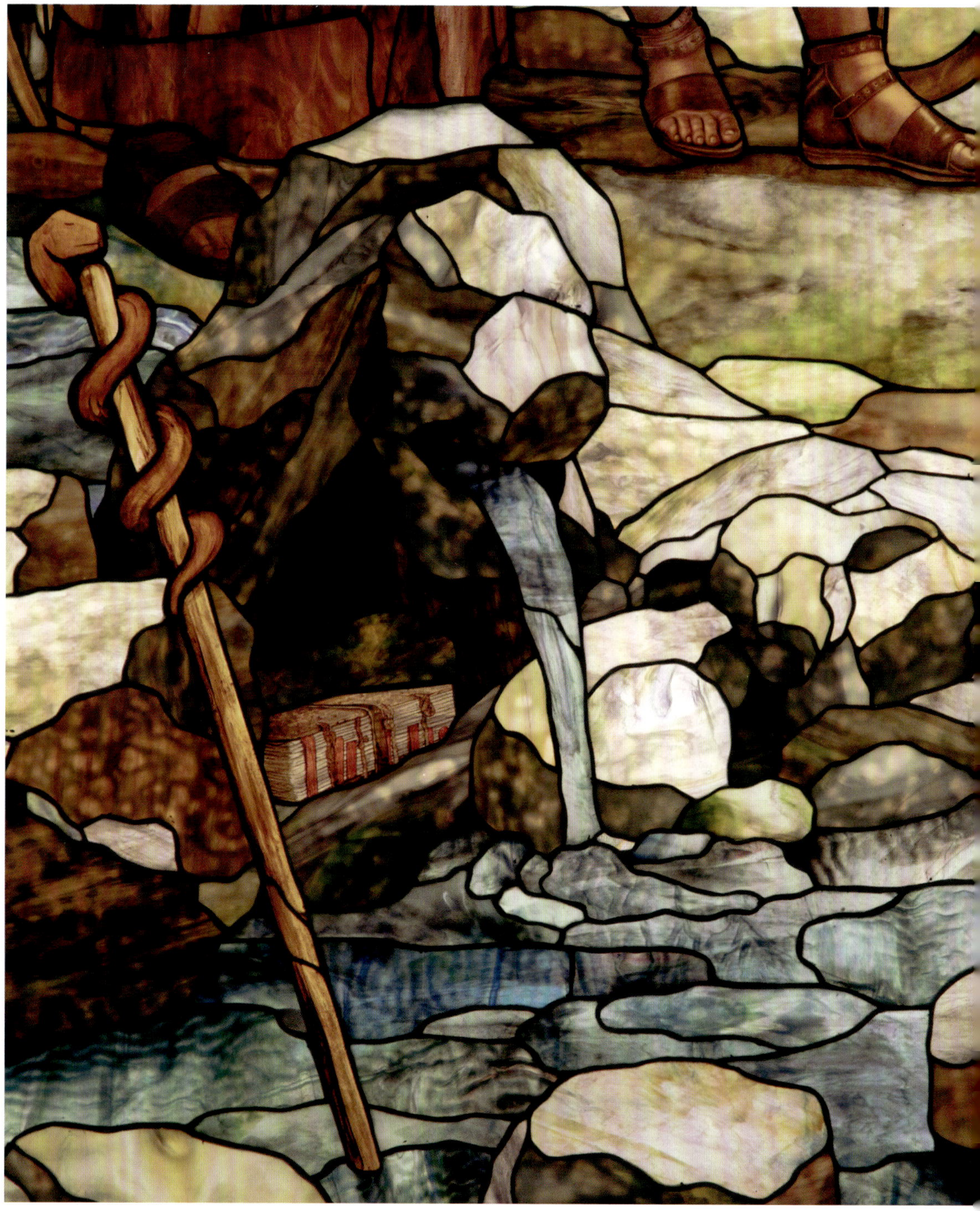

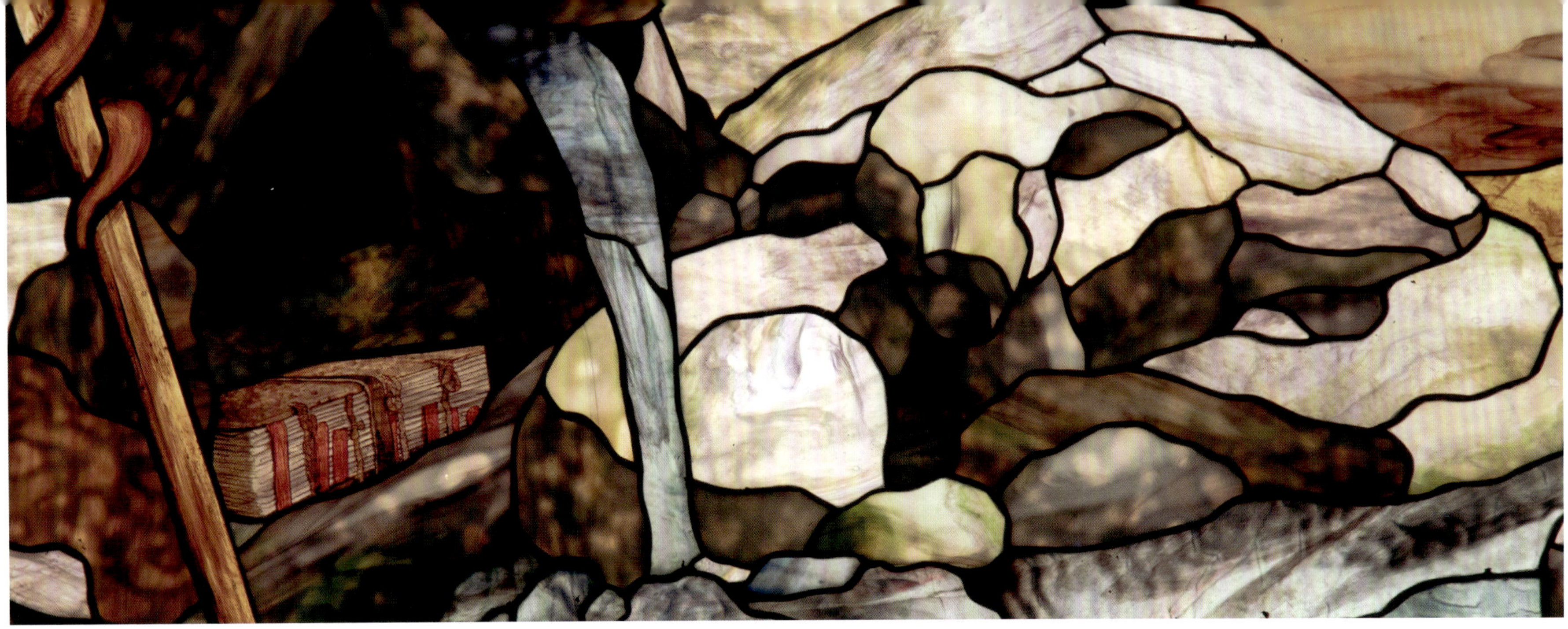

12. LAMB OF GOD

When Adam and Eve were expelled from the Garden of Eden, "the Lord God made garments of skin for Adam and his wife and clothed them" (Genesis 3:21). Innocent animals had to die for Adam and Eve to have garments of skins. From the beginning of time, they were learning symbolic lessons about the solution to their problems who would be born thousands of years later and willingly lay down His life to cover all of humanity in a garment of grace. In John's vision in Revelation 5, immediately after seeing the Lion of the Tribe of Judah, John "saw a Lamb, looking as if it had been slain, standing at the center of the throne" (v. 6). Paul invited the Roman saints to "put aside the deeds of darkness and put on the armor of light" (Romans 13:12). After listing off some of their dark deeds, Paul concluded, "Clothe yourselves with the Lord Jesus Christ, and do not think about how to gratify the desires of the flesh" (v. 14). In the window, you see these two animals who are often seen as opposites both symbolizing different attributes, roles, and names of Jesus Christ, both lying down together in peace (see Isaiah 11:6). We need both His lion-like attributes to protect and defend us just as much as we need the lamb whose sacrifice would clothe us "with garments of salvation" and array us "in a robe of his righteousness" (Isaiah 61:10).

13. CLEANSING WATERS

Faithful Jews in the first century were careful to maintain ritual purity. One of the ways they accomplished this was through immersing themselves in *mikva'ot*, or ritual baths. A mikvah could be small or it could be a very large public pool that thousands of people could use. In John 5, Jesus went to a very large public mikvah, called Bethesda, where a "great number of disabled people used to lie" (v. 3). He found a man who had been lame for 38 years and asked if he wanted to be healed. The man complained that he didn't have anyone to put him in the cleansing water at the appointed time. Jesus simply responded, "Get up! Pick up your mat and walk" (v. 8). In John 9, Jesus was departing from the temple when He spat on the ground and made mud, which He put on a blind beggar's eyes before telling him to go and wash in another large mikvah, the Pool of Siloam. The blind man would have passed multiple smaller, more convenient pools and water sources on his way to Siloam, but he dutifully obeyed Christ's instruction to go and wash and he was healed. This is like the miracle of Naaman the leper, who was told by Elisha to go and wash seven times in the Jordan River (see 2 Kings 5). There were many other better water sources available, but Naaman did as Elisha had instructed, and he was cleansed from his leprosy. Centuries later, Jesus would go to John

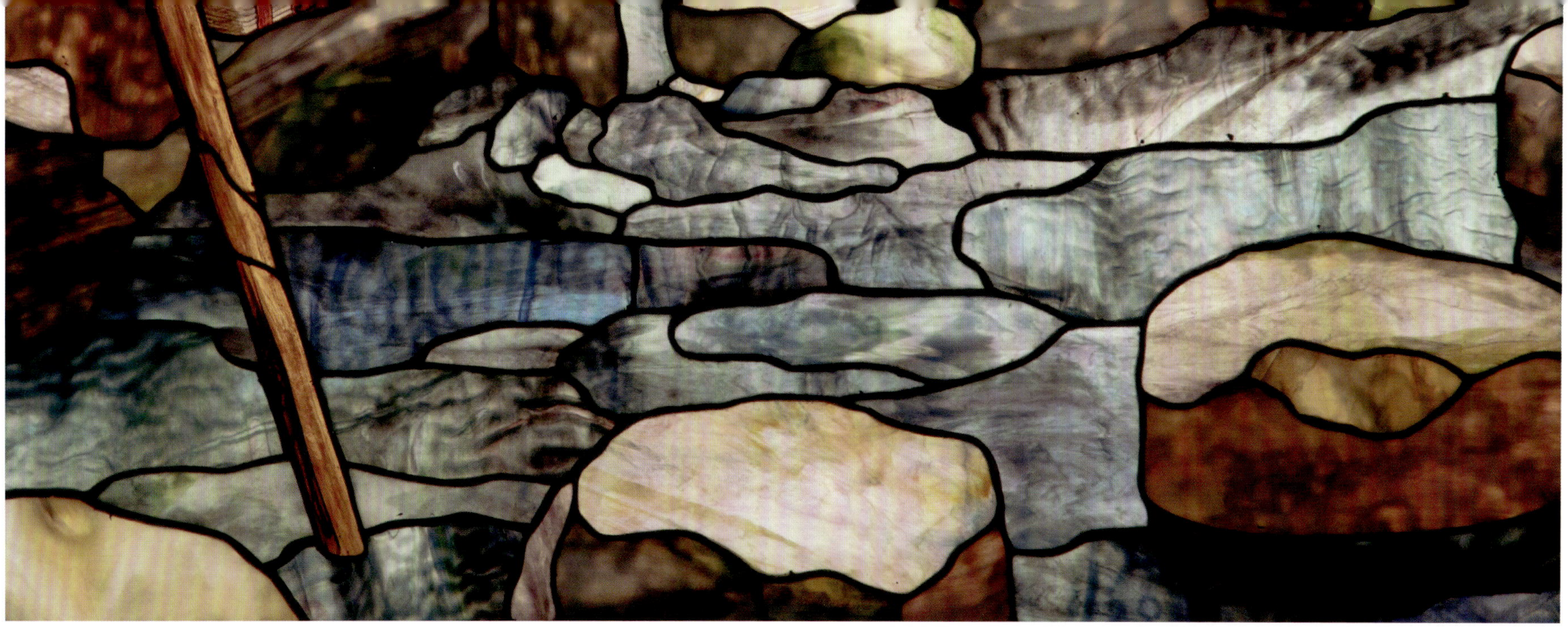

the Baptist to be baptized in that same river. In these experiences, it wasn't the water that had healing or cleansing power, it was God; but God often uses water, with its powerful cleansing symbolism, to allow people to exercise their faith in Him. The beautiful water depicted in the lower-left corner of the window is reminiscent of a symbolic rebirth (see John 3:5) and the spiritual cleansing Christ offers through baptism that is mentioned in many New Testament passages (see Matthew 3:6, 11; John 3:5; Acts 2:38; 8:12–13; 18:8; Romans 6:1–5; Galatians 3:26–27; Colossians 2:12; and 1 Peter 3:21).

14. STONES IN THE WATER AS PRINCIPLES OF THE GOSPEL

On the first Pentecost after Jesus's resurrection, many believers were touched deeply by Peter's message and asked, "What shall we do?" (Acts 2:37). Peter's response was, "Repent and be baptized, every one of you, in the name of Jesus Christ for the forgiveness of your sins. And you will receive the gift of the Holy Spirit" (Acts 2:38). The New Testament has many examples of people who followed a similar pattern; they exercised their faith in God (see Hebrews 11), repented of their sins, were baptized, and then received the Gift of the Holy Spirit (see Matthew 3:6–11; Acts 8:12–17; 19:1–7). In the bottom-left corner of the window, the artists have placed four stones in the water, each representing a part of the "narrow gate" that Jesus referenced in His Sermon on the Mount, cautioning that "only a few find it" (Matthew 7:13–14). The window portrays many people who are at various phases of seeking to come unto Christ by exercising their faith in Him, repenting of their sins, seeking baptism, and living by the light of the Holy Spirit that He promises.

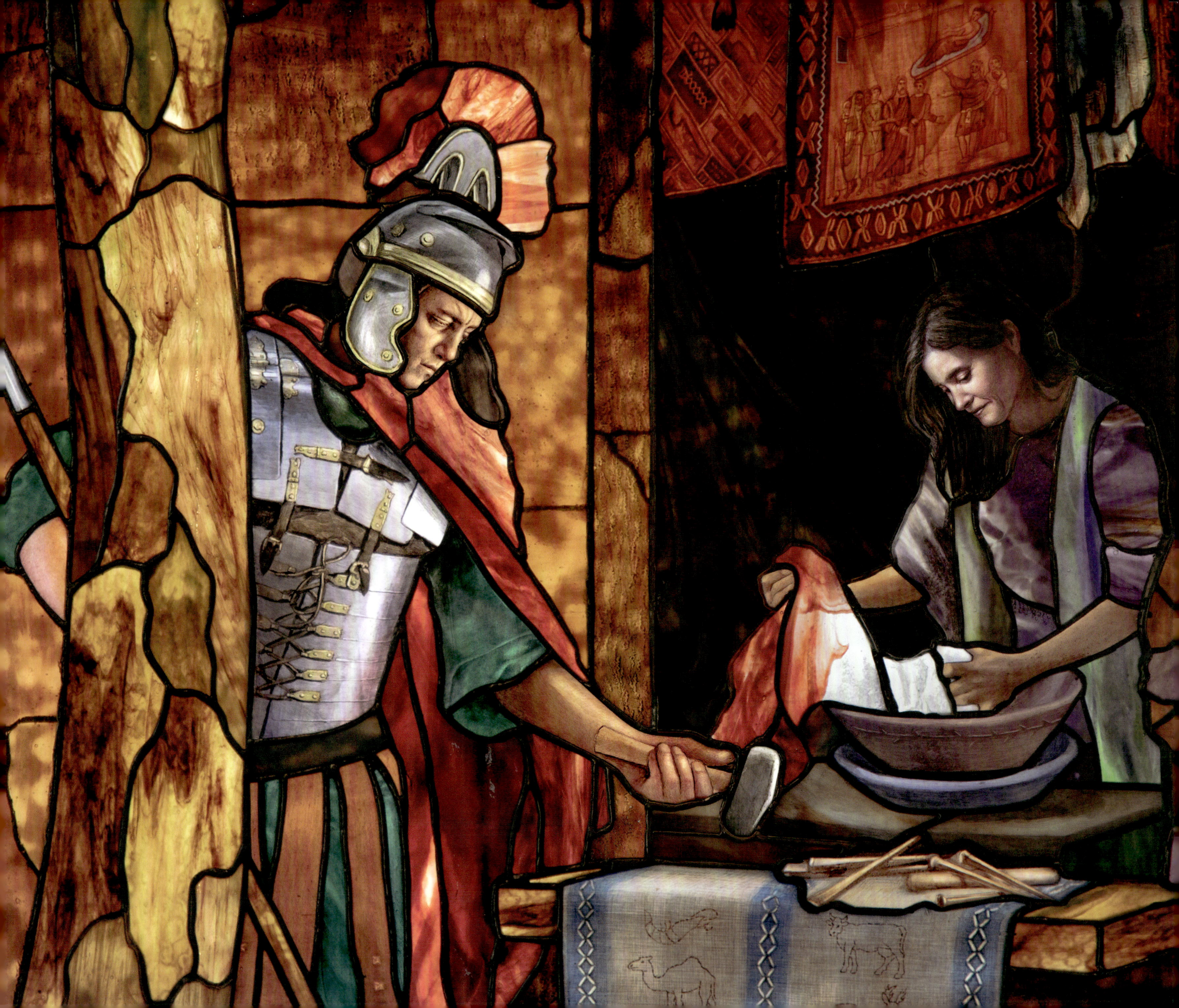

Panel B

Featuring Cornelius and Lydia

REPENTANCE, CONVERSION, AND THE GOSPEL BEING TAKEN TO ALL THE WORLD | 12

1. Zacchaeus the publican or Simon the Zealot
2. Tapestry of man lowered through a roof
3. Cornelius and other centurions
4. Lydia, seller of purple
5. Red cloak becoming white
6. Fig tree
7. Nails and hammer
8. Sheet seen by Peter
9. Stone manger
10. Stem of Jesse
11. Goat separated from the sheep

REPRESENTATIONS OF PAUL | 18

12. Athens and the Acropolis
13. Saul having a vision on the road to Damascus
14. Man holding the stones to kill Stephen and Paul
15. Satchel near Saul
16. Sword on the ground

PROPHETS POINTING TOWARD CHRIST | 20

17. Scroll from the revelation of John
18. Scrolls of Isaiah
19. Handel's *Messiah*
20. A chosen vessel
21. "The Lord Is My Shepherd"
22. Symbols of the twelve tribes of Israel
23. Camel hair, sandals, and honeycomb
24. Praise Psalms
25. Baptism by water and fire
26. Tongs with hot coal
27. Actual gemstones like those on the high priest's breastplate
28. Actual sand from the Holy Land

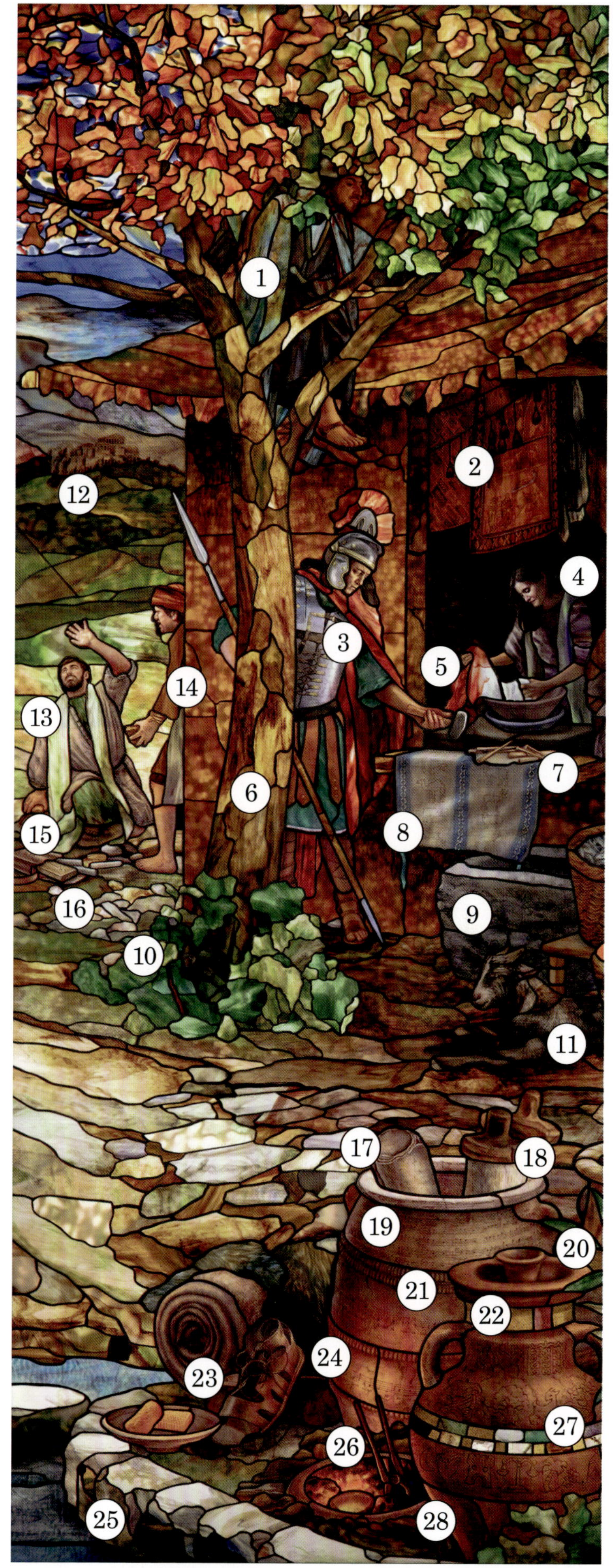

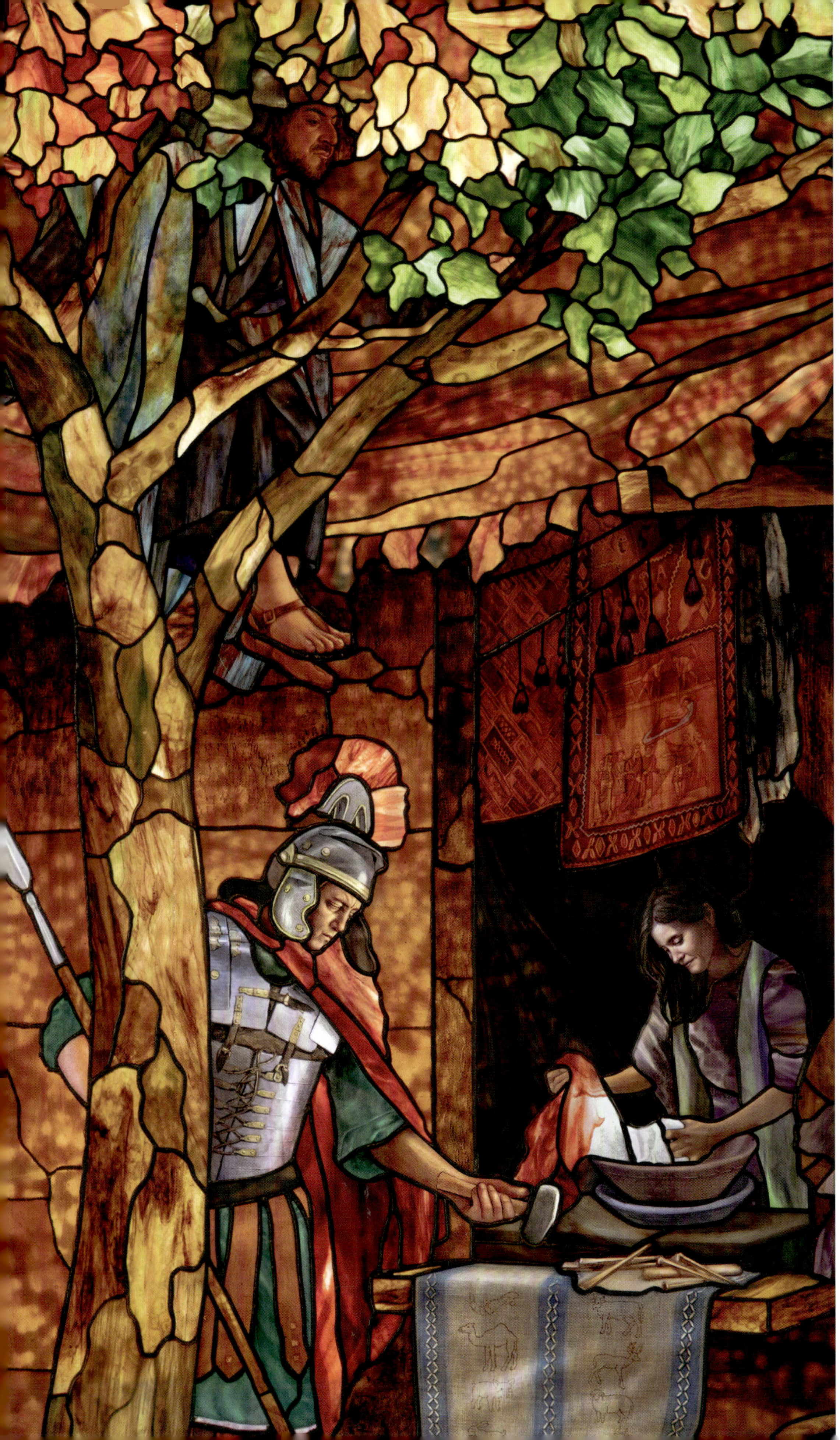

REPENTANCE, CONVERSION, AND THE GOSPEL BEING TAKEN TO ALL THE WORLD

1. ZACCHAEUS THE PUBLICAN OR SIMON THE ZEALOT

If you look closely at the fig tree near the top of panel B, you will notice a man, hidden in the leaves, who is trying to get a glimpse of Jesus. This man, Zacchaeus, was a chief tax collector. People in the Jericho crowd that day would not have looked kindly on the wealthy Zacchaeus or given him an opportunity to get a better view. Because he was short, he chose to climb the tree, perhaps thinking Jesus would simply pass underneath. "When Jesus reached the spot, he looked up and said to him, 'Zacchaeus, come down immediately. I must stay at your house today'" (Luke 19:5). This caused no small stir among the people who had judged Zacchaeus as "a sinner" (Luke 19:7). Zacchaeus seemed to feel unworthy and perhaps a bit apologetic. After defending his honesty and integrity, Jesus promised him that salvation had come to his house, "for the Son of Man came to seek and to save the lost" (Luke 19:10). This interchange became even more significant when we consider that this was the last time Jesus passed through Jericho before ascending to Jerusalem to ultimately be crucified. In our day, what trees are available for us to climb to get a better view of Jesus? How have we been surprised by Him calling out to us in various ways to fulfill His requests? The man in the tree is also a good representation of one of the lesser-known apostles of Jesus, Simon the Zealot (see Matthew 10:4; Mark 3:18; Luke 6:15). In this context, the man has a knife ready to use, symbolic of the Zealots who lurked in the shadows, waiting for opportunities to cause trouble for their Roman occupiers. Simon and Zacchaeus might have been on two opposite extremes of the Jewish spectrum regarding support for Rome, but both were able to find their identity as disciples of Jesus Christ.

2. TAPESTRY OF MAN LOWERED THROUGH A ROOF

In the shop below the tree, there is a beautiful tapestry hanging from the ceiling that depicts the story of a paralyzed man being lowered through the roof so Jesus could heal him. It was impossible for this man to approach Jesus himself, but his friends could bring him. Imagine the effort it took to carry him to the top of the house, make a hole in the roof, and lower him down without dropping him. "When Jesus saw their faith, He said to the man, 'Friend, your sins are forgiven'" (Luke 5:20). How surprised everyone must have been to hear this declaration. In their culture, many believed that a physical ailment or disability was a sign of divine disfavor because of sin. This man had likely been the recipient of many probing questions about what terrible things he or his parents had done to deserve such a debilitating punishment from God. Jesus helped refute their false assumptions by spiritually healing the man without first healing him physically. This caused some in the group to complain about Him claiming authority to forgive sins. Jesus plainly said, "I want you to know that the Son of Man has authority on earth to forgive sins. . . . I tell you, get up, take your mat and go home" (Luke 5:24). This man experienced two miracles that day, a healing for his body and a healing for his soul.

3. CORNELIUS AND OTHER CENTURIONS

Underneath the fig tree stands a roman soldier who represents many different centurions in the New Testament (see Luke 7:1–10; Matthew 27:54; Acts 22:25–29; 23:23; and 27:1–28:16) but the main character portrayed in this instance is Cornelius, the first Gentile convert to Christianity (see Acts 10). Immediately preceding Christ's ascension into heaven, He told His apostles, "Go and make disciples of all nations, baptizing them in the name of the Father and of the Son and of the Holy Spirit" (Matthew 28:19). For a Jew to reach out to Gentiles and welcome them into full religious fellowship was a significant reversal from a law of Moses tradition that dominated Israelite culture for nearly 1,500 years. Years after the Ascension, the apostles still had not taken the gospel to any Gentiles. God accelerated that effort by sending an angel to the "devout and God-fearing" (Acts 10:2) centurion named Cornelius. He was directed to send for Peter, who came and taught him the gospel and then baptized him and many others who were with him. The window portrays Cornelius picking up a hammer that was sitting next to some large nails, symbolic of him accepting Jesus's crucifixion and reminding us of another centurion's words at the cross, "Surely he was the Son of God!" (Matthew 27:54). The spear in his other hand is pointing at a representation of the city of Athens, the cultural embodiment of learning and philosophy in his day. Cornelius has chosen to turn his back on all that Athens represents and in so doing, he symbolically took upon himself the whole armor of God rather than the armor of Rome so imposingly displayed. Artists have filled the window with multiple examples of people either turning toward Christ or embracing the things of the world. In this way the window represents the past, but also becomes a powerful mirror for our lives in the present as well.

4. LYDIA, SELLER OF PURPLE

In keeping with the theme of "firsts" in the New Testament, the woman in the shop represents Lydia, the first European convert mentioned (see Acts 16:13–15). On Paul's second missionary journey, he was directed by the Lord to cross over from modern-day Türkiye to Philippi, located in northern Greece today. After many days of preaching without success, Paul and his companions left the city on the Sabbath and went down to a place of prayer by the river and began speaking with some women assembled there. Lydia, a dealer in purple cloth, was there that day to worship God. "The Lord opened her heart to respond to Paul's message" (Acts 16:14), and she and her household were baptized. Purple dye was so expensive, the cloth was usually associated with royalty and the richest people in society. However, the finest cloth that Lydia's industry could produce couldn't compare with the garment that Christ offers: "I delight greatly in the Lord; my soul rejoices in my God. For he has clothed me with garments of salvation and arrayed me in a robe of his righteousness" (Isaiah 61:10).

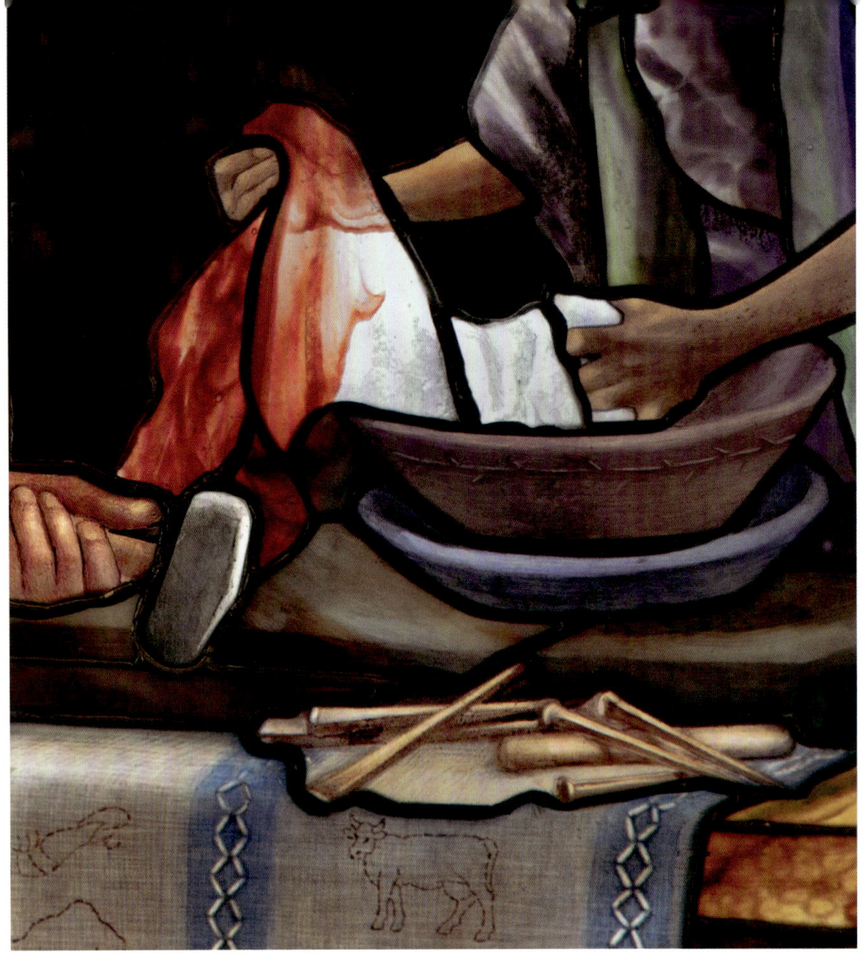

5. RED CLOAK BECOMING WHITE

The woman representing Lydia is washing a piece of red cloth in a bowl. The cloth which is stained red is turning white through the cleansing process. The Lord taught Isaiah, "Though your sins are like scarlet, they shall be as white as snow; though they are red as crimson, they shall be like wool" (1:18). The red and white metaphors are repeated in the vision of John the Revelator when he "saw heaven standing open and there before me was a white horse, whose rider" judges and wages war while wearing many crowns on his head, dressed in a "robe dipped in blood, and his name is the Word of God" (Revelation 19:11–13). Christ, as the heavenly warrior clad in red, is followed by a heavenly throng "riding on white horses and dressed in fine linen, white and clean" (v. 14). The bowl has sharp thorns carved around the outside that symbolize the crown of thorns worn by the King of Kings on the cross. We stain His raiment through our sin and wrongdoing. In return, Jesus can cleanse us and our garments because of His suffering and death. "Surely he took up our pain and bore our suffering. . . . He was pierced for our transgressions, he was crushed for our iniquities; the punishment that brought us peace was on him, and by his wounds we are healed" (Isaiah 53:4–5). The entire window is a reminder that all souls who trust Jesus enough to offer Him their mortal weakness and sins will, in return, be cleansed by His grace and perfection.

6. FIG TREE

The fig tree shows great contrast in the window. Looking at the upper branches, the artists have portrayed all four seasons of the year. Moving from right to left, the leaves and branches all witness of Christ being with us through all phases of our lives. Even when the leaves are dying on the lefthand side and we don't see any fruit, we can now more easily see the branches of the tree that can help us contemplate the wooden cross. Just like the cross, those wooden branches point both heavenward and outward. This creates visual reminders of how Christ demonstrated the two great commandments to turn upward through our love of God and to turn outward in our love of our neighbors (see Mark 12:28–31; Matthew 22:37–39). This fig tree is also symbolic of the fall of Adam and Eve. Once they had partaken of the forbidden fruit, "the eyes of both of them were opened, and they realized they were naked; so they sewed fig leaves together and made coverings for themselves" (Genesis 3:7). Because fig leaves are large, they dry out and shrivel quickly. They also have scratchy hair follicles and would not have been the most comfortable thing to use for clothing, but it was the best they could do. God lovingly replaced their feeble efforts with "garments of skin" (3:21). This implies that an animal had to die to provide a covering for their nakedness. That animal had surely done nothing wrong and didn't deserve to die. And so it is, that even before they had been banished from the Garden of Eden, they were learning their first tangible lessons about their redemption that would come through the sacrifice of the Lamb of God, even Christ the Lord. In the overall window, contrast the branches of the fig tree in the upper-left corner with the beautiful Easter lilies in the bottom-right corner. The line connecting these two symbols, like everything else that really matters, passes through Jesus Christ and His tomb in the center of the window.

7. NAILS AND HAMMER

The nails on the table and the hammer in the centurion's hand remind us of the suffering that Jesus endured at the hands of cruel men. The artists placed the nails in a strategic way. Directly behind them, we see the bowl with thorns, in which we see Lydia washing a stained cloth. As part of the preparations for His crucifixion, the Roman soldiers scourged Him, placed a crown of thorns on His head, and mockingly covered Him with a robe. Matthew said it was scarlet (see 27:27–28) while Mark (see 15:16–17) and John (see 19:1–2) both identify it as a purple robe. Both colors are symbolized in that part of the window. Lydia is a seller of purple, and the cloth she is purifying is blood red. After arriving at Golgotha, the soldiers took His clothes (see John 19:23) and nailed Him to the cross. The irony of that moment is that Jesus, the Word of God, had created all things in the heavens and the earth, including the wood for that cross and the elements that would become those nails and hammer. Now they were being used as the instrument of death for the great Creator. Considering His power and abilities over the elements of His creation, was it really the nails that held Him bound to the cross that day? Or was it something much more powerful and lasting than steel? His perfect love for us held Him fastened there until He could say, "It is finished" (John 19:30) and give up His spirit.

8. SHEET SEEN BY PETER

It was noon on the day after Cornelius had seen the angel and sent three men to find Simon Peter in Joppa. Peter was at the house of Simon the tanner where he went up on the roof to pray. There, he "fell into a trance. He saw heaven opened and something like a large sheet being let down to earth by its four corners. It contained all kinds of four-footed animals" (Acts 10:10–12). A voice told Peter to "kill and eat" (v. 13). The problem with this command was that many of the animals in the sheet were considered unclean under the Mosaic law of that day. Peter was revolted by the idea of eating non-kosher meat. The voice responded, "Do not call anything impure that God has made clean" (v. 15). The same vision and dialogue recurred three times, and left Peter puzzling over the vision until Cornelius's three servants arrived at the door asking for him. For nearly 1,500 years, faithful Israelites had limited their contact and interactions with Gentiles. Welcoming them into one's home or traveling with them and staying in their homes would cause a person to be considered unclean. Worse yet would be to share a meal with them. The interpretation of Peter's vision soon became clear—the unclean animals in the vision were symbolic placeholders for the Gentiles. The time had finally come for Peter to break with all the old traditions of the law and treat all people as being worthy of God's love. In the window, the cloth on the table next to Cornelius shows a variety of embroidered animals, with those that were considered unclean on the left and those considered clean on the right. The sheet is in the style of a blue-and-white prayer shawl representing the house of David and signifying the prayers that were offered by both Cornelius and Peter. This symbol of cleansing connects the nails above with the stone manger below showing that Christ was born to heal and save through His sacrifice. This singular event opened the door for the preaching of His gospel in all the world, which continues to this day.

9. STONE MANGER

Underneath Peter's cloth sheet, artists have portrayed a stone manger—or feeding trough for animals. In the Holy Land where wood is scarce, mangers were made of stone. Because there was no room for Mary and Joseph in the inns of Bethlehem, the couple was relegated to a stable where Mary brought forth her firstborn son (see Luke 2:7). After Jesus was born, Mary wrapped Him in cloth before placing Him in a manger. The sheet above the manger reminds us of His sacred arrival, the stars shining down on the scene, and the angel proclaiming His birth to the shepherds seen in panel A. The Lord willingly left His heavenly throne to join us in a simple manger in a stable. He was Immanuel, which means "God with us" (Matthew 1:23), who truly descended below all things. He became one of us to take upon Himself all the effects of the Fall of Adam and Eve that we experience. Another symbolic connection is displayed in the window with the stone altar to the unknown God in panel I. The baby Jesus was truly an unknown God to all but a small handful of people and the heavenly throng that first night. One day all will know Him. Long after the baby grew, that crude cradle was a silent witness that "God so loved the world that he gave his one and only Son, that whoever believes in him shall not perish but have eternal life" (John 3:16). The empty cradle, along with an empty tomb, testifies that even though He ascended to heaven nearly 2,000 years ago, He would still be Immanuel for us: "And surely I am with you always, to the very end of the age" (Matthew 28:20).

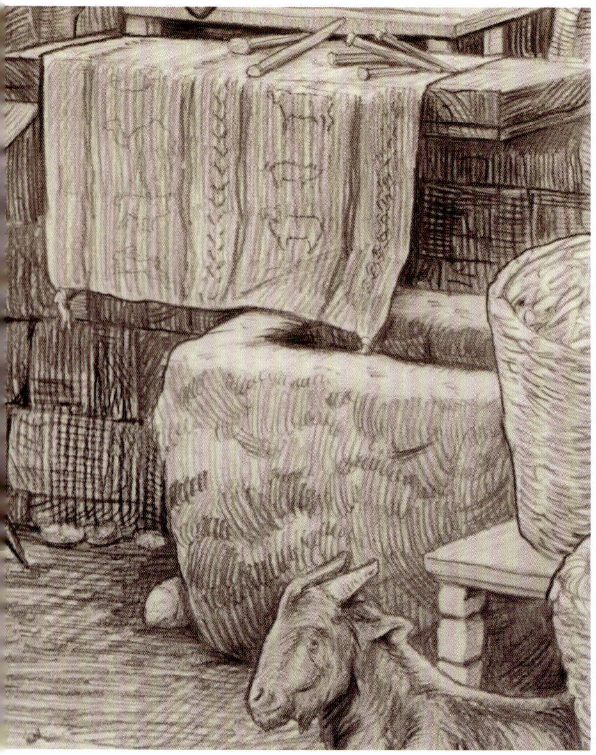

10. STEM OF JESSE

Near the base of the fig tree is a small shoot growing out of the roots. Isaiah prophesied that "a shoot will come up from the stump of Jesse; from his roots a Branch will bear fruit" (Isaiah 11:1). Jesse was the father of King David. David was promised that his posterity would reign in Israel forever and God would raise up a righteous descendent to secure all the covenant promises (see 2 Samuel 7; Ezekiel 34:23). In Matthew 1, Joseph was instructed to take Mary and the Son of God as his own and name Him (vv. 20–21). Joseph is shown to be a direct descendent of King David (v. 6). Jesus Christ is the stem that would grow out of the root of Jesse, even after the House of Israel was cut down, and all hope was seemingly lost for redemption. The whole panoramic window shows countless examples of Isaiah's additional prophecies of what Jesus would do. Truly the earth will be filled with the knowledge of the Lord (see Isaiah 11:2–5, 9).

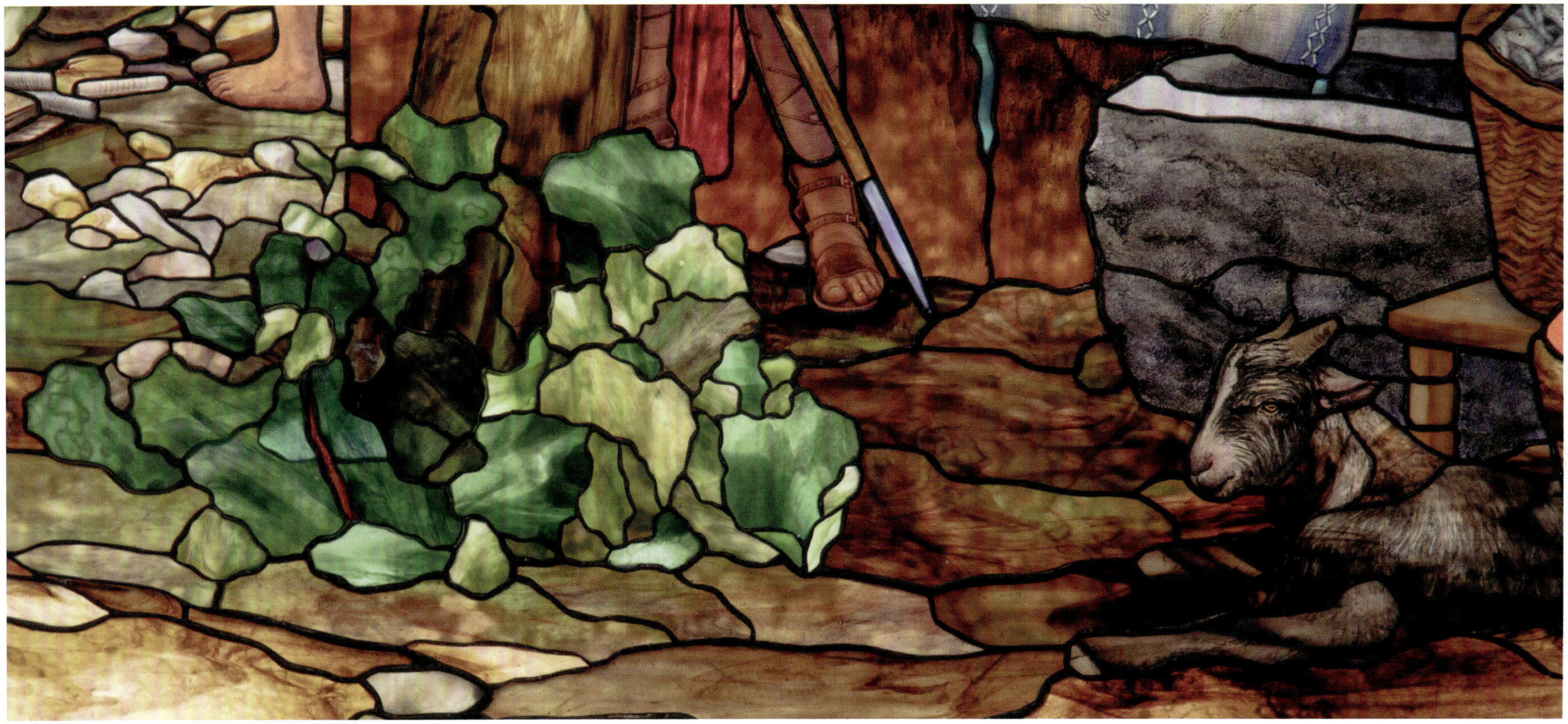

11. GOAT SEPARATED FROM THE SHEEP

Near the end of His life, Jesus gave indications that He would soon be departing, but He promised that He would come again at the end of time. In private, His disciples asked Him when that would occur and what signs they should look for (see Matthew 24:3). He gave them a long list of prophecies followed by three parables to help disciples better prepare for His coming. He introduced the third parable by saying, "When the Son of Man comes in his glory, . . . he will separate the people one from another as a shepherd separates the sheep from the goats. He will put the sheep on his right and the goats on his left" (Matthew 25:31–33). He describes the sheep as those who fed Him when He was hungry, welcomed Him when He was a stranger, clothed His nakedness, ministered to Him when sick, and visited Him in prison. When no one could remember doing any of that for the Lord, "The King will reply, 'Truly I tell you, whatever you did for one of the least of these brothers and sisters of mine, you did for me'" (Matthew 25:40). The goats in the parable were those who did none of those loving things to their fellow beings. On the right side of panel F, we see a sheep attentively standing in contrast to the goat passively lying on the ground on the left side of the window in panel B. These two animals represent two opposite approaches we can choose to take when presented with people having various needs every day. This contrast reminds us that *love* is much more than just a feeling to be absorbed—it is an action to be shared and magnified.

REPRESENTATIONS OF PAUL

12. ATHENS AND THE ACROPOLIS

The might of Rome and the wisdom of mankind are both symbolically portrayed in the Greco-Roman city on the hill in the background of panel B. Greek philosophies and architecture permeated the Mediterranean world of that day. The Romans had adopted much of the Greek worldview, as reflected in the language, politics, theater, pagan worship, and culture that dominated the Jews at the time of Christ. Near the bottom of panel I, we see the altar to the unknown god—the ultimate embodiment of the pagan religion and culture of that day. An imaginary line runs between that altar and the Acropolis in panel B, where the altar was found on Mars Hill by Paul. That same line passes through "the Messiah, the Son of the living God" (Matthew 16:16). The world today continues to offer us a pantheon of gods to worship, but none of these counterfeit gods or worldly pursuits can offer us anything that will ultimately last or connect us with the only One who has power to save us.

13. SAUL HAVING A VISION ON THE ROAD TO DAMASCUS

As Saul approached the city of Damascus to take prisoners of the early followers of Christ, "suddenly a light from heaven flashed around him" (Acts 9:3). He fell to the ground as portrayed by the man on the left in panel B. Thus began one of the greatest conversions in scripture. Saul, the devout Jewish pharisee who was a persecutor of Christians, would soon begin using his Roman name of Paul and become one of the most powerful witnesses for Christ in all the world. This story shows us that one's level of conviction to a cause is not always an indicator of ultimate truth. Saul was confident that he was on the Lord's errand by persecuting Christians. However, he was to be taught: "'My thoughts are not your thoughts, neither are your ways my ways,' declares the Lord. 'As the heavens are higher than the earth, so are my ways higher than your ways and my thoughts than your thoughts'" (Isaiah 55:8–9). The window portrays Saul as looking up to the light. His experience on the road to Damascus started this upward-looking process for Paul, and he kept looking up throughout the rest of his life, especially when he experienced terrible setbacks, pains, and trials (see 2 Corinthians 11:24–26). One of those trials occurred on Paul's first missionary journey in Lystra, when he found himself on the ground again, this time surrounded by angry men stoning him (see Acts 14:19). Ironically, Saul had stood by and watched as an angry mob had "laid their coats at [Saul's] feet" (Acts 7:58) and stoned Stephen. The man in the window has one hand on a stone and one hand stretched heavenward, representing the two contrasting parts of Paul's life and representing the Savior's offer to all: to help us become new creations in Him (see 2 Corinthians 5:17).

14. MAN HOLDING THE STONES TO KILL STEPHEN AND PAUL

The man standing to the left of the centurion represents all those men who stoned both Stephen (see Acts 7:54–60) and Paul (see Acts 14:19). The man is partially hidden behind the building, symbolizing the shame that comes whenever we fight against the work of God. Wrapped around the man's left wrist is a snake bracelet, symbolizing the devil's power to tempt. This also symbolizes Satan's attempts to counterfeit the healing power of God as modeled by Moses holding up the brass snake on a pole (see Numbers 21:8).

15. SATCHEL NEAR SAUL

To the left of Saul, there is a satchel filled with arrest warrants and a copy of the scriptures. Both items in the satchel represent his work as a Pharisee and his deep study of the Hebrew Bible. As he turned his life over to Jesus, the scrolls and books then represent the many epistles he wrote and the scriptures he studied and taught. The satchel is marked with the famous symbol of the Roman Empire, signifying

Paul's Roman citizenship. That certification would allow him to do things that other Jews and Christians of that day could not. For instance, Paul and Silas were arrested, beaten, and imprisoned in Philippi, which should not have happened to Roman citizens. They used this injustice to further the work in that city (see Acts 16:25–40). Near the end of his ministry, Paul was being judged of Festus when he invoked a privilege only afforded to Roman citizens, appealing to be judged by Caesar in Rome (see Acts 25:7–12). Paul could have used his citizenship to great personal advantage, but instead he chose to use it in ways that would cost him dearly but would further God's work.

16. SWORD ON THE GROUND

Near the satchel is a sword on the ground. This is a foreshadowing that one day Paul would face a martyr's death. The fallen world has always resisted the truth from God and sought to silence the followers of Christ through the threat of violence or death. Gratefully, the Lord invites His followers to "be strong in the Lord and in his mighty power. Put on the full armor of God, so that you can take your stand against the devil's schemes. For our struggle is not against flesh and blood, but against the rulers, against the authorities, against the powers of this dark world and against the spiritual forces of evil in the heavenly realms" (Ephesians 6:10–12). Paul's description of the whole armor of God consists mostly of defensive armor (vv. 14–17). There is only one predominantly offensive weapon he mentions: "The sword of the Spirit, which is the word of God" (v. 17). The epistle to the Hebrews describes the word of God as "alive and active. Sharper than any double-edged sword, it penetrates even to dividing soul and spirit, joints and marrow" (Hebrews 4:12). Although the sword portrayed on the ground has power to take mortal life, the sword of the Spirit has the power to penetrate spiritual hearts and help followers of Christ to "stand firm" in their faith (Ephesians 6:14), even when that faith might cost them dearly from a worldly perspective.

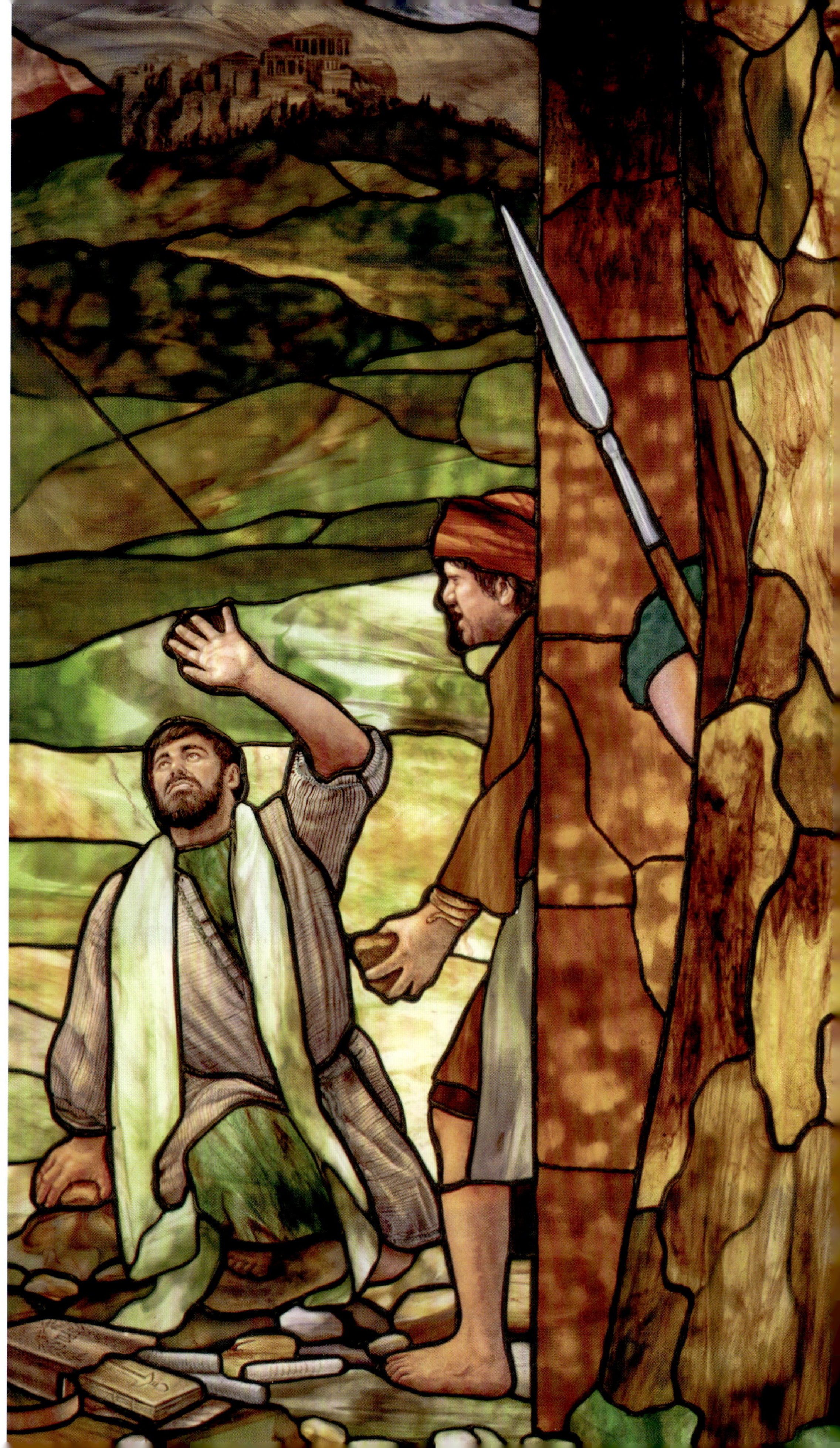

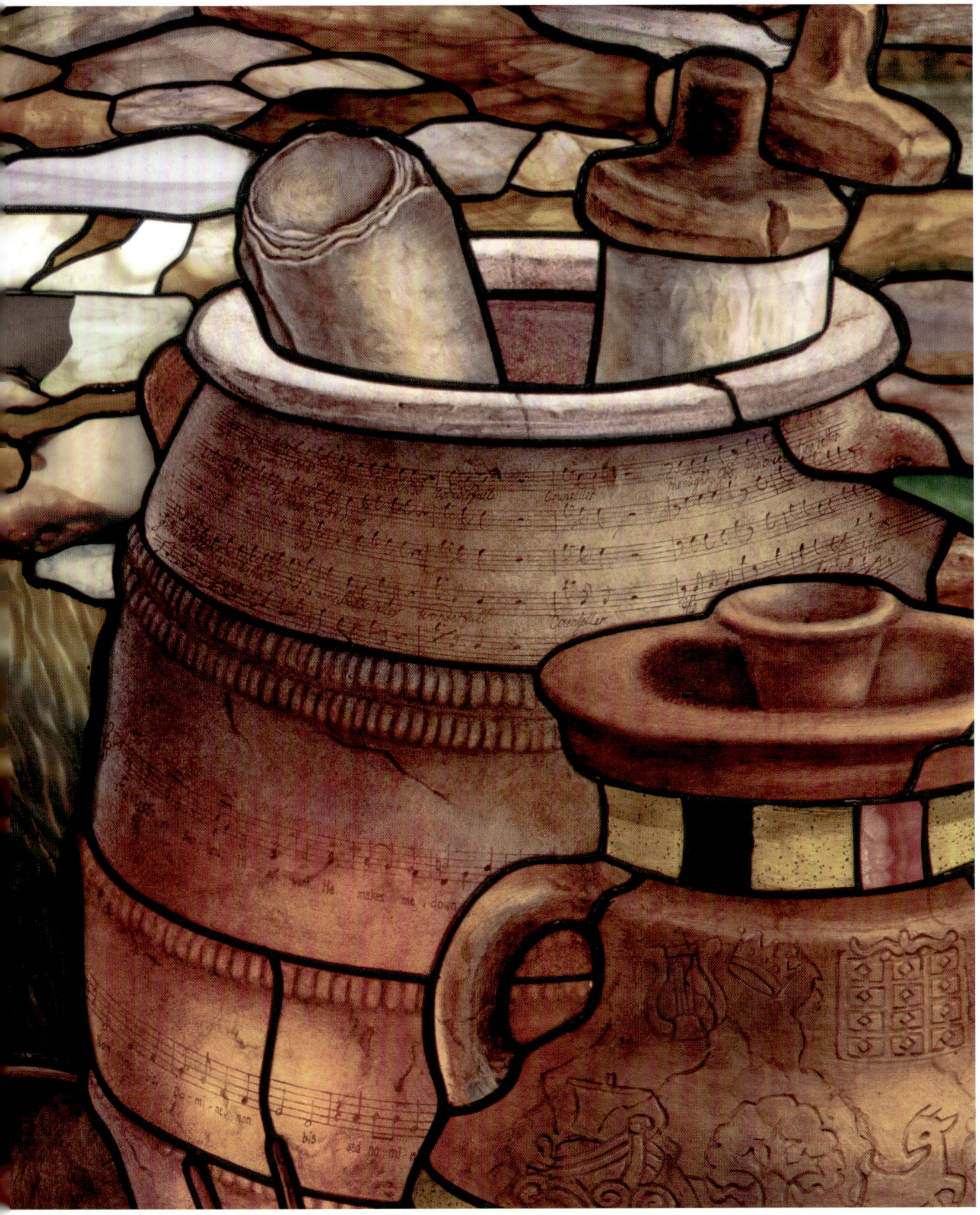

PROPHETS POINTING TOWARD CHRIST

17. SCROLL FROM THE REVELATION OF JOHN

In John's vision of heaven, he "saw in the right hand of him who sat on the throne a scroll with writing on both sides and sealed with seven seals" (Revelation 5:1). At first, there was none found in heaven or the earth who could open the scroll and allow the history of the earth to unfold. John was comforted when one of the elders in the vision informed him that the Lion of the tribe of Judah would triumph to open the seals. When John looked, however, he saw a lamb who "went and took the scroll from the right hand of him who sat on the throne" (v. 7) and opened the seals, one by one. Later in the vision, John sees another little scroll being held by an angel who tells him to eat it. It was sweet in his mouth but bitter in his stomach (see Revelation 10:9–10). To the left of the jar holding the scroll, we see a depiction of honey to represent this part of the vision. How many things in life cause us to experience moments of sweetness but include hardships? The opposite is also true. Often, we experience trials and setbacks that are bitter but in the long run become sweet. Both are learning opportunities that connect us with God.

18. SCROLLS OF ISAIAH

The window portrays a large scroll in the clay jar next to the Revelation scroll. Beginning in 1947, large clay pots began to be discovered in caves at Qumran that contained many sacred writings dating back to the centuries right before and after the time of Christ. These writings, now known as the Dead Sea Scrolls, largely consisted of Old Testament books. One of the first discovered, and the one that ended up being the largest and most complete writing found in the collection, was the Great Isaiah Scroll. Isaiah is also one of the most quoted prophets of all time. The apostle Paul taught that a person's mind would be made dull, and they would read the Old Testament through a veil unless they were clearly looking for Christ in the symbols and prophecies from the past (see 2 Corinthians 3:14). This is especially true when studying Isaiah's words. The large scroll in the window is a reminder to read Isaiah's words and look for their ultimate fulfilment in Christ's life and teachings.

19. HANDEL'S *MESSIAH*

Few works of music are more recognizable in the Christian world than George Frideric Handel's *Messiah*. The person who assembled the scriptures for that great work was Charles Jennens. He used King James Version passages from 14 different biblical books, but none more than Isaiah (21 separate verses). Around the top of the clay jar, the artists have portrayed the music from Handel's work that highlights the text from Isaiah 9:6: "For unto us a child is born." The specific words that appear are from the same verse, "His name shall be called Wonderful, Counsellor, The mighty God, The everlasting Father." The beginning and the ending parts of that significant verse did not fit on the visible part of the jar. Those words, though not visible in the window, reveal significant elements of Christ's identity and mission, "For unto us a child is born, unto us a son is given," which is portrayed by the manger as well as the cloth that wrapped up God's gift of love for us, depicted above the jar. "And the government shall be upon his shoulder" is a stark reminder that all worldly leaders and governments will one day be overthrown and replaced by Jesus Christ Himself. This is symbolically portrayed by following the line created by the spear in the soldier's hand that, if extended, connects the words on this jar with the city of Athens representing all kingdoms and glories of the world. The last phrase of this verse is also missing from the jar but is majestically portrayed not in words but by the central feature of the window—Jesus Christ, "the Prince of Peace."

20. A CHOSEN VESSEL

Vessels and instruments are often used in the Bible to represent servants of the Lord who are called to do His work or to carry something special to the world or a specific group of people. Paul was called a "chosen vessel unto me, to bear my name before the Gentiles, and kings, and the children of Israel" (KJV, Acts 9:15). Abraham and Sarah were such vessels and instruments in the Lord's hands in ancient times. The decorative pot sitting to the right of the clay pot represents this significant couple who were promised a large posterity, great lands, and great influence throughout the world (see Genesis 17:3–8). Four thousand years later, we all have access to those great promises given to the father and mother of all the faithful. Few were more faithful than a young handmaid of the Lord who became one of history's greatest chosen vessels for the son she would bear and bring forth for all of God's children. All these people are symbolic reminders of the greatest chosen vessel of all time: Jesus Christ. He embodies all that is true, noble, right, pure, lovely, admirable, excellent, or praiseworthy (see Philippians 4:8).

21. "THE LORD IS MY SHEPHERD"

Halfway down the clay pot on the left, the artists have included the words and music to a second song, "The Lord Is My Shepherd," from Psalm 23. Many elements from panels A and B are reflected in that psalm: shepherds, green pastures, quiet waters, refreshing foods, right paths, a dark valley, a rod and staff, and a table prepared in the presence of enemies. Having been raised as an active participant in Jewish traditions and feasts, Jesus was no stranger to the songs in the book of Psalms, and He quoted from them more than any other book in the Old Testament. He was familiar with the praise psalms. He would have also known the songs of Thanksgiving and the songs of ascension at the temple. On the cross, He quoted Psalm 22:1, "My God, my God, why have you forsaken me?" That verse continues: "Why are you so far from saving me, so far from the cries of anguish?" This part of the window is a recognition that some of the gospel's greatest truths cannot be communicated with prose alone, and that is why God has given us the gift of inspired poetry and music to help open additional windows to our soul.

22. SYMBOLS OF THE TWELVE TRIBES OF ISRAEL

On the beautiful jar to the right of the clay pot, the artists have portrayed one version of many possible symbols used to represent the twelve tribes of Israel or sons of Jacob. The symbols are described from top to bottom and left to right as follows: The harp and the crown are the symbols for Judah because of one of his most famous descendants, King David. The breastplate with twelve stones represents the tribe of Levi, whose direct descendants would be appointed to be the high priest and wear this breastplate as part of their priestly responsibilities in the tabernacle and, later, in the temple. The boat represents Zebulon because his tribal land was between the Sea of Galilee and the Mediterranean Sea. The olive tree represents the tribe of Asher because they were known for their olive oil production. The gazelle represents Naphtali who were traditionally known as fast runners. The mandrakes represent Reuben because they symbolize fertility, and he was the firstborn son. Issachar is represented by a sun and moon because his tribe was known for their gift of scholarship and for creating the Israelite calendar. The jug and ladle represent Benjamin, the smallest tribe and the last-born son of Jacob. The tower represents the warlike might of Simeon. Dan, whose name in Hebrew means *judge*, is represented by the scales of justice and judgment. Joseph's tribe was divided in two when Israel adopted his two sons Manasseh and Ephraim. Before that division, Joseph is symbolized by a palm tree and fruit because "the righteous will flourish like a palm tree" (Psalm 92:12) and be a fruitful bough. The tent represents Gad because they settled on the east of the Jordan River and frequently defended the land from outside armies.

Symbolic representation lies at the heart of pieces of art like this window. Every object and person you see in these panels is a placeholder for the real thing they represent. Our very lives can likewise become symbolic placeholders for those around us to see more and more of Christ's goodness shining through as we increasingly believe in Him and follow Him.

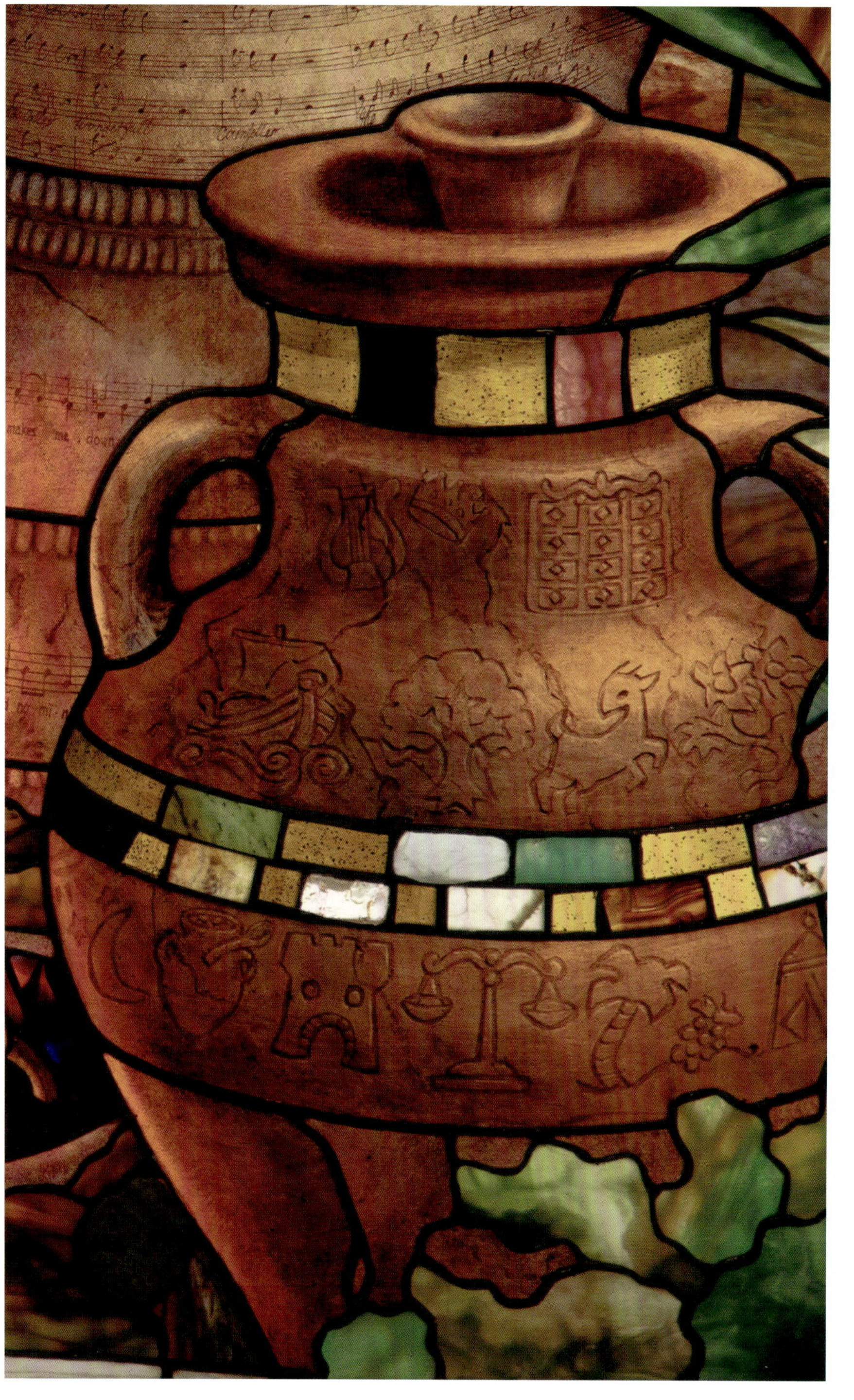

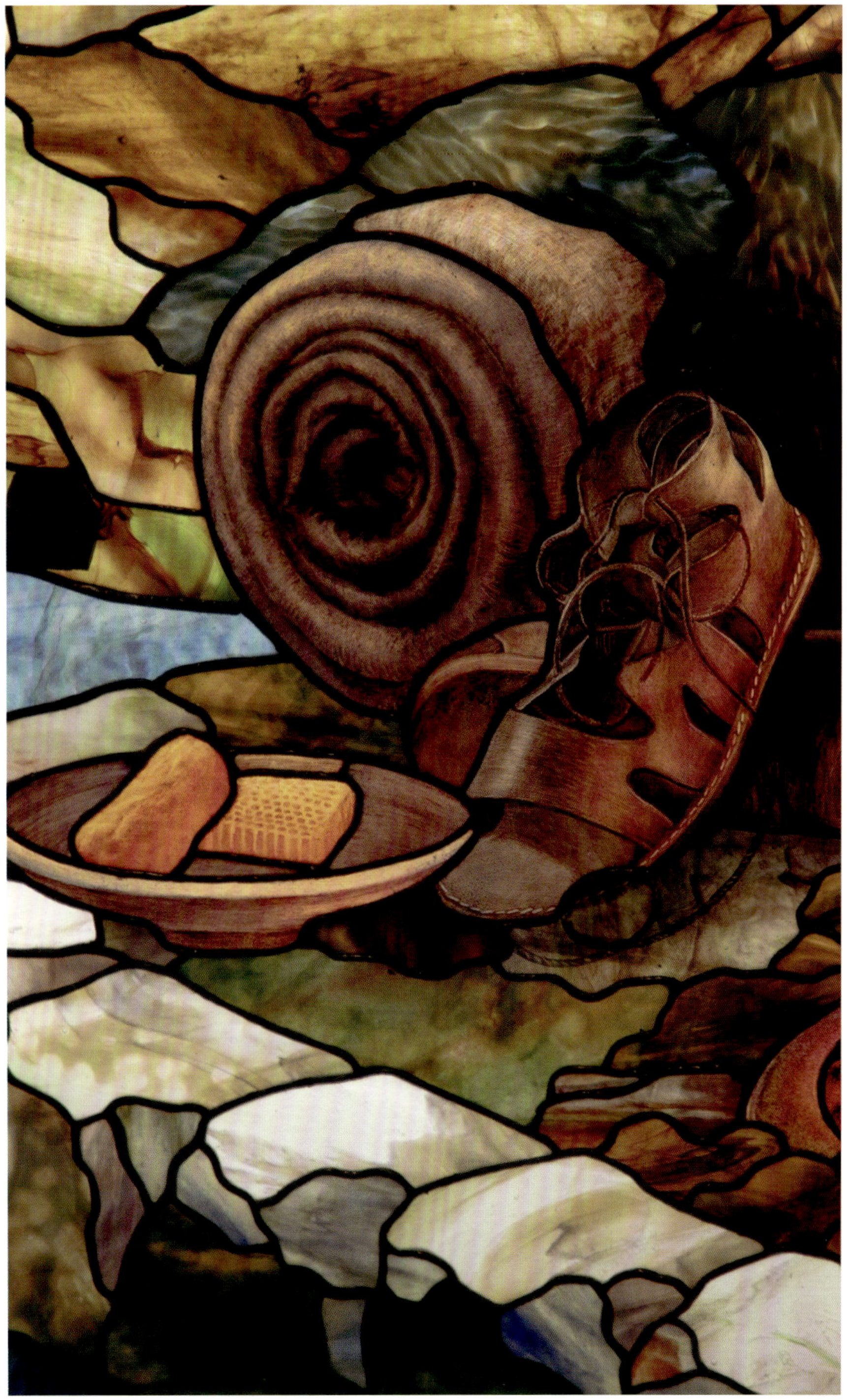

23. CAMEL HAIR, SANDALS, AND HONEYCOMB

Near the water's edge, the artists have placed certain objects together that all represent John the Baptist. John's mission was to be the forerunner of Jesus and prepare the way before Him. He lived in the wilderness, hence the bedroll. He dressed in camel's hair. He ate locusts and wild honey (see Matthew 3:4). When Jesus was ready to begin His ministry, He came to John, who claimed that he was not worthy to even carry Jesus's sandals, which can be seen to the right of the honeycomb. "As soon as Jesus was baptized, he went up out of the water. At that moment heaven was opened, and he saw the Spirit of God descending like a dove and alighting on him. And a voice from heaven said, 'This is my Son, whom I love; with him I am well pleased'" (Matthew 3:16–17). Of this man who didn't enjoy any of the fineries of this world or the societal comforts of his day, Jesus said, "Truly I tell you, among those born of women there has not risen anyone greater than John the Baptist" (Matthew 11:11). John summed up his whole life's purpose and gave us something to consider applying to ourselves as well when he said, "[Jesus] must become greater; I must become less" (John 3:30).

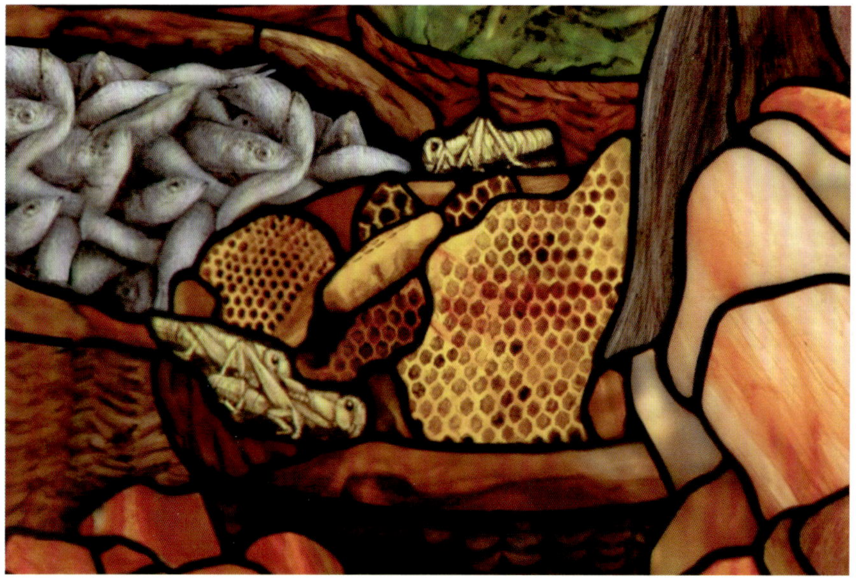

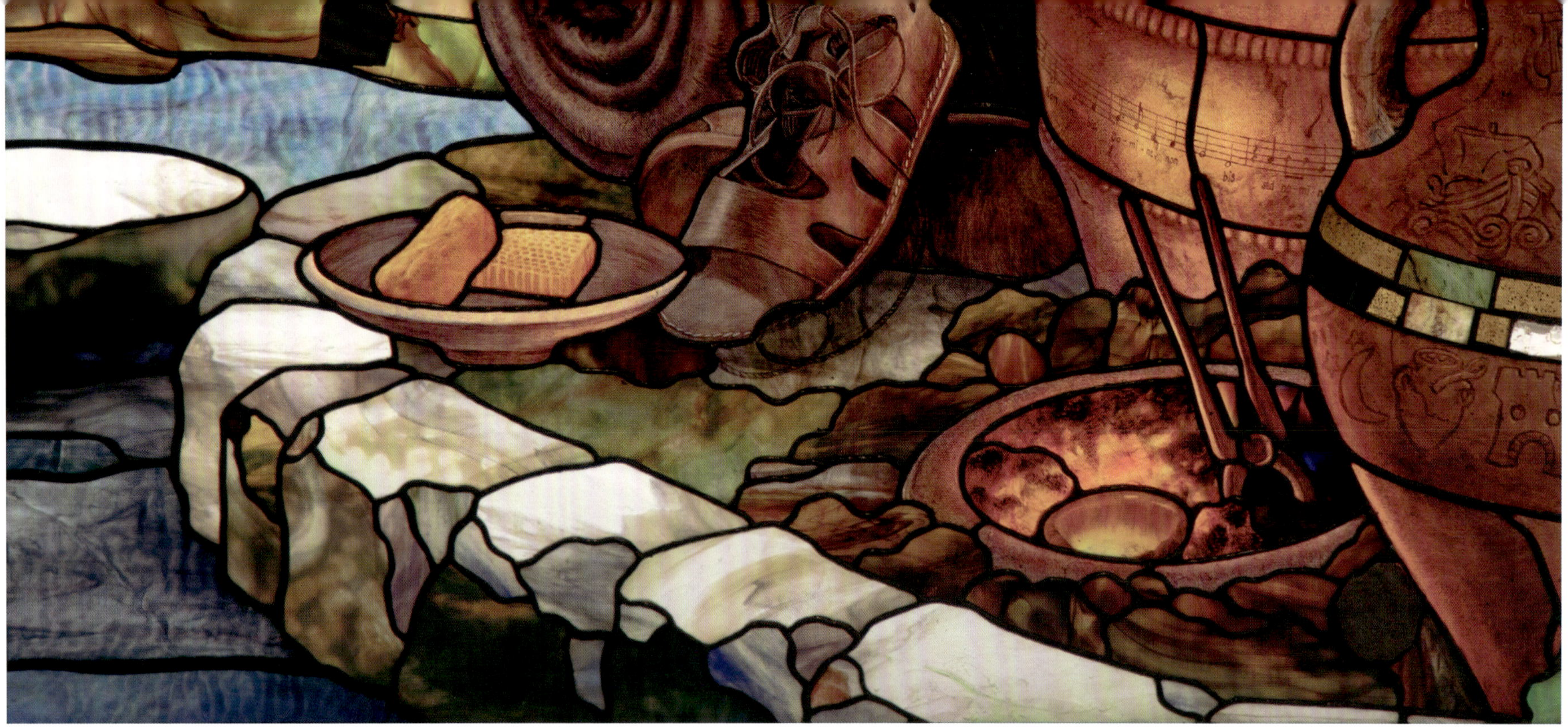

24. PRAISE PSALMS

Next time you hear the Hallelujah Chorus from Handel's *Messiah*, ponder the significance of the word. *Hallel* means "to praise" and *Jah* is the root for "Jahweh," or the name of God in the Old Testament. *Hallelujah* literally means to "praise Jehovah." At every feast or festival of each year, including at His Last Supper, Jesus would have sung the Hallel hymns (Psalms 113–118; 136). On the large clay pot, the artists have included a few lines from Psalm 115, "To your name be the glory" (v. 1). The rest of that psalm contrasts the living God with His power and mercy alongside the false idols of that day who could not speak, see, hear, or move. It is meaningful to carefully read through the Hallel hymns and recognize how much God has done for us. The act of worshipfully praising God benefits us far more than it benefits Him!

25. BAPTISM BY WATER AND FIRE

Near the bottom of panel B, we see the purifying waters of baptism located near purifying coals of a fire at the base of the pots. The symbolism of both baptisms reminds us of a two-step purifying process. Water can cleanse external soil and stains, but fire has the capacity to purge and purify internal and microscopic impurities. John the Baptist promised his disciples that Jesus would extend his baptism of water by baptizing them "with the Holy Spirit and fire" (Matthew 3:11).

26. TONGS WITH HOT COAL

The artists have depicted some metal tongs in the fire with the hot coals. When Isaiah was having his vision of God in the Temple, he was intimidated by the glory of God represented by angels and smoke that filled the temple. He cried aloud that he was "a man of unclean lips and [lived] among a people of unclean lips" (Isaiah 6:5). One of the angels in the temple "flew to [Isaiah] with a live coal in his hand, which he had taken with tongs from the altar" (v. 6). He touched the live coal to Isaiah's mouth and reassured him that through the Atonement of Christ his guilt was purged (see v. 7). Fire can destroy and consume or purify and cleanse depending on the object it touches. For those who love the Lord and want to follow Him, the baptism of fire is purifying. For the wicked who reject His love and teachings, His presence will be "a consuming fire" (Hebrews 12:29). The Psalmist asked the question, "Who may ascend [to the temple]? Who may stand in his holy place?" (Psalm 24:3). The response applies to Isaiah and can apply to all of us as well: "The one who has clean hands and a pure heart, who does not trust in an idol or swear by a false god" (v. 4).

27. ACTUAL GEMSTONES LIKE THOSE ON THE HIGH PRIEST'S BREASTPLATE

The window contains actual gemstones like those found on the high priest's breastplate in Moses's time. Each stone had one of the names of the twelve sons of Israel written on it (see Exodus 28:15–21). Additionally, the high priest carried two other stones on his shoulders with six tribal names inscribed on each (see Exodus 28:9–12). These tribes have been scattered through time, and the promises are that Christ will gather them all back to Him in our time. The epistle to the Hebrews teaches: "Since we have a great high priest who has ascended into heaven, Jesus the Son of God, let us hold firmly to the faith we profess. For we do not have a high priest who is unable to empathize with our weaknesses, but we have one who has been tempted in every way, just as we are—yet he did not sin" (Hebrews 4:14–15). Jesus Christ has borne our sins on His shoulders and carries us in His heart as He enters the ultimate Holy of Holies, Heaven. The epistle continues, "Let us then approach God's throne of grace with confidence, so that we may receive mercy and find grace to help us in our time of need" (Hebrews 4:16). Jesus came into the world to be *our* high priest, to save, redeem, reclaim, and carry us.

28. ACTUAL SAND FROM THE HOLY LAND

When God established His covenant with Abraham and Sarah (see Genesis 12, 15, and 17), many promises were made to that faithful couple. Those promises were reestablished with their son Isaac, "I will be with you and will bless you. . . . I will make your descendants as numerous as the stars in the sky and will give them all these lands, and through your offspring all nations on earth will be blessed" (Genesis 26:3–4). God continued the covenant promises to Jacob, Abraham's grandson, as well, saying, "I will surely make you prosper and will make your descendants like the sand of the sea, which cannot be counted" (Genesis 32:12). These must have seemed like lofty promises indeed for the ancient patriarchs and matriarchs. The stars in the sky and the sands of the sea invoke imagery of incomprehensible numbers. Looking at the world today, three major religious traditions claim Abraham as their ancestor: Jews, Christians, and Muslims. In the window, the artists have included some grains of sand on the glass from the Holy Land as a reminder of the far-reaching effects of the promises God made 4,000 years ago to an aged couple with no children who were well beyond the child-bearing years. God keeps His promises!

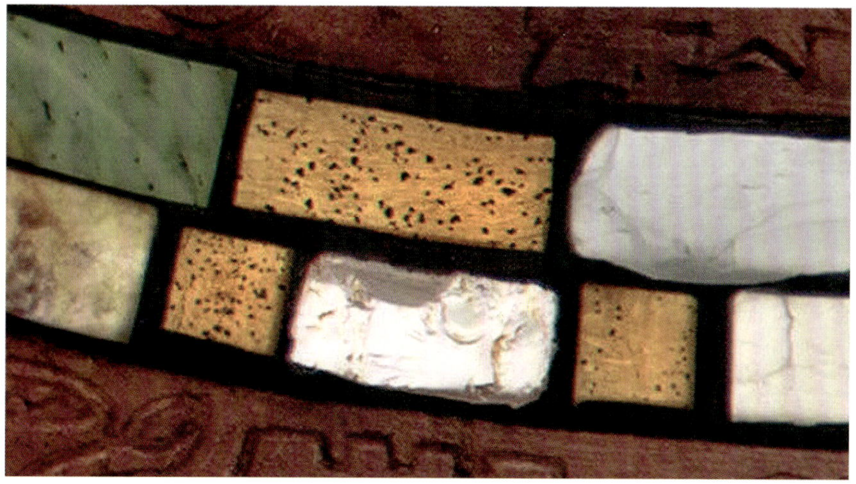

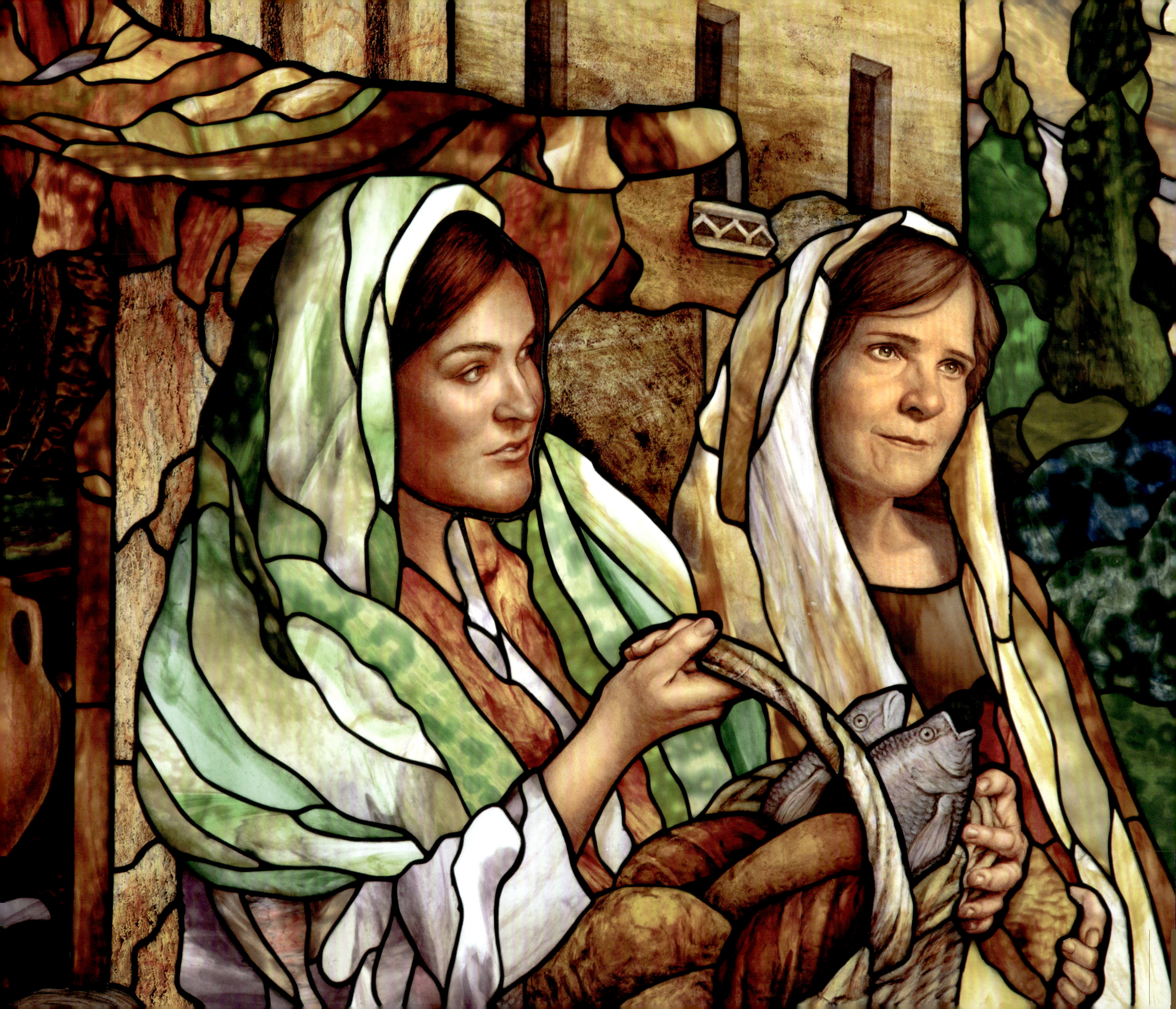

Panel C

Featuring Mary and Martha

CHRIST'S ANCESTRY, HOME, AND TIMES | 28

1. Barren fig tree
2. Roman soldier
3. *Dalet vav dalet*, Hebrew for "David"
4. Net calling to mind the Sea of Galilee

SYMBOLIC FOOD, DRINK, AND CLOTHING | 30

5. The rich young ruler
6. New bottles for new wine
7. Purple robe
8. Parable of the marriage feast
9. Wild honey and locusts
10. Pomegranates

CHOICES AND MIRACLES | 32

11. Martha troubled about many things
12. Mary choosing the good part
13. Coin in fish's mouth
14. Fish from the Sea of Galilee
15. Bread of Life
16. Jairus's daughter

VESSELS AND PLANTS | 36

17. Wine representing Communion and Christ's first recorded miracle
18. Lion of Judah
19. Modern-day hyssop plants
20. Young olive tree with grafts
21. New Testament hyssop plants

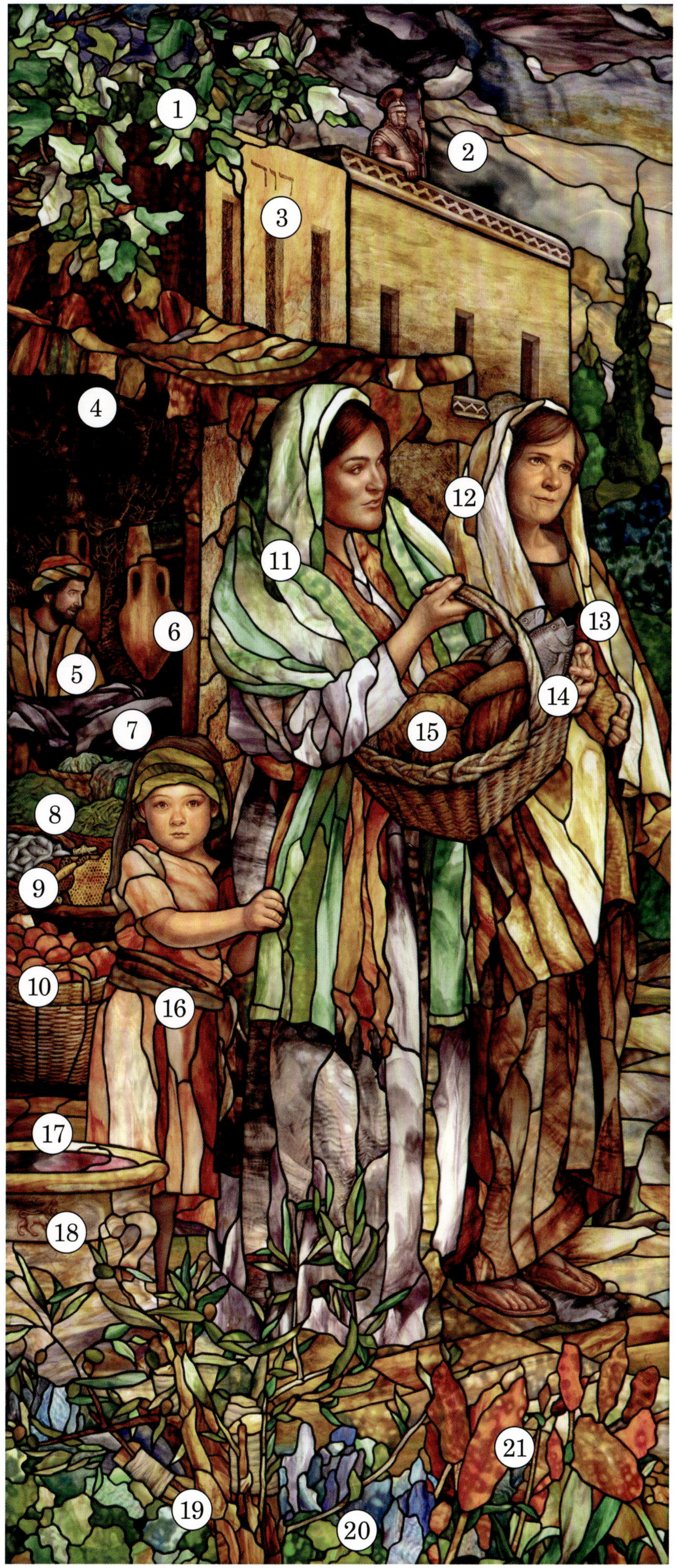

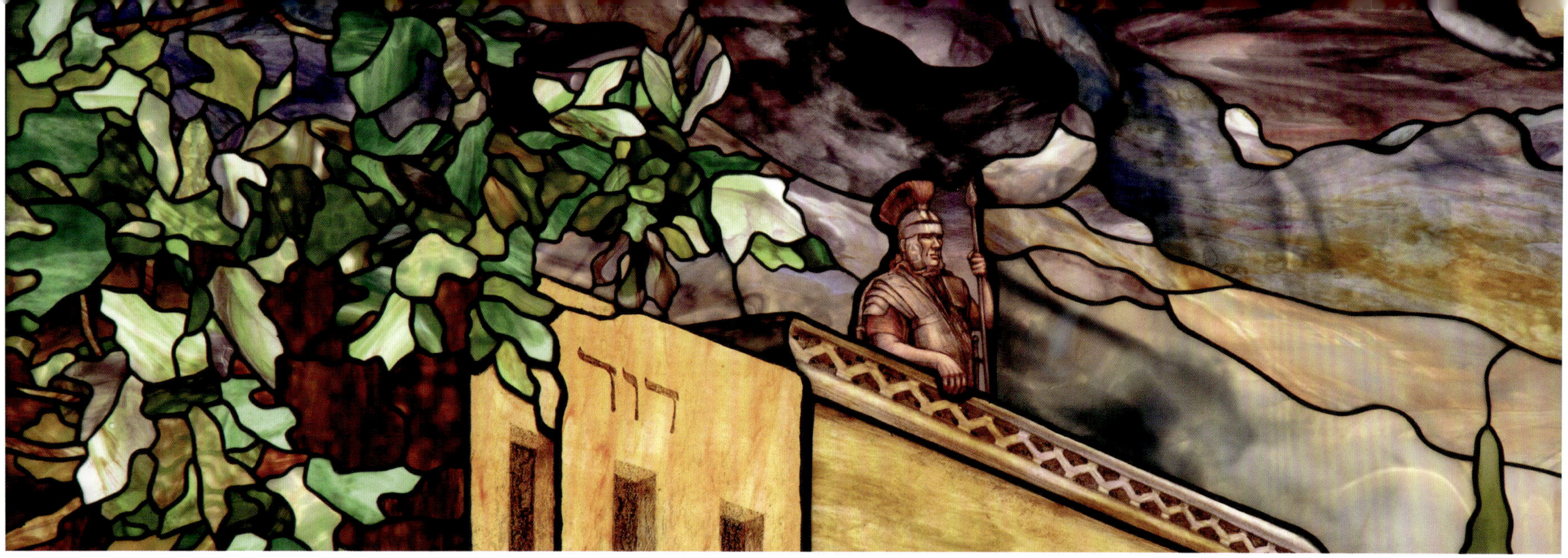

CHRIST'S ANCESTRY, HOME, AND TIMES

1. BARREN FIG TREE

It is discouraging to go to the effort of preparing soil, planting a seed, nurturing the plant, and then not reap the anticipated harvest. Christ shared this type of disappointment in a parable: "A man had a fig tree growing in his vineyard, and he went to look for fruit on it but did not find any. So he said to the man who took care of the vineyard, 'For three years now I've been coming to look for fruit on this fig tree and haven't found any. Cut it down! Why should it use up the soil?'" (Luke 13:6–9). In this case, the missing fruit to which Christ referred was the lack of understanding, humility, and repentance in the lives of many Jewish leaders. They had great knowledge of the scriptures but could not see how they testified of Christ. Their lives were full of hypocrisy. In the window you will notice fig leaves have a beautiful and unique shape. You will also see that some leaves are beginning to wither and die because the tree was cursed: "Early in the morning, as Jesus was on his way back to the city, he was hungry. Seeing a fig tree by the road, he went up to it but found nothing on it except leaves. Then he said to it, 'May you never bear fruit again!' Immediately the tree withered" (Matthew 21:18–19). The tree, like some Jewish leaders, was all show and no fruit. Perhaps the cursing was one way of showing His disciples that He had power of life and death—that when He would die, it would be of His own choosing and not because hypocritical Jewish leaders demanded it.

2. ROMAN SOLDIER

The Jews hated the Roman soldiers. The soldiers assigned to crucify Christ were cruel men intent on mocking Christ as well as killing Him: "Then the governor's soldiers took Jesus into the Praetorium and gathered the whole company of soldiers around him. They stripped him and put a scarlet robe on him, and then twisted together a crown of thorns and set it on his head. They put a staff in his right hand. Then they knelt in front of him and mocked him. 'Hail, king of the Jews!' they said. They spit on him, and took the staff and struck him on the head again and again. . . . Then they led him away to crucify him" (Matthew 27:27–31). For early Christian disciples, it must have been devastating to witness their Lord and Savior abused and tormented by the Romans and be powerless to help. Christ could have stopped it at any time. Yet He was stoic and silent. Even while hanging on the cross, Christ said, "Father, forgive them, for they do not know what they are doing" (Luke 23:34). Not long after uttering those remarkable words, Christ declared that He had completed what He was sent to do and died. The earth responded violently, shaking and tearing stones apart. "When the centurion and those with him who were guarding Jesus saw the earthquake and all that had happened, they were terrified, and exclaimed, 'Surely he was the Son of God!'" (Matthew 27:54). We will all one day make the same acknowledgment. May it be in love and worship rather than fear and regret. After Christ's death, a soldier thrust a spear into His side. He was making sure Christ was dead but also fulfilling prophecy: "These things happened so that the scripture would be fulfilled: 'Not one of his bones will be broken,' and, as another scripture says, 'They will look on the one they have pierced'" (John 19:36–37).

3. *DALET VAV DALET,* HEBREW FOR "DAVID"

In the Old Testament, God promised that Jesus would come through David's posterity (see 2 Samuel 7:13; Acts 13:22–23). When Matthew began his gospel, he proclaimed Christ's Davidic descent and condensed Christ's genealogy to three sets of fourteen generations (see Matthew 1:17). It seems he used a literary technique found in Hebrew called *gematria*, in which letters are given numeric value based on their order in the alphabet. Thus, *dalet vav dalet*, the Hebrew letters for D, V, and D equal 14 because *dalet* is the fourth letter in the Hebrew alphabet and *vav* is the sixth. Taken together, D (4) + V (6) + D (4) = 14. By using three sets of 14 generations, Matthew seems to have made a purposeful connection between King David and Jesus, the Son of David (see Luke 1:32).

4. NET CALLING TO MIND THE SEA OF GALILEE

Although modern fishing nets are made of different materials than those in Christ's time, the shape of the nets hasn't changed significantly. However, notice the floats in the window are in the shape of the Sea of Galilee where Christ had many poignant experiences during His mortal ministry. It was there that Christ called His first apostles.

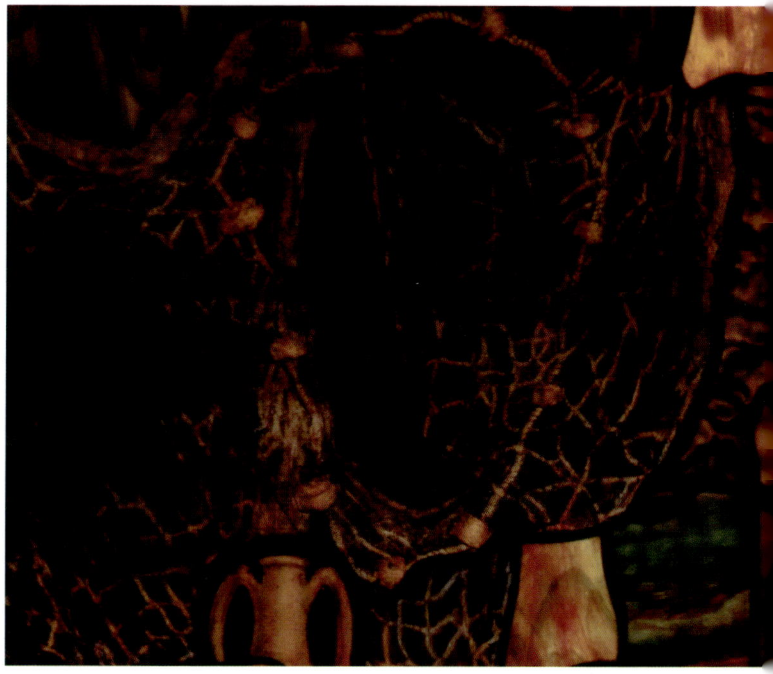

At the end of an extremely unsuccessful attempt at fishing, Christ invited Peter to "put out into deep water and let down the nets for a catch" (Luke 5:4). There was no logical reason to do so except that the Master had commanded. Peter obeyed and gathered an extraordinary number of fish in his nets. It was then that Christ called Peter and his brother, Andrew, along with James and his brother, John: "Come, follow me, . . . and I will send you out to fish for people" (Matthew 4:18). These men immediately left their boats and nets—their livelihoods—to follow Christ and learn from Him how to gather God's children. They witnessed firsthand the Savior's teachings and learned from His example. They saw Him perform miracles with the audacious expectation that they would one day perform similar miracles. As apostles of the Lord Jesus Christ, they devoted their lives to testifying of His divinity and role as Savior and Redeemer.

SYMBOLIC FOOD, DRINK, AND CLOTHING

5. THE RICH YOUNG RULER

One of the more surprising things the disciples heard the Lord say was, "Truly I tell you, it is hard for someone who is rich to enter the kingdom of heaven. Again I tell you, it is easier for a camel to go through the eye of a needle than for someone who is rich to enter the kingdom of God" (Matthew 19:23–24). They had just witnessed a wealthy young man who claimed to be seeking eternal life walk away saddened because he could not obey Christ's direction: "If you want to be perfect, go, sell your possessions and give to the poor, and you will have treasure in heaven. Then come, follow me" (Matthew 19:21). At that time the young man was not willing to part with his earthly treasures. If we foolishly do the same, we will not be able to follow the Savior either. Notice in the window how the shopkeeper is shown surrounded by earthly possessions, such as the lavish and expensive purple cloth that he holds in his hands. The Lord knows that giving up such things is difficult, but He said, "What is impossible with man is possible with God" (Luke 18:27). He will strengthen and sustain us as we strive to turn our lives over to Him in humility, obedience, and love. There is far more to be gained than lost in such a process.

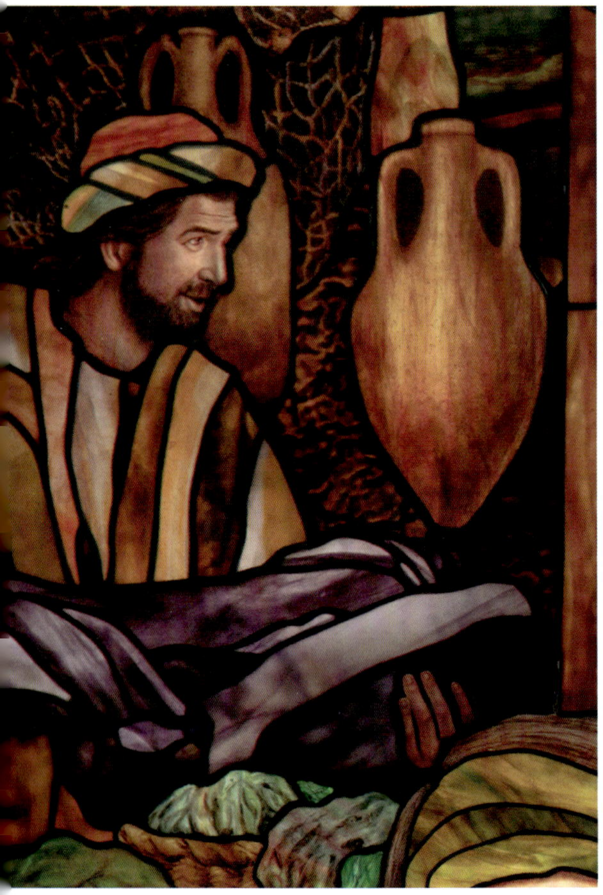

6. NEW BOTTLES FOR NEW WINE

"No one pours new wine into old wineskins. Otherwise, the new wine will burst the skins; the wine will run out and the wineskins will be ruined. No, new wine must be poured into new wineskins" (Luke 5:37–39). Christ was not giving instruction on how to keep wine fresh. He was speaking about bringing a new law and a new covenant to fulfill the old. Our hearts, like wineskins, must be new and able to accept the new law. They can't be stiff and unyielding when we encounter additional understanding. If so, the joy and blessings the Savior offers for living in a higher and holier way will spill out on the ground, as it were, and be lost. The wine bottle portrayed hanging on the wall in the window is a new one ready to be filled.

7. PURPLE ROBE

Purple has long been associated with royalty because few others could afford clothing of that color. Anciently, the process to dye cloth purple required materials that were extremely rare. Yet, the soldiers somehow obtained a purple robe to drape over Christ (see John 19:5). We read in Luke: "Then Herod and his soldiers ridiculed and mocked him. Dressing him in an elegant robe, they sent him back to Pilate" (Luke 23:11). Herod and his soldiers used the robe to deride and belittle Christ. Little did they know that they were in the presence of the King of Kings and Lord of Lords.

8. PARABLE OF THE MARRIAGE FEAST

"The kingdom of heaven is like a king who prepared a wedding banquet for his son. He sent his servants to those who had been invited to the banquet to tell them to come, but they refused to come. Then he sent some more servants and said, 'Tell those who have been invited that I have prepared my dinner: My oxen and fattened cattle have been butchered, and everything is ready. Come to the wedding banquet.' But they paid no attention and went off—one to his field, another to his business. The rest seized his servants, mistreated them and killed them" (Matthew 22:1–4). The artists filled the baskets portrayed in the window with fish, fruits, and vegetables to represent this bounty generously offered by the king. Think of the bitter disappointment and hurt the king must have felt when his guests turned against him, rejected his selfless gift, and even murdered his servants. Instead of retaliating against them, the king told his servants, "'The wedding banquet is ready, but those I invited did not deserve to come. So go to the street corners and invite to the banquet anyone you find'" (Matthew 22:8–9). Think of the blessing the original guests missed because of their selfishness and wickedness. Think of the joy felt by those who accepted the invitation. God's gospel and grace is a bounteous feast—a gift freely given that must also be freely received.

9. WILD HONEY AND LOCUSTS

John the Baptist testified of Christ throughout his life and even before his birth. The angel Gabriel announced to John's father, Zechariah, that His son would "be filled with the Holy Spirit even before he is born" (Luke 1:15), and so it was: "At that time Mary got ready and hurried to a town in the hill country of Judea, where she entered Zechariah's home and greeted Elizabeth. When Elizabeth heard Mary's greeting, the baby leaped in her womb, and Elizabeth was filled with the Holy Spirit" (Luke 1:39–41). As an adult, John preached in the wilderness of Judea saying, "Repent, for the kingdom of heaven has come near" (Matthew 3:1–2). His words were a fulfilment of Isaiah's prophecy of the voice calling "in the wilderness prepare the way for the Lord; make straight in the desert a highway for our God" (Isaiah 40:3). John's clothes were made of camel hair, and he had a leather belt around his waist. His food was locusts and wild honey. People went out to him from Jerusalem and all Judea and the whole region of the Jordan, confessing their sins and being baptized by him in the Jordan River (see Matthew 3:1–6). John would be the one to help Christ "fulfill all righteousness" by baptizing Him even though he felt unworthy to even untie the Lord's sandals (see Matthew 3:13–15). John the Baptist is a remarkable example of one willing to fulfill his mission. In the artwork, among the baskets laden with produce and fish there is one full of honeycomb with locusts on the edges to remind viewers of John and his integral role in the Savior's life and ministry.

10. POMEGRANATES

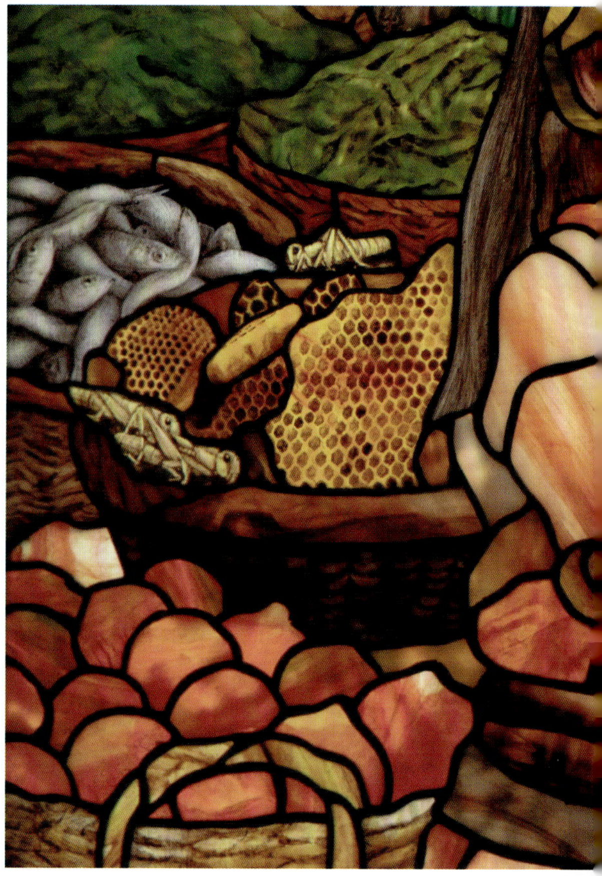

Pomegranates were a common harvest in Israel and were an indication of prosperity in a culture. It meant they had fertile soil with plenty of sunshine and water. Pomegranates are a symbol of righteousness, knowledge, and wisdom and a reflection of God's love for His people. The bright red color and quantity of the seeds reflect Christ's blood willingly given and the new life He brings. When the Israelites found themselves suffering in the wilderness, they asked Moses and Aaron: "Why did you bring the Lord's community into this wilderness, that we and our livestock should die here? Why did you bring us up out of Egypt to this terrible place? It has no grain or figs, grapevines or pomegranates" (Numbers 20:4–5). The lack of pomegranates seemed like evidence that God had abandoned them. In the artwork, the presence of pomegranates is to show the opposite—that God is very much aware of us, and He has not and will not forsake us. Christ came to love, save, heal, exalt, preserve, protect, and bless all who sincerely seek Him. He willingly gave His blood because He could see the seeds of potential within us.

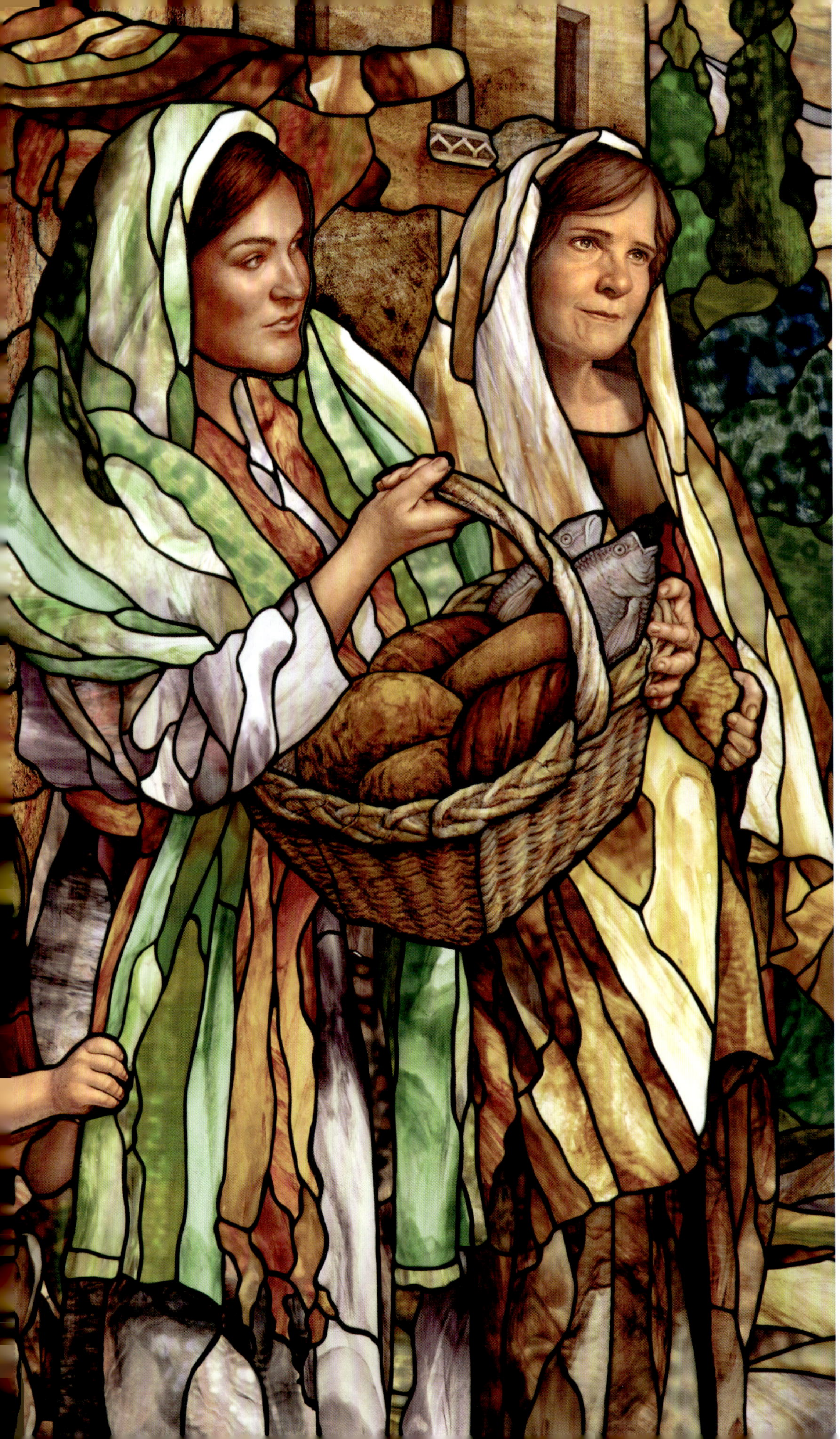

CHOICES AND MIRACLES

11. MARTHA TROUBLED ABOUT MANY THINGS

Jesus taught about the crucial skill of placing priorities: "As Jesus and his disciples were on their way, he came to a village where a woman named Martha opened her home to him. She had a sister called Mary, who sat at the Lord's feet listening to what he said. But Martha was distracted by all the preparations that had to be made. She came to him and asked, 'Lord, don't you care that my sister has left me to do the work by myself? Tell her to help me!' 'Martha, Martha,' the Lord answered, 'you are worried and upset about many things, but few things are needed—or indeed only one. Mary has chosen what is better, and it will not be taken away from her'" (Luke 10:38–41). The artists chose to show Martha burdened by some of life's demands—carrying a basket laden with food to be prepared and tending a young child clinging to her skirt. The Lord was not saying that what Martha was doing was not important. He was simply saying some things are more important than others. At death, we take nothing with us but our spirits, and if we have not made consistent efforts to strengthen our connection with God, then we will have missed the most important thing in mortality. Despite showing Martha as laden with responsibilities, the artists chose to put her gaze toward the Savior as a hopeful encouragement for all of us to seek Him—especially when life's demands are intense.

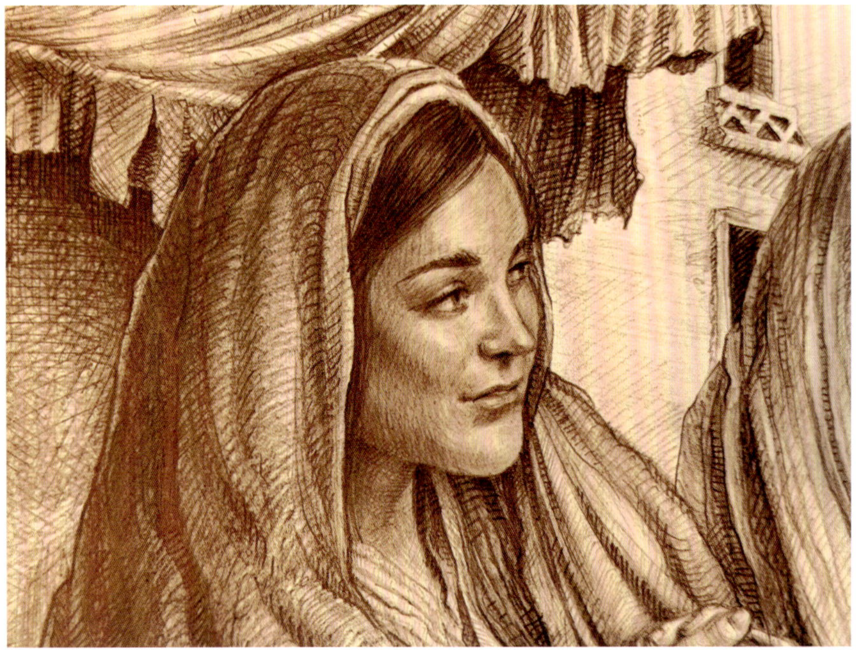

12. MARY CHOOSING THE GOOD PART

The apostle John proclaimed, "And we have seen and testify that the Father has sent his Son to be the Savior of the world" (1 John 4:14). And Jesus, Himself, said, "For the Son of Man came to seek and to save the lost" (Luke 19:9). Christ's most crucial role is to save God's beloved children from the destructive effects of sin and death so that we may return to dwell with Him eternally. This is what Jesus was teaching when He stated, "Few things are needed—or indeed only one. Mary has chosen what is better, and it will not be taken away from her" (Luke 10:41). Jesus validated Mary's choice to put aside all other cares to put herself physically, mentally, and spiritually in a place to draw closer to Christ. What Martha mistook as laziness or apathy was Mary recognizing the rare opportunity before her to learn at the Savior's feet. She saw it for the extraordinary gift it was, and she chose to embrace it. The reason her choice could not be taken from her is because choices inevitably shape character. Similarly, Christ told His apostles that, after His departure, "I will see you again and you will rejoice, and no one will take away your joy" (John 16:22). Christ's Atonement is infinite and eternal. The blessings that come through Him are everlasting. The joy they bring cannot be taken away from us. In the artwork, viewers see Mary's face full of peace, joy, and gratitude. She holds a loaf of bread symbolizing the "bread of life" (John 6:35) that is her priority.

13. COIN IN FISH'S MOUTH

"After Jesus and his disciples arrived in Capernaum, the collectors of the two-drachma temple tax came to Peter and asked, 'Doesn't your teacher pay the temple tax?' 'Yes, he does,' he replied. When Peter came into the house, Jesus was the first to speak. 'What do you think, Simon?' he asked. 'From whom do the kings of the earth collect duty and taxes—from their own children or from others?' 'From others,' Peter answered. 'Then the children are exempt,' Jesus said to him. 'But so that we may not cause offense, go to the lake and throw out your line. Take the first fish you catch; open its mouth and you will find a four-drachma coin. Take it and give it to them for my tax and yours'" (Matthew 17:24–27). Christ provided a way to meet an obligation that clearly wasn't His. He helped Peter to meet the same obligation, which he did owe. And He did both in a miraculous manner. This is true of Christ's entire life and mission. He was born to pay a price He did not owe for all those who could not pay. "Greater love has no one than this: to lay down one's life for one's friends" (John 15:13). In the art glass, the coin in the mouth of the fish in the basket is a genuine silver coin from Christ's time, which would have been used to pay taxes.

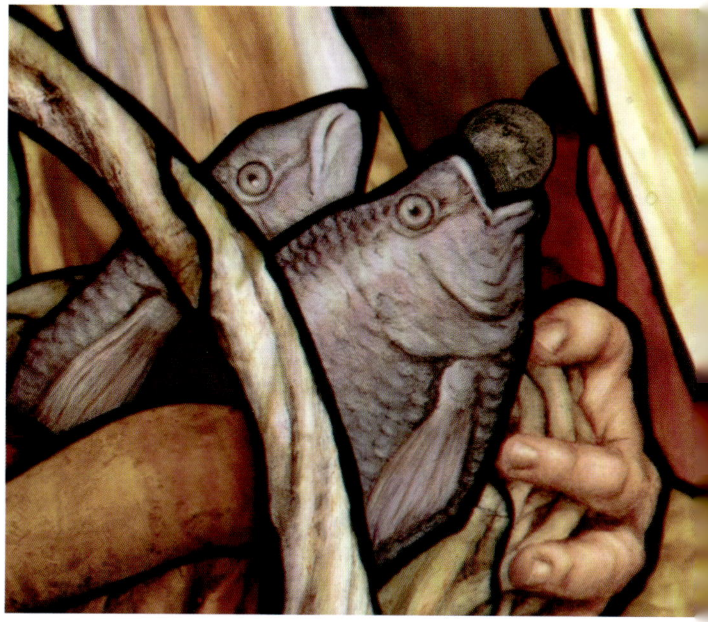

14. FISH FROM THE SEA OF GALILEE

Tilapia, often called St. Peter's fish today, is a hearty species of fish that thrives in the fresh, warm waters of the Sea of Galilee. Many Biblical scholars conclude it is likely the fish that filled Peter's nets at the time of his call to be an apostle (see Luke 5:1–11) as well as the fish that was part of the miracle of the loaves and fishes (see Matthew 14:17–21).

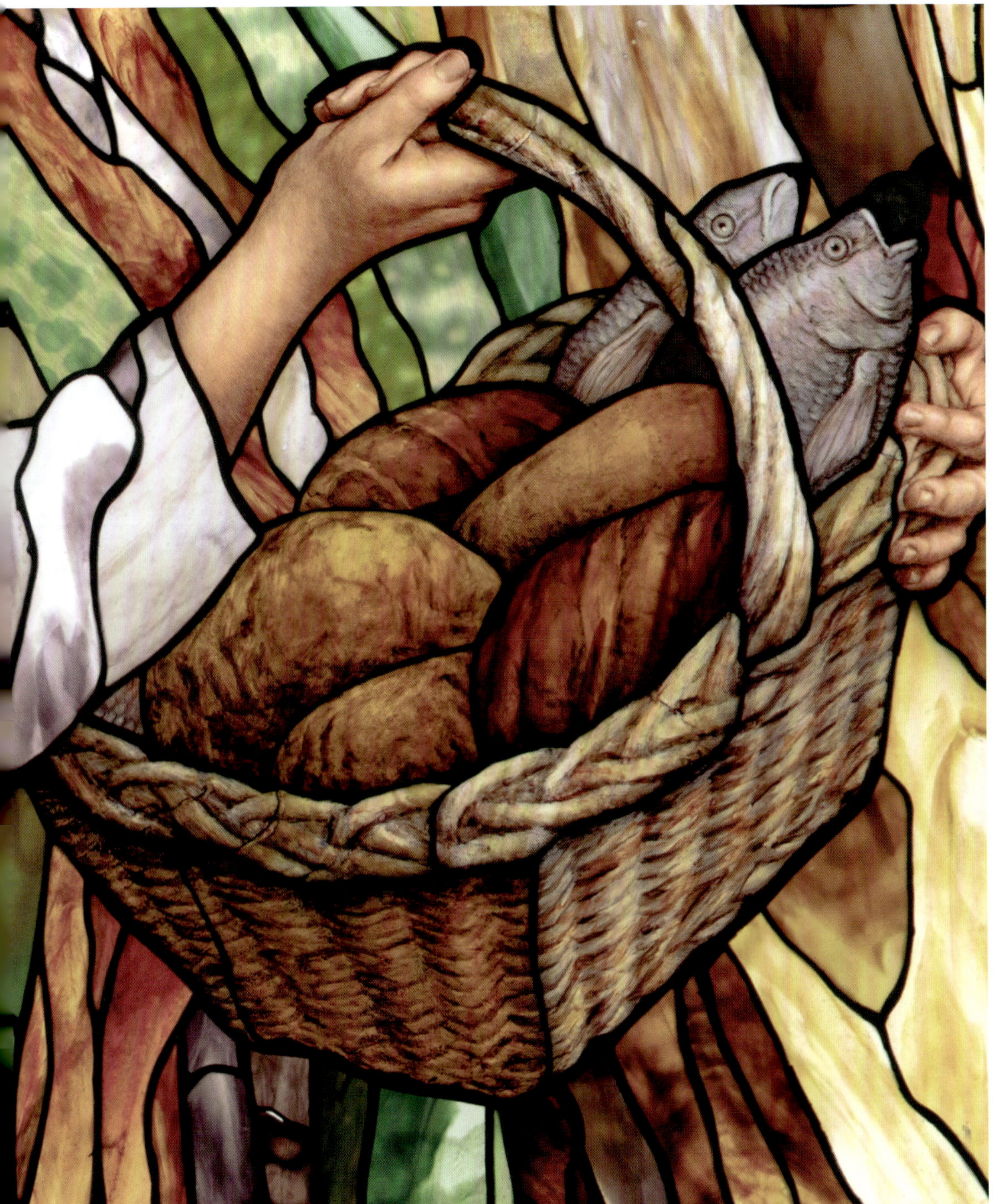

15. BREAD OF LIFE

"Jesus declared, 'I am the bread of life. Whoever comes to me will never go hungry, and whoever believes in me will never be thirsty'" (John 6:35). Christ taught that He is the staple needed for eternal sustenance. He used bread to institute Communion: "And he took bread, gave thanks and broke it, and gave it to them, saying, 'This is my body given for you; do this in remembrance of me'" (Luke 22:19). It was the food mentioned by Satan to tempt the Savior: "If you are the Son of God, tell these stones to become bread" (Matthew 4:3). One of the more memorable instances in the Savior's life that involved bread happened near the shores of the Sea of Galilee. Christ had just received word of John the Baptist's death, and He sought solace to grieve. Yet, instead of demanding privacy, He chose to bless and teach the vast multitude that had followed Him. After some time, when the apostles suggested that the very large crowd be sent away to get food for themselves, the Savior told His apostles to provide something for them all to eat. They explained that they had but a few loaves and fishes among them that had been brought by a boy (see John 6:9). "'Bring them here to me,' he said. And he directed the people to sit down on the grass. Taking the five loaves and the two fish and looking up to heaven, he gave thanks and broke the loaves. Then he gave them to the disciples, and the disciples gave them to the people. They all ate and were satisfied, and the disciples picked up twelve basketfuls of broken pieces that were left over. The number of those who ate was about five thousand men, besides women and children" (Matthew 14:18–21). Christ took a simple offering and enhanced and magnified it to bless God's children physically and spiritually.

16. JAIRUS'S DAUGHTER

The young girl clinging to the woman's skirt in the window is small and vulnerable. She needs protection and care. Parents brought their children to the Savior during His lifetime just as parents bring their children to Him today. They knew He could provide things for their precious little ones that they could not. Jesus called the children to Him and said, "Let the little children come to me, and do not hinder them, for the kingdom of God belongs to such as these. Truly I tell you, anyone who will not receive the kingdom of God like a little child will never enter it" (Luke 18:16–17). We must accept Christ into our lives with the love and humility of a little child. This young girl is also reminiscent of the daughter of Jairus: "Then one of the synagogue leaders, named Jairus, came, and when he saw Jesus, he fell at his feet. He pleaded earnestly with him, 'My little daughter is dying. Please come and put your hands on her so that she will be healed and live.' So Jesus went with him" (Mark 5:22–24). Along the way, however, Christ was waylaid by the needs of another, and Jairus's daughter died. One can imagine the disappointment, grief, and even frustration that Jairus felt. Jairus had the faith to ask the Lord to heal his daughter from sickness but likely couldn't even imagine that anything might be done to help her now. Jesus said to him as He says to us, "Don't be afraid; just believe" (Mark 5:36). Jairus would soon learn there is no problem that is beyond the power of God and Christ. "For everyone who asks receives; the one who seeks finds; and to the one who knocks, the door will be opened" (Matthew 7:8). In the window, this child is the only image who looks directly at the viewer. In this way the artists invite viewers into the scene. It is as if the young girl is asking each of us, "What do you think about the Messiah?" (Matthew 22:42). If we had been given the opportunity to be present in His day, where would our focus have been? Would it have been on the Savior or on our daily tasks? Would we have honored Him or despised or ignored Him? Where is our focus today?

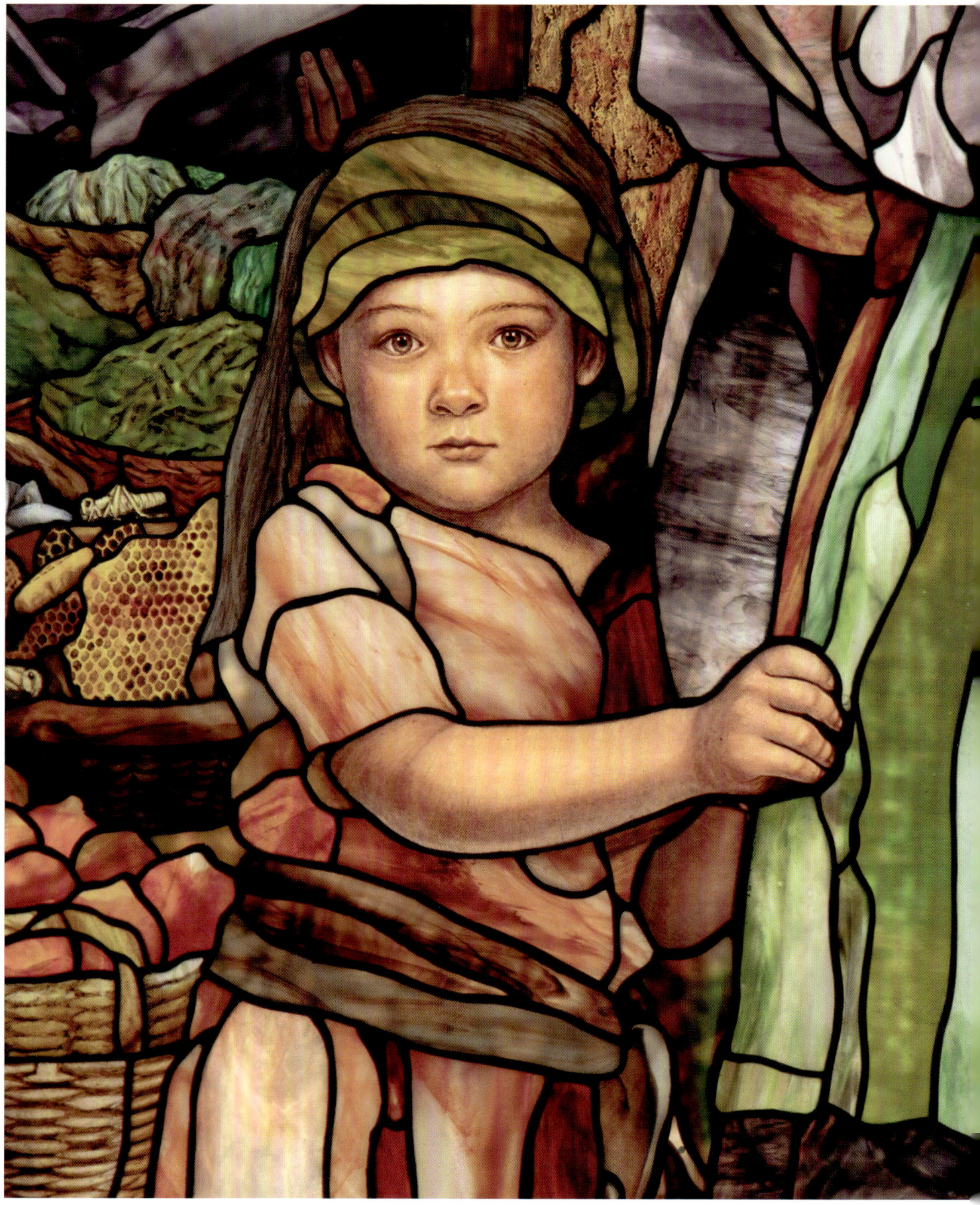

VESSELS AND PLANTS

17. WINE REPRESENTING COMMUNION AND CHRIST'S FIRST RECORDED MIRACLE

Notice in the window a common water jug that is not filled with common water. It is filled with wine. Wine is what Christ used to institute Communion. It was also the beverage to serve to esteemed guests at wedding feasts. To run out of wine at a wedding celebration would have been seen as an insult. This is why Christ's mother asked for His help that day in Cana. Mary had absolute faith and confidence that Jesus could do something to solve that very problem. She told the servants to do whatever Jesus said, no questions asked: "Nearby stood six stone water jars, the kind used by the Jews for ceremonial washing, each holding from twenty to thirty gallons. Jesus said to the servants, 'Fill the jars with water'; so they filled them to the brim. Then he told them, 'Now draw some out and take it to the master of the banquet.' They did so, and the master of the banquet tasted the water that had been turned into wine. He did not realize where it had come from, though the servants who had drawn the water knew. Then he called the bridegroom aside and said, 'Everyone brings out the choice wine first and then the cheaper wine after the guests have had too much to drink; but you have saved the best till now'" (John 2:6–10). In His first recorded miracle Christ was announcing that He had the power to change things—even things we think are impossible to change. It was miraculous that one compound could be transformed into another by His command, but it is also miraculous that something ordinary could be made extraordinary. Water had become wine of superb quality in containers that held water used for cleaning hands and feet! There is nothing beyond Christ's capacity to change, magnify, purify, and improve. None of us are too filthy, too ordinary, or too far gone for His miraculous redemption.

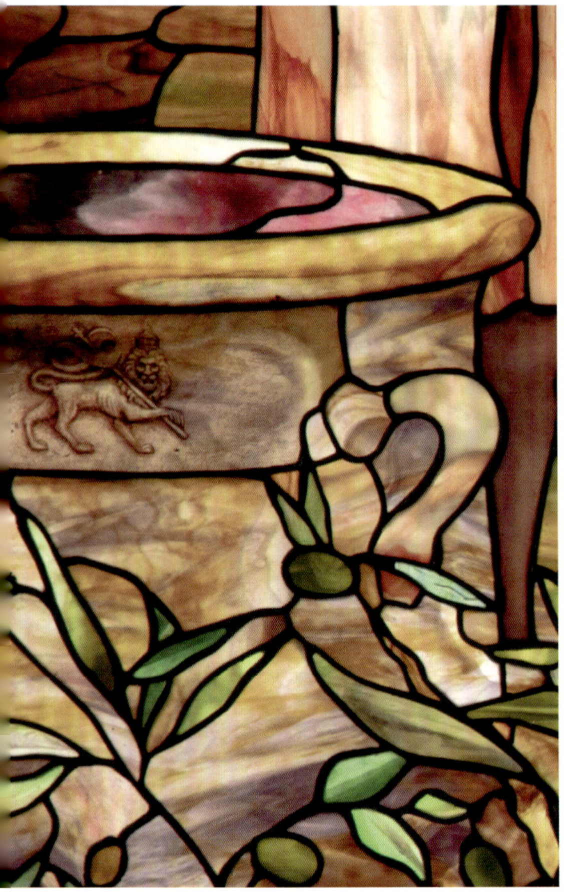

18. LION OF JUDAH

One symbol of the tribe of Judah has been a lion since the time Jacob told his son, "You are a lion's cub, Judah; you return from the prey, my son. Like a lion he crouches and lies down, like a lioness—who dares to rouse him?" (Genesis 49:9). Christ was born in the tribe of Judah through the lineage of King David (see Matthew 1:1). The lion is known as the king of beasts and Jesus is the King of Kings. Like a lion, Christ is noble, strong, protective, majestic, and powerful: "Do not weep! See, the Lion of the tribe of Judah, the Root of David, has triumphed. He is able to open the scroll and its seven seals" (Revelation 5:5).

19. MODERN-DAY HYSSOP PLANTS

Hyssop is mentioned many times throughout the Bible. The Israelites were told to use it to mark their doorways with the blood of a lamb so that death would pass over them (see Exodus 12:21–23). King David spoke about using it to be cleansed (see Psalm 51:7). In modern times, the hyssop plant is slightly different than the varieties referred to in Biblical times and would not be as useful in sopping up liquid. Today, hyssop is a perennial herb with small purple flowers and has a spicy, mildly bitter taste. It is used for cooking and medicinal purposes. It can be a reminder of the Messiah who came to nourish and heal.

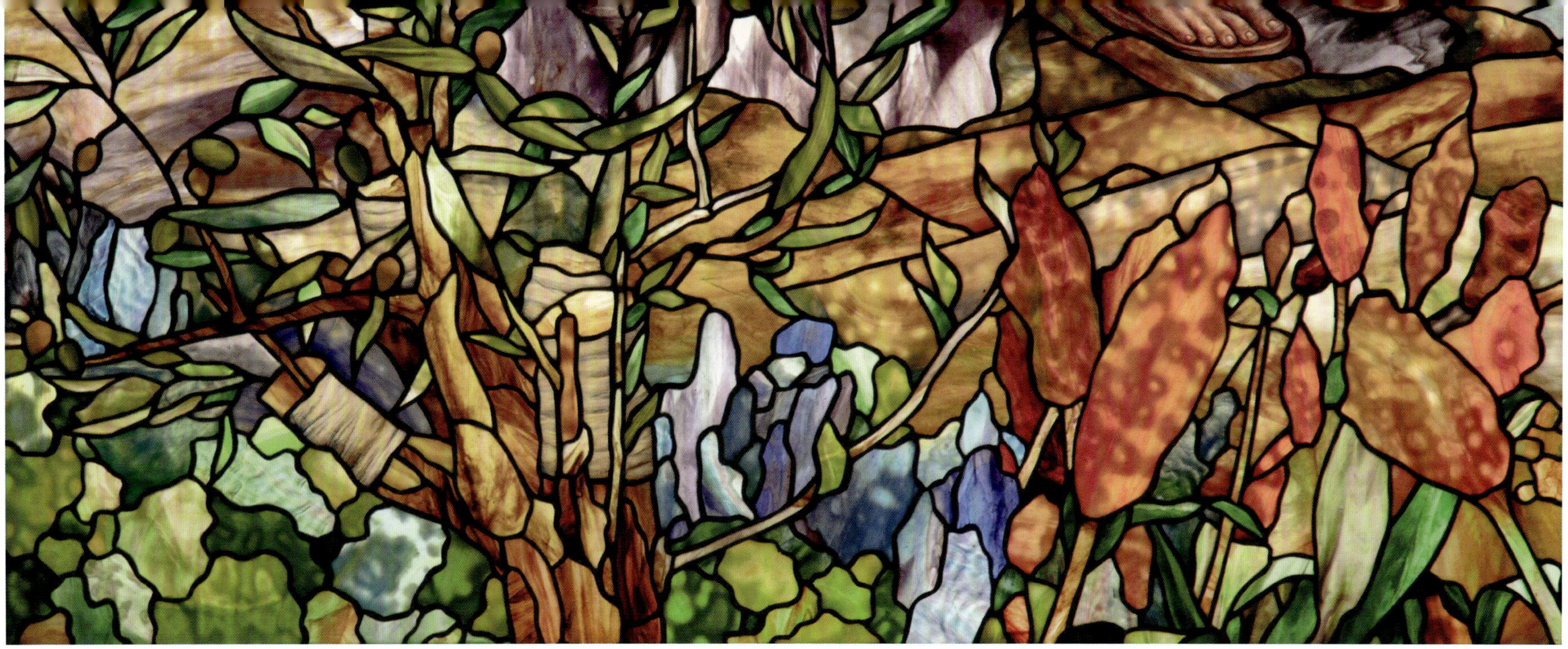

20. YOUNG OLIVE TREE WITH GRAFTS

Christ frequently taught using olive trees, grapevines, fields of wheat, and other living, growing things as object lessons. He said, "I am the true vine, and my Father is the gardener. He cuts off every branch in me that bears no fruit, while every branch that does bear fruit he prunes so that it will be even more fruitful. You are already clean because of the word I have spoken to you. Remain in me, as I also remain in you. No branch can bear fruit by itself; it must remain in the vine. Neither can you bear fruit unless you remain in me" (John 15:1). Christ came to offer His gospel to the children of Israel, but He was rejected by many. The same blessing was then offered to those outside the House of Israel, and many accepted. Paul spoke to the recent converts to Christianity who were in Rome after the Savior's death and reminded them that, like a branch grafted onto a flourishing tree, they had a genuine right to the blessings of the gospel. He told them, "If some of the branches have been broken off, and you, though a wild olive shoot, have been grafted in among the others and now share in the nourishing sap from the olive root, do not consider yourself to be superior to those other branches. If you do, consider this: You do not support the root, but the root supports you. You will say then, 'Branches were broken off so that I could be grafted in.' Granted. But they were broken off because of unbelief, and you stand by faith. Do not be arrogant, but tremble. For if God did not spare the natural branches, he will not spare you either" (Romans 11:17–21). Notice how the artists showed a young and healthy olive tree sprouting up near the pots on the bottom-left side. Look closely at the branch that has been successfully grafted with the support of the wrap around it. The wrap represents the covenants and ordinances of Christ's gospel, which help keep us growing and flourishing.

21. NEW TESTAMENT HYSSOP PLANTS

In the New Testament the hyssop plant (a stalk with rust-colored flowers) was used to offer sour wine (vinegar) to the Savior when He suffered on the cross: "Later, knowing that everything had now been finished, and so that Scripture would be fulfilled, Jesus said, 'I am thirsty'" (John 19:28–29). His life and ministry had fulfilled many prophecies, and what happened next fulfilled yet another. In Psalm 69:21 we read, "They put gall in my food and gave me vinegar for my thirst." In John 19:29–30 we read, "A jar of wine vinegar was there, so they soaked a sponge in it, put the sponge on a stalk of the hyssop plant, and lifted it to Jesus' lips."

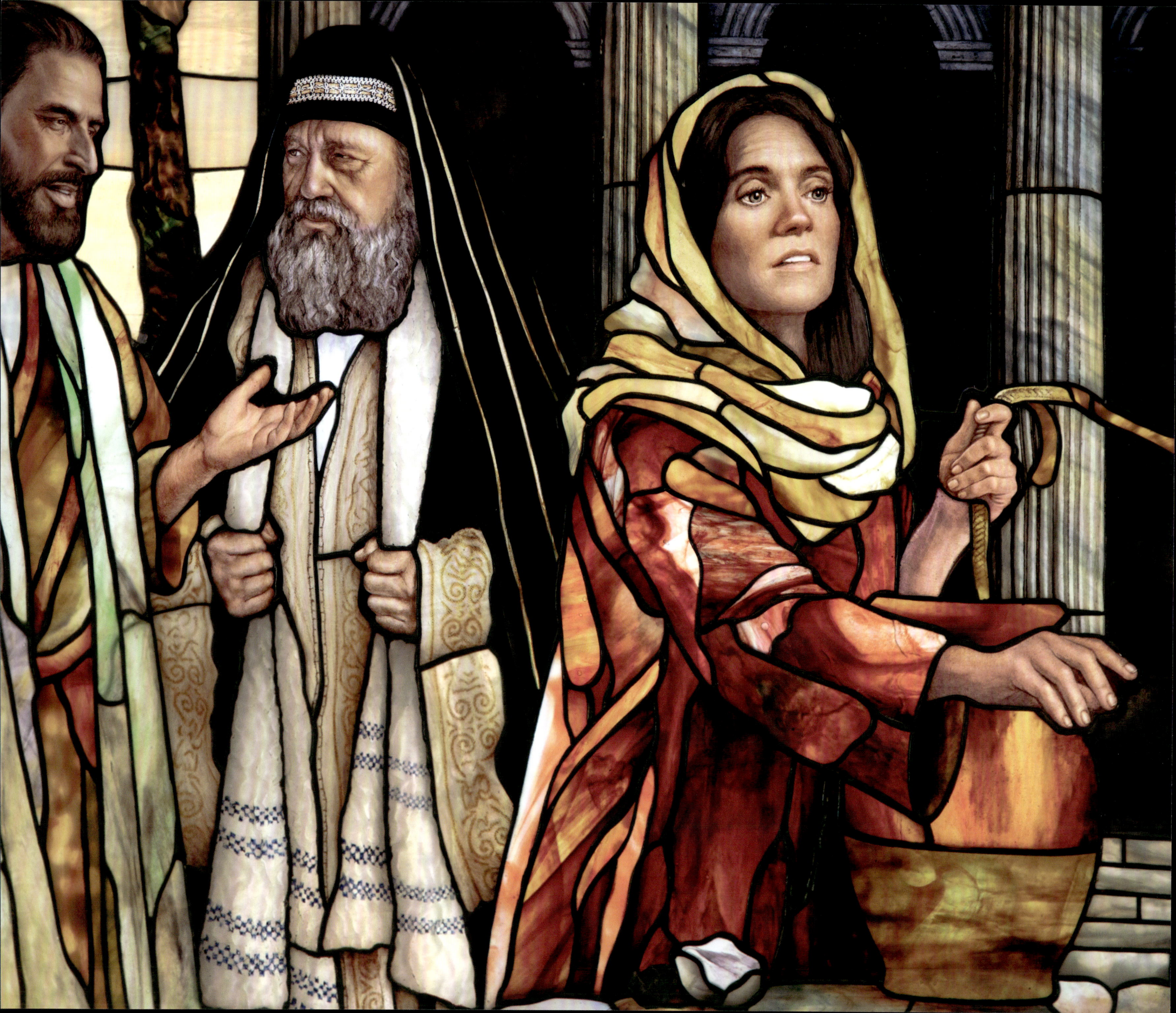

Panel D

Featuring the Woman at the Well

LIGHTS AND GIFTS | 40

1. Star, sign of Christ's birth
2. Depiction of last supper
3. Palm branches recalling Christ's triumphal entry
4. Design of interlocking olive branches
5. Greek for "Come to me"
6. Three mountains where light has been offered despite apostasy
7. His yoke is easy, and His burden is light
8. The law and the prophets
9. Heaven and earth

TURNING POINTS | 44

10. Three crosses
11. Widow of Nain
12. Son of the widow of Nain; also representing Lazarus
13. Seventy with scrolls; also representing the humble publican
14. Nicodemus the Pharisee; also representing the wicked husbandman
15. Woman at the well, woman with issue of blood, and woman taken in adultery
16. Stones recalling the only One without sin
17. Well and container representing Living Water
18. "He called a little child to him"
19. Seeds symbolizing the message of the gospel
20. Toy boat recalling the Sea of Galilee

SYMBOLS FROM NATURE | 50

21. Old Testament hyssop plants
22. Myrrh
23. Actual bits of frankincense
24. Almond blossom symbolizing Aaronic priesthood

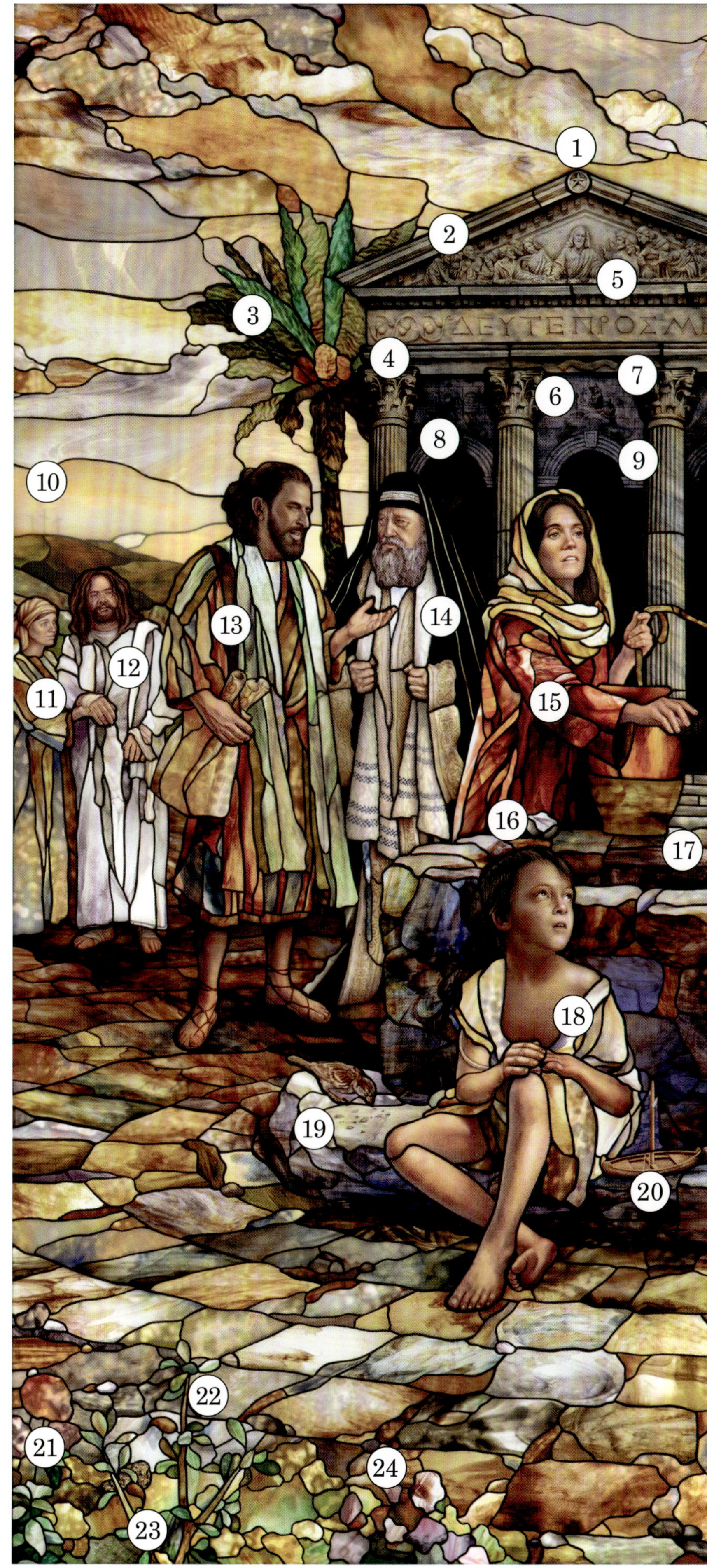

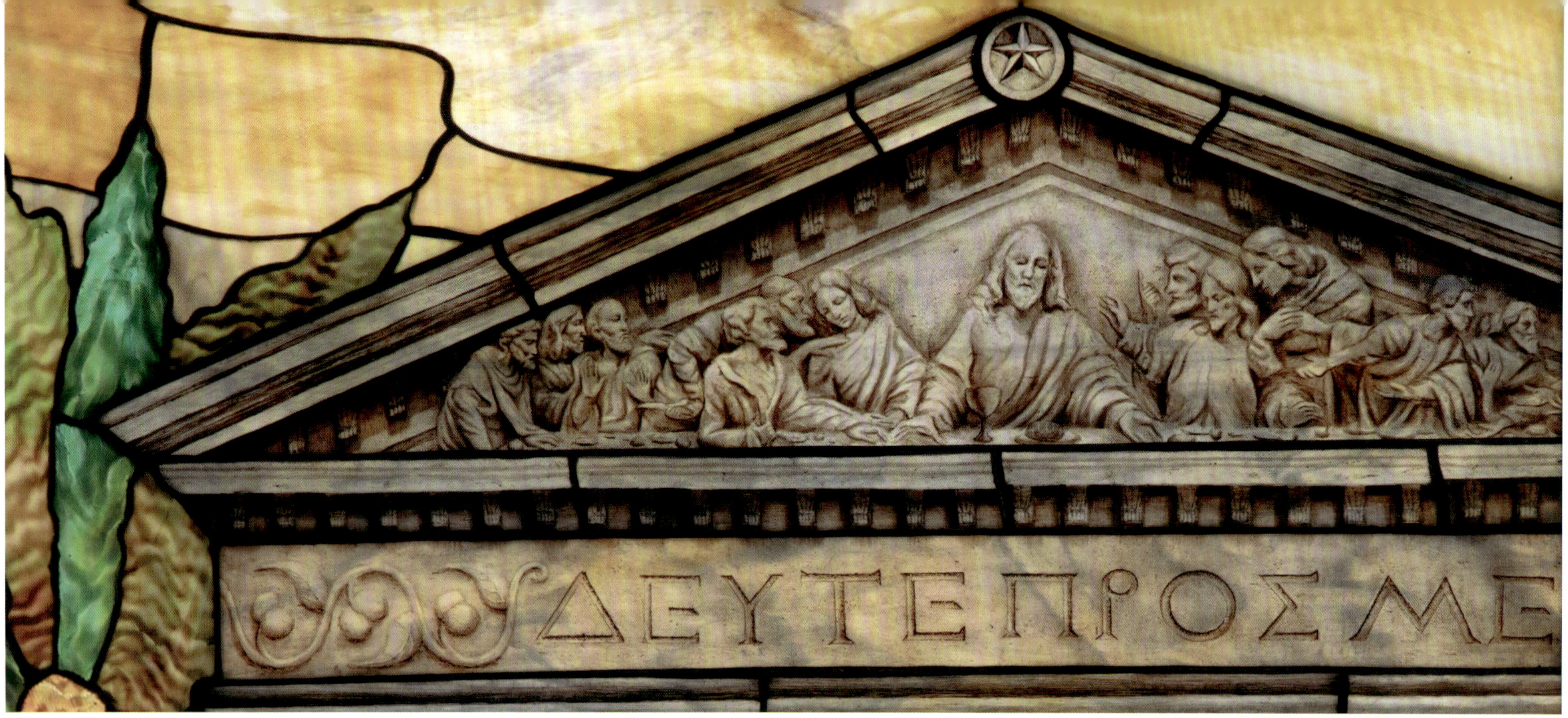

LIGHTS AND GIFTS

1. STAR, SIGN OF CHRIST'S BIRTH

"After Jesus was born in Bethlehem in Judea, during the time of King Herod, Magi from the east came to Jerusalem and asked, 'Where is the one who has been born king of the Jews? We saw his star when it rose and have come to worship him'" (Matthew 2:1–2). How beautiful that a star was one of the signs of Christ's birth. After all, "God is light; in him there is no darkness at all" (1 John 1:5). "In him was life, and that life was the light of all mankind. The light shines in the darkness, and the darkness has not overcome it" (John 1:4–5). Light is life. Without it, we are lost, and we perish. Stained glass is an art form that is completely dependent on light. Like stained glass, we cannot reach our potential without light to fill our souls, hearts, and lives. Christ can be the light that shines through us.

2. DEPICTION OF LAST SUPPER

The institution of holy Communion was a pivotal moment in the Savior's ministry. Not only because it took place right after Judas had left to betray Christ into the hands of His accusers, but because it introduced a critical ordinance that would bless the lives of the faithful and forever remind us of Christ's love and sacrifice: "While they were eating, Jesus took bread, and when he had given thanks, he broke it and gave it to his disciples, saying, 'Take and eat; this is my body.' Then he took a cup, and when he had given thanks, he gave it to them, saying, 'Drink from it, all of you. This is my blood of the covenant, which is poured out for many for the forgiveness of sins'" (Matthew 26:26–28). Humans can quickly forget, so as we choose to partake of Communion regularly it gives us the opportunity to refocus our lives on Christ and receive His divine help. It is a sacred moment when we can feel more closely connected to the Savior and give thanks for His atoning sacrifice. Leonardo DaVinci's portrayal of the Last Supper is known across the world. Thus the creators of the window chose to honor DaVinci and include elements of his fresco as a sculpted frieze at the top of the mausoleum.

3. PALM BRANCHES RECALLING CHRIST'S TRIUMPHAL ENTRY

In ancient Greece, palm branches represented victory and triumph and were awarded to athletic champions. The Romans embraced that tradition as did those under their rule. Thus, people waved palm branches when Christ entered Jerusalem: "They took palm branches and went out to meet him, shouting, 'Hosanna! Blessed is he who comes in the name of the Lord! Blessed is the king of Israel!'" (John 12:13). *Hosanna* means "save now we pray." The people were greeting Christ as a victor, Savior, and King. This joyful experience fulfilled the prophecy of the Old Testament: "Rejoice greatly, Daughter Zion! Shout, Daughter Jerusalem! See, your king comes to you, righteous and victorious, lowly and riding on a donkey" (Zechariah 9:9). Most that day hoped Christ would save them from Rome and reign as king over an independent Jewish nation as David once had. Few recognized that the salvation Christ would secure was from the tyranny of death and sin. Palm Sunday is observed throughout the Christian world as a reminder of that significant moment—the beginning of the last week of the Savior's mortal ministry. It was the gateway to the Atonement, which is the most triumphant victory the world will ever know. The tree portrayed in the art to the left of the mausoleum isn't just any palm; it is a King Palm to remind all of the King of Kings.

4. DESIGN OF INTERLOCKING OLIVE BRANCHES

Ancient Greek design often used repeating patterns in long chains. Waves, leaves, palms, and geometric shapes were all used to create borders for fabric, wall art, and in other architecture. The design of the border carved along the top of the mausoleum demonstrates this. It is made of an olive branch woven in an interlocking pattern. In the center of each circle created by the weave are two olives, side by side, representing a husband and wife together. The Savior, the true vine (see John 15:1), came to gather and connect the human family—all of God's children—as one: "All the believers were one in heart and mind" (Acts 4:32). "Make my joy complete by being like-minded, having the same love, being one in spirit and of one mind" (Philippians 2:2). Christ made possible immortality and eternal life. The border shows what loving one another (see John 13:34) can do for a marriage, a family, a community, and the world. Christ makes things beautiful and makes them last: "He has made everything beautiful in its time. . . . I know that everything God does will endure forever" (Ecclesiastes 3:11, 14).

5. GREEK FOR "COME TO ME"

Christ said "Come to me" multiple times as recorded in the New Testament (see Matthew 11:28, Luke 14:26, John 5:40; 6:37, 44). Coming to Christ is the first step on the path of discipleship, the beginning of a life focused on God's will and blessed by His spirit. Christ is "the way and the truth and the life" (John 14:6). No one can return to the Father except through the Savior (see John 14:6–7). Although Christ preached in Judea during His mortal ministry, His gospel is for all of God's children throughout the world. After Christ's resurrection, He instructed His apostles, "Go into all the world and preach the gospel to all creation" (Mark 16:15). He said, "Go and make disciples of all nations, baptizing them in the name of the Father and of the Son and of the Holy Spirit, and teaching them to obey everything I have commanded you. And surely I am with you always, to the very end of the age" (Matthew 28:19–20). In the artwork, the building behind the Savior is a representation of Greek architecture used throughout the ancient world. The words carved there are also Greek—the international language of the ancient world. However, the message is from Christ: "Come to me" (Matthew 11:28). It is the invitation Christ and His disciples gave and continued to give to all the world.

6. THREE MOUNTAINS WHERE LIGHT HAS BEEN OFFERED DESPITE APOSTASY

Mountains have traditionally been seen as places where heaven and earth meet. The three mountains depicted in the window are examples of that sacred connection. Mount Sinai on the left is where the Lord spoke to Moses and delivered the lower law (see Exodus 19–23). The Mount of Beatitudes in the middle is where Jesus delivered the Sermon on the Mount to His followers. There He gave the higher law that focused on purifying attitudes, desires, and motivation as well as behavior (see Matthew 5–7). The Mount of Transfiguration on the right was where keys of the kingdom and a special witness of Christ's divinity were delivered to the apostles who would continue to direct the work after Christ's death (see Matthew 17:1–8; Mark 9:2–8; Luke 9:28–36; and 2 Peter 1:16–19).

7. HIS YOKE IS EASY, AND HIS BURDEN IS LIGHT

One of the Savior's most tender and hopeful invitations is found in Matthew 11:28–30, where we read, "Come to me, all you who are weary and burdened, and I will give you rest. Take my yoke upon you and learn from me, for I am gentle and humble in heart, and you will find rest for your souls. For my yoke is easy and my burden is light." In the artwork, a yoke is portrayed on the building just under the words *Come to me* written in Greek. Just as a yoke links two work animals together, our covenants yoke us with Christ. As we turn our wills over to Him, His strength becomes our own, and we can do together with Him what we could never do alone. Our load is made easy, and we find rest in Him: "And the peace of God, which transcends all understanding, will guard your hearts and your minds in Christ Jesus" (Philippians 4:7).

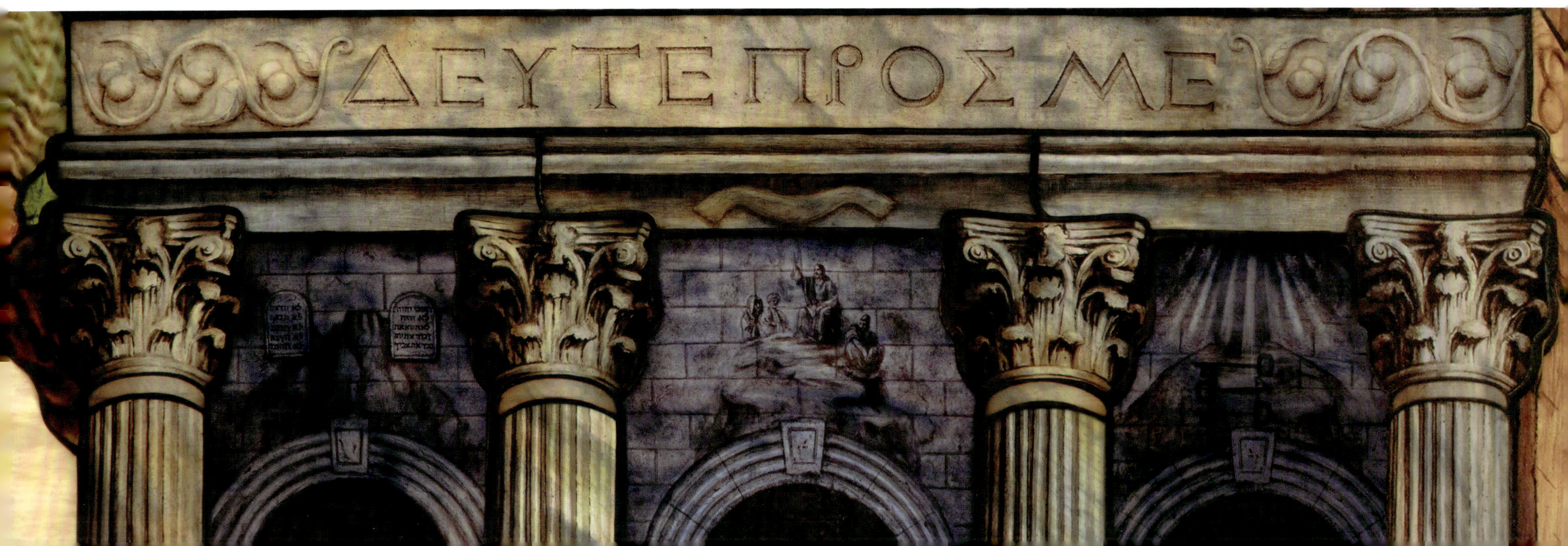

8. THE LAW AND THE PROPHETS

"When the Lord finished speaking to Moses on Mount Sinai, he gave him the two tablets of the covenant law, the tablets of stone inscribed by the finger of God" (Exodus 31:18). "Moses turned and went down the mountain with the two tablets of the covenant law in his hands. They were inscribed on both sides, front and back. The tablets were the work of God; the writing was the writing of God, engraved on the tablets" (Exodus 32:15–16). The scriptures clearly describe *how* we received the law. However, we must also understand *why*. God gives laws to His children because He loves us and wants us to be happy. Through His laws, He teaches us how He lives so we can be more like Him. When Christ came, He offered a higher law: "'Do not think that I have come to abolish the Law or the Prophets; I have not come to abolish them but to fulfill them'" (Matthew 5:17). He taught His followers, "'Love the Lord your God with all your heart and with all your soul and with all your mind.' This is the first and greatest commandment. And the second is like it: 'Love your neighbor as yourself.' All the Law and the Prophets hang on these two commandments" (Matthew 22:37–40). Christ was trying to lift people to live in a higher and holier way. He not only cared about their behavior, but also their hearts. He knew that if people sincerely embraced and lived the two great commandments, they would also be living and embracing all ten. More important, they would be doing the right thing for the right reasons.

9. HEAVEN AND EARTH

The square enclosing a circle is not a new design concept. It is found in art and architecture throughout the world. In a spiritual setting, the square can represent the four corners of the earth and the circle can represent the infinite or eternal nature of God. Together, as seen on the mausoleum arches in the window, they teach that Christ has provided the way to bring earth and heaven together or "to bring unity to all things in heaven and on earth under Christ" (Ephesians 1:10).

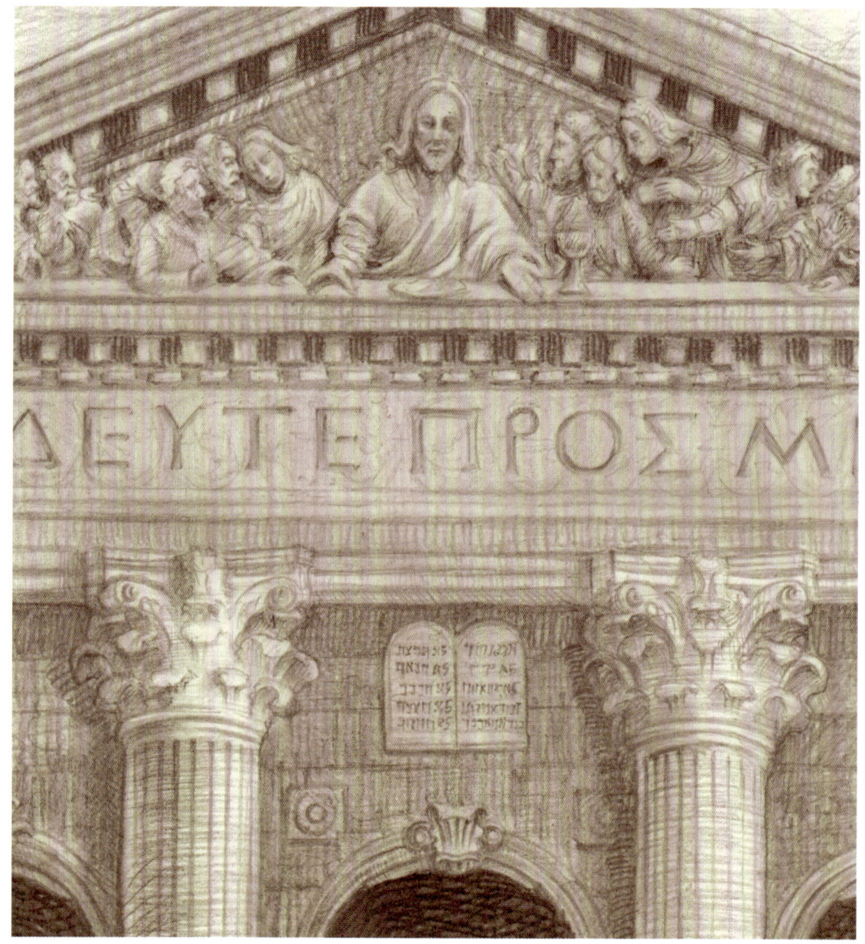

TURNING POINTS

10. THREE CROSSES

To the left of the mausoleum in the window, viewers see three crosses in the distance—barely noticeable at first amid other more clear and obvious images. Subtle though they may be, they carry a significant reminder of the magnitude of what the Savior willingly endured as He gave His life for us. His death is the greatest injustice in the history of the world. Never has a more innocent and perfect soul suffered a more humiliating and brutal death. The irony of Christ's crucifixion was that all the while He faced this prolonged torture, He had the power to stop it. His life was not being taken but willingly given. He said to Peter, "Do you think I cannot call on my Father, and he will at once put at my disposal more than twelve legions of angels? But how then would the Scriptures be fulfilled that say it must happen in this way?" (Matthew 26:53–54). The Son, the Only Begotten of the Father, the Prince of Peace stoically endured every appalling moment of suffering out of love for His Father and for us (see John 15:13). He willingly descended below all things so that He could "be familiar in all . . . ways" of human suffering (Psalm 139:3) to completely understand us and help us. The three crosses remind us that Christ was crucified between two convicted thieves. One taunted Jesus to save Himself and them if He were truly the Messiah. The other found an unexpected source of hope during their excruciating suffering. He cried, "We are punished justly, for we are getting what our deeds deserve. But this man has done nothing wrong." Then he begged, "'Jesus, remember me when you come into your kingdom.' Jesus answered him, 'Truly I tell you, today you will be with me in paradise'" (Luke 23:41–43). In the window, this event has not yet taken place. The crosses are bathed in soft light and stand empty, foreshadowing that the Light of the World would overcome all, allowing the thieves and each of us to eventually return to our heavenly home.

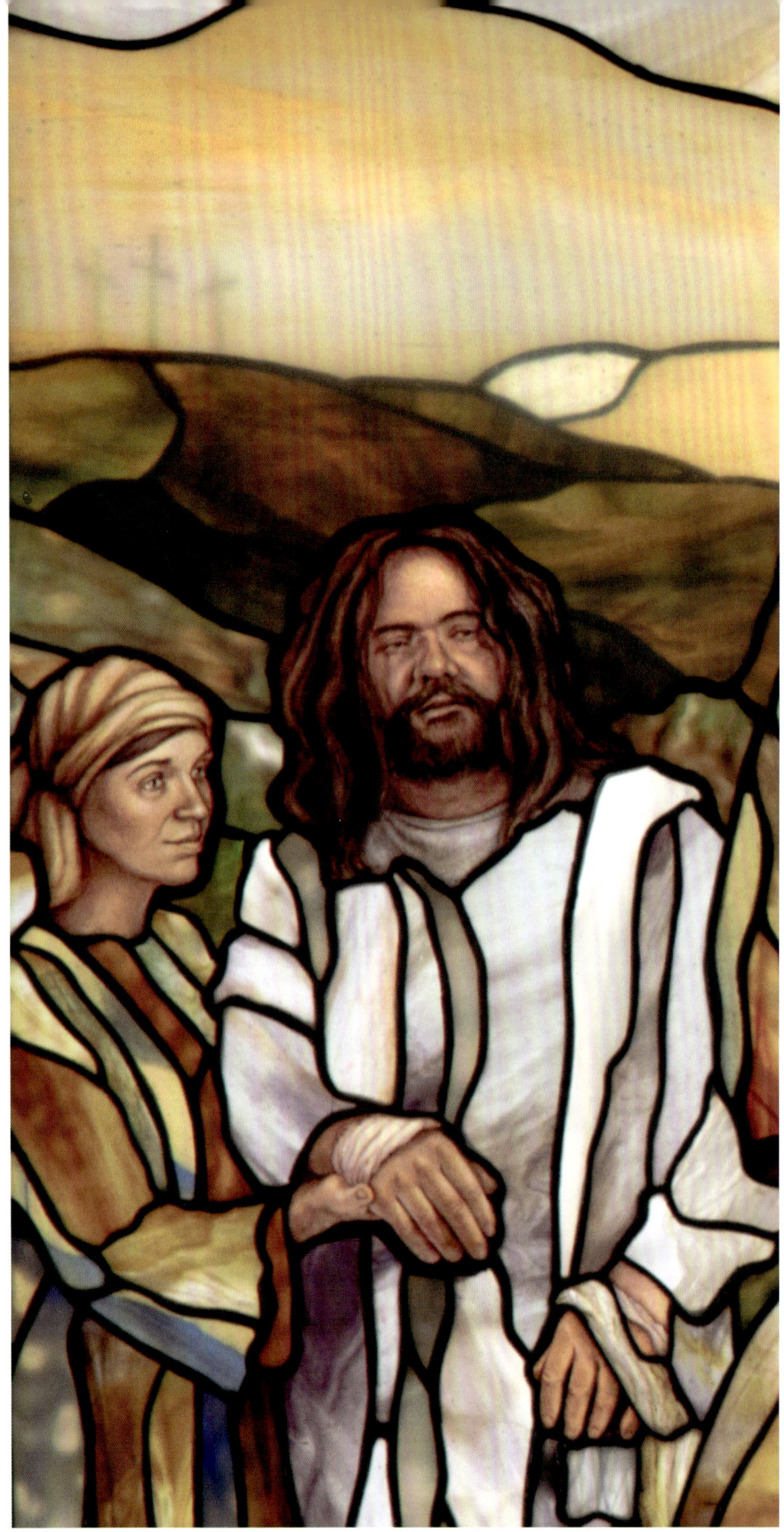

11. WIDOW OF NAIN

Christ was often found ministering to individuals who needed the peace and healing only He could give. The widow of Nain is one such soul: "Jesus went to a town called Nain, and his disciples and a large crowd went along with him. As he approached the town gate, a dead person was being carried out—the only son of his mother, and she was a widow. And a large crowd from the town was with her. When the Lord saw her, his heart went out to her and he said, 'Don't cry'" (Luke 7:11–13). Christ recognized the real and valid grief of this woman. She grieved the loss of her child, but also the loss of her support and sustenance because he was her only son. She grieved for the loss of a future daughter-in-law and possible grandchildren. The Savior understood and felt her pain, fear, and despair. "Then he went up and touched the bier they were carrying him on, and the bearers stood still. He said, 'Young man, I say to you, get up!' The dead man sat up and began to talk, and Jesus gave him back to his mother" (vv. 14–15). This was a moment of perfect compassion. There is no loss that Christ cannot understand and ultimately make right. It also interesting to note that this was the woman's *only* son, just as Jesus is God's only Son begotten in the flesh. Christ would die but, like the son of the widow, live again. When the people saw the young man arise, they were astonished: "They were all filled with awe and praised God. 'A great prophet has appeared among us,' they said. '*God has come to help his people*'" (v. 16; emphasis added). Indeed, Jesus had come not just to help this widow and her son, but to help all His people. Christ's Atonement and grace are for the salvation of all of God's children, throughout time and across all cultures. Christ loves and is keenly aware of everyone. In the work of art, the widow of Nain is helping to hold up her son who was just brought back from the dead. The artists intentionally left her feet not visible. It is almost as if she is floating. God sends angels, unseen and seen, to help support us in our trials. "Keep on loving one another as brothers and sisters. Do not forget to show hospitality to strangers, for by so doing some people have shown hospitality to angels without knowing it" (Hebrews 13:1–2).

12. SON OF THE WIDOW OF NAIN; ALSO REPRESENTING LAZARUS

The Bible tells of two different men who had died and were brought back to life through Christ's miraculous power. One was the son of the widow of Nain. The other was the brother of Mary and Martha from Bethany. His name was Lazarus, and Christ loved the family (see John 11:5). When the Savior arrived too late to save Lazarus from dying, Martha proclaimed her deep testimony of Christ's divinity and His power to have healed Lazarus had He arrived in time. Jesus said to her, "I am the resurrection and the life. The one who believes in me will live, even though they die; and whoever lives by believing in me will never die" (John 11:25–26). "Jesus called in a loud voice, 'Lazarus, come out!' The dead man came out, his hands and feet wrapped with strips of linen, and a cloth around his face. Jesus said to them, 'Take off the grave clothes and let him go'" (vv. 43–44). As amazing as it is that Christ raised the son of the widow as well as His friend Lazarus, both would ultimately die again, as would the widow and Mary and Martha. Christ's testimony to Martha is a testimony to all: He is the resurrection and the life for all mankind: "And the God of all grace, who called you to his eternal glory in Christ, after you have suffered a little while, will himself restore you and make you strong, firm and steadfast" (1 Peter 5:10).

13. SEVENTY WITH SCROLLS; ALSO REPRESENTING THE HUMBLE PUBLICAN

Notice in the window the individual next to the Pharisee who is holding a bag of scrolls. He is an illustration of those called to testify of Christ: "After this the Lord appointed seventy-two others and sent them two by two ahead of him to every town and place where he was about to go. He told them, 'The harvest is plentiful, but the workers are few. Ask the Lord of the harvest, therefore, to send out workers into his harvest field'" (Luke 10:1–2). It is no small task to share the good news of the gospel of Jesus Christ with the world. It is both a privilege and a responsibility. However, we are not left alone. Christ sent forth those He called two by two because "every matter must be established by the testimony of two or three witnesses" (2 Corinthians 13:1). As we choose to accept the work of gospel harvest, we are never alone. Along with earthly companions, the Spirit will also accompany us: "And it is the Spirit who testifies, because the Spirit is the truth" (1 John 5:6). The same male image in the window is reminiscent of the parable of the Pharisee and the tax collector or publican: "Two men went up to the temple to pray, one a Pharisee and the other a tax collector. The Pharisee stood by himself and prayed: 'God, I thank you that I am not like other people—robbers, evildoers, adulterers—or even like this tax collector. I fast twice a week and give a tenth of all I get.' But the tax collector stood at a distance. He would not even look up to heaven, but beat his breast and said, 'God, have mercy on me, a sinner.' I tell you that this man, rather than the other, went home justified before God. For all those who exalt themselves will be humbled, and those who humble themselves will be exalted" (Luke 18:10–14).

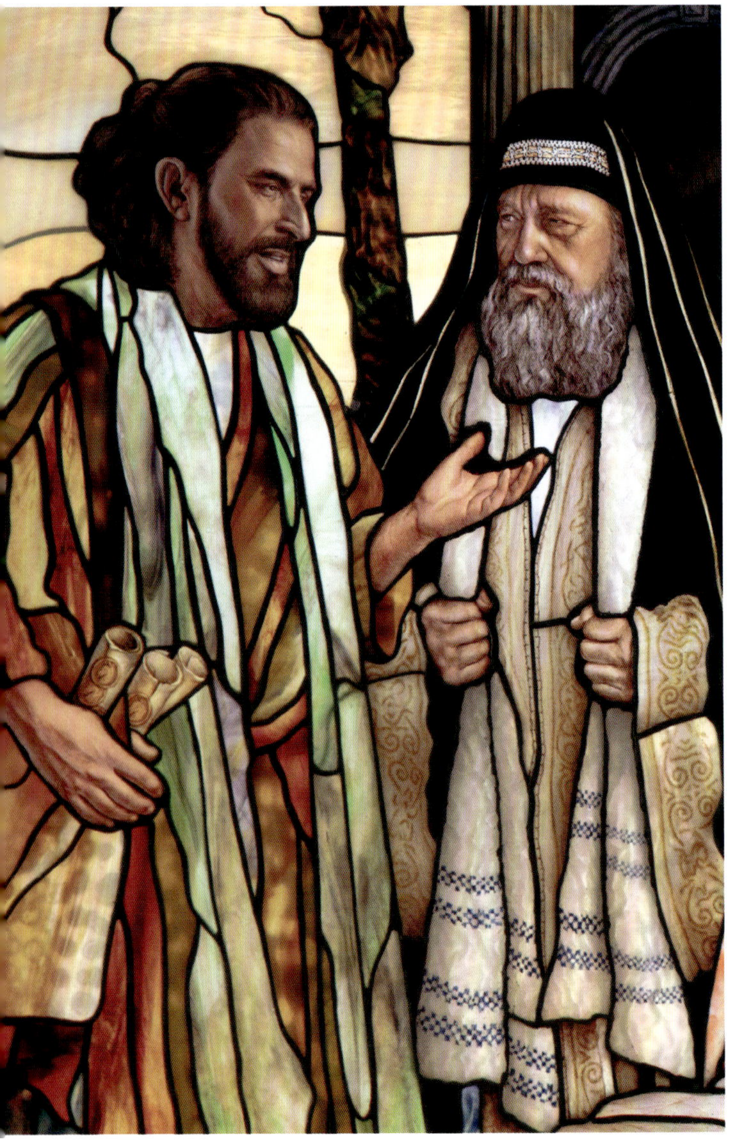

14. NICODEMUS THE PHARISEE; ALSO REPRESENTING THE WICKED HUSBANDMAN

"Now there was a Pharisee, a man named Nicodemus who was a member of the Jewish ruling council. He came to Jesus at night and said, 'Rabbi, we know that you are a teacher who has come from God. For no one could perform the signs you are doing if God were not with him'" (John 3:1–2). It is quite remarkable that Nicodemus chose to approach the Savior with a sincere desire to learn and understand. Most of the Pharisees and other Jewish leaders completely rejected Christ and were like the wicked husbandman in Christ's parable who persecuted and stoned God's servants and even killed God's Son (see Matthew 21:33–40). Nicodemus had more of an open heart than others in his position, and his questions allowed the Savior to teach him—and though him, all of us. In the art, this individual is holding onto his prayer shawl in a way that suggests he is torn between letting go of faulty beliefs and traditions and pondering what he would need to change to truly accept Christ.

15. WOMAN AT THE WELL, WOMAN WITH ISSUE OF BLOOD, AND WOMAN TAKEN IN ADULTERY

Although there is only one woman pictured by the well in the artwork, she represents three distinct women from the Savior's ministry. She holds a water jug reminiscent of the Samaritan woman at the well. Her hand is stretched out towards the hem of Christ's robe like the woman with the issue of blood, and she is dressed in red, with two stones beside her, to illustrate the woman taken in adultery. Each one of these daughters of God found themselves in front of the Savior for a unique reason. The Samaritan woman had simply been at the well to collect water, while the woman with the long-term illness sought the Savior for healing. The woman taken in adultery was forcefully brought before Christ by those who condemned her. One commonality between all these women is that they were in a position of need and vulnerability. Whether or not they knew it initially, they all needed to be made whole. Christ didn't just give water to the Samaritan woman but gave her the gift of testimony and conversion. He didn't just heal the woman of her condition, but He validated her faith and gave her back her place in the community. To the woman caught in adultery, He gave compassion, forgiveness, and counsel to move forward in righteousness. Each woman found hope regardless of the disappointments of her life. "Praise be to the God and Father of our Lord Jesus Christ! In his great mercy he has given us new birth into a living hope through the resurrection of Jesus Christ from the dead, and into an inheritance that can never perish, spoil or fade. This inheritance is kept in heaven for you. . . . In all this you greatly rejoice, though now for a little while you may have had to suffer grief in all kinds of trials" (1 Peter 1:3–4, 6).

16. STONES RECALLING THE ONLY ONE WITHOUT SIN

The stones portrayed on the rim of the well refer to the words of Jesus to the accusers of the woman taken in adultery: "The teachers of the law and the Pharisees brought in a woman caught in adultery. They made her stand before the group and said to Jesus, 'Teacher, this woman was caught in the act of adultery. In the Law Moses commanded us to stone such women. Now what do you say?' They were using this question as a trap, in order to have a basis for accusing him" (John 8:3–6). If Jesus said to let her go, they would call Him a lawbreaker. If Jesus said she was not guilty, they would call Him a liar. The response they had not considered was Christ's willingness to forgive and show compassion. He said, "Let any one of you who is without sin be the first to throw a stone at her" (John 8:7). The Savior was the only sinless one and, therefore, the only one with the right to cast a stone, yet He did not. Nor did He condone the wrongdoing. Instead, He counseled her, "Go now and leave your life of sin" (John 8:11).

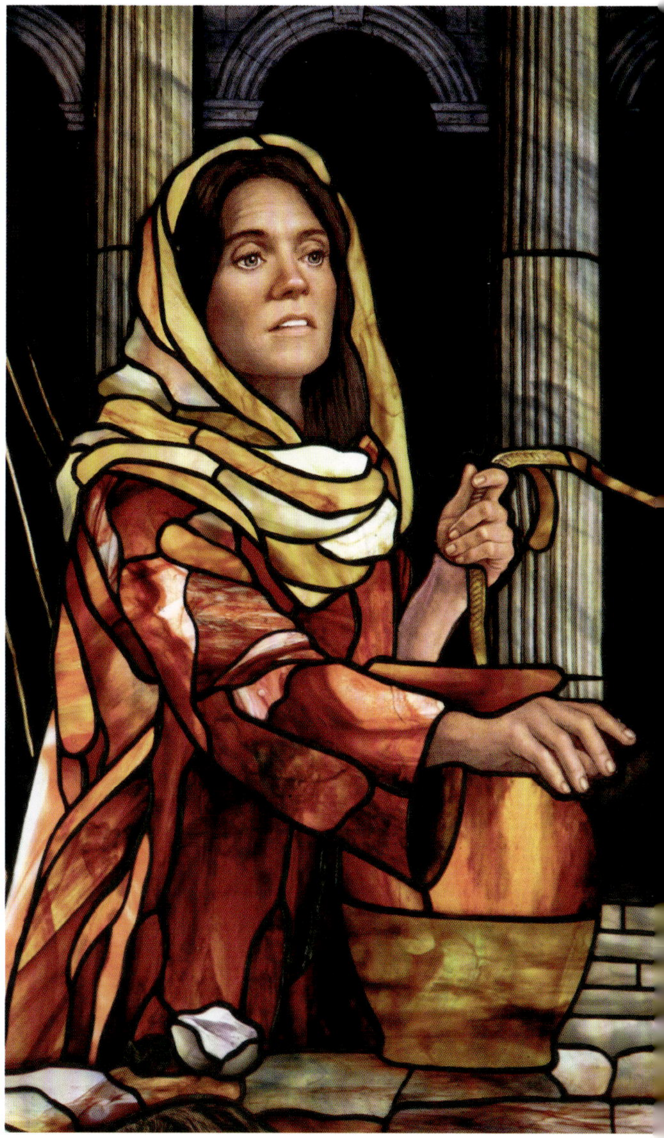

17. WELL AND CONTAINER REPRESENTING LIVING WATER

All living things require water for survival. This is why the Samaritan woman had come, as she did every day, to gather water in her jug from the well. Christ broke cultural taboos by beginning a conversation with the Samaritan woman. He asked for water. Jesus then taught her, "If you knew the gift of God and who it is that asks you for a drink, you would have asked him and he would have given you living water" (John 4:10). Truly, Jesus is the Living Water. He said, "Let anyone who is thirsty come to me and drink. Whoever believes in me, as Scripture has said, rivers of living water will flow from within them" (John 7:37–38). To those who accept Christ, He is enough and more. The scriptures teach of His role as Savior and Redeemer. They teach of His love—enough to quench the spiritual thirst of every human soul. He brings hope and peace to balance the injustices of life. Allowing Him into our lives will transform our perspective, our motives, and our desires. We need not bring a jug like the one held by the woman near the well in the art. We need only to bring our hearts, open and ready to be filled.

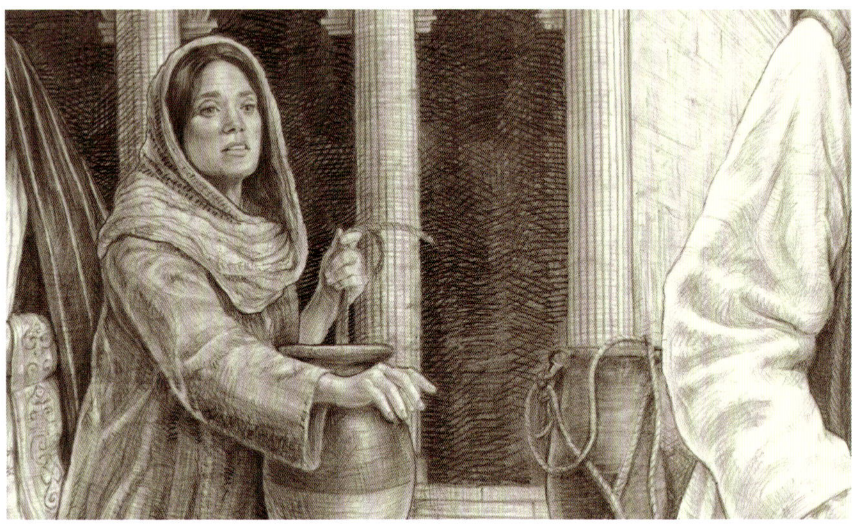

18. "HE CALLED A LITTLE CHILD TO HIM"

"He called a little child to him, and placed the child among them. And he said: 'Truly I tell you, unless you change and become like little children, you will never enter the kingdom of heaven. Therefore, whoever takes the lowly position of this child is the greatest in the kingdom of heaven. And whoever welcomes one such child in my name welcomes me'" (Matthew 18:2–5). The small boy sitting at the well represents the children of whom the Master spoke. He brought with him a toy boat he carved in hopes of finding water in which to float it. He is innocent, humble, and genuinely content with little. He represents those of whom the Lord said, "For those who exalt themselves will be humbled, and those who humble themselves will be exalted" (Matthew 23:12). Notice the boy's gaze is on Christ. Had the lad heard stories of how this man walked on water, turned water to wine, and calmed the raging sea? Or does he simply sense His goodness and desires to know Him better? One way or the other, the boy's face is filled with awe. If he could speak his thoughts, we would see the fulfillment of Matthew's words: "From the lips of children and infants you, Lord, have called forth your praise" (Matthew 21:16).

19. SEEDS SYMBOLIZING THE MESSAGE OF THE GOSPEL

Christ intentionally taught parables using people, places, and things with which His listeners were familiar. For example, during His mortal ministry, many people were fishermen, animal herders, or farmers: "A farmer went out to sow his seed. As he was scattering the seed, some fell along the path, and the birds came and ate it up. Some fell on rocky places, where it did not have much soil. It sprang up quickly, because the soil was shallow. But when the sun came up, the plants were scorched, and they withered because they had no root. Other seed fell among thorns, which grew up and choked the plants. Still other seed fell on good soil, where it produced a crop—a hundred, sixty or thirty times what was sown" (Matthew 13:3–8). The gospel, as the seed, has the potential to yield astounding results if it is planted into a heart that is humble, open, and ready to accept it. If, instead, it lands with those whose hearts are closed, hard, shallow, or otherwise unprepared, it will not grow as it should. In each case the seed is good. It is the soil that varies. In the art, some of the seeds are shown on the ground being eaten by a bird because there was no good soil in which to take root and flourish. Sadly, Christ knew that some of God's children would be like the stones—unwilling to receive His gospel at that time. The Parable of the Sower is one of the few parables Christ explained to His disciples. Typically, He left it to His listeners to have ears to hear. Those who took responsibility for their own learning were able to recognize the spiritual messages.

20. TOY BOAT RECALLING THE SEA OF GALILEE

Like the fishing net with floats in the shape of the Sea of Galilee hanging in the shop at the left of the well, this handcrafted toy boat belonging to the young boy sitting at the well is a reminder of that special body of water. The miracles of walking on water (see Matthew 14:25–27) and calming the storm (see Mark 4:35–41) testify of Christ's divine power. Additionally, the Sea of Galilee is where Christ called His first apostles. Thus, the artists included a Greek inscription on the side of the boat that reads "I will make you fishers of men" (KJV, Matthew 4:19) as a reminder that Peter, Andrew, James, and John immediately left their nets and followed Him.

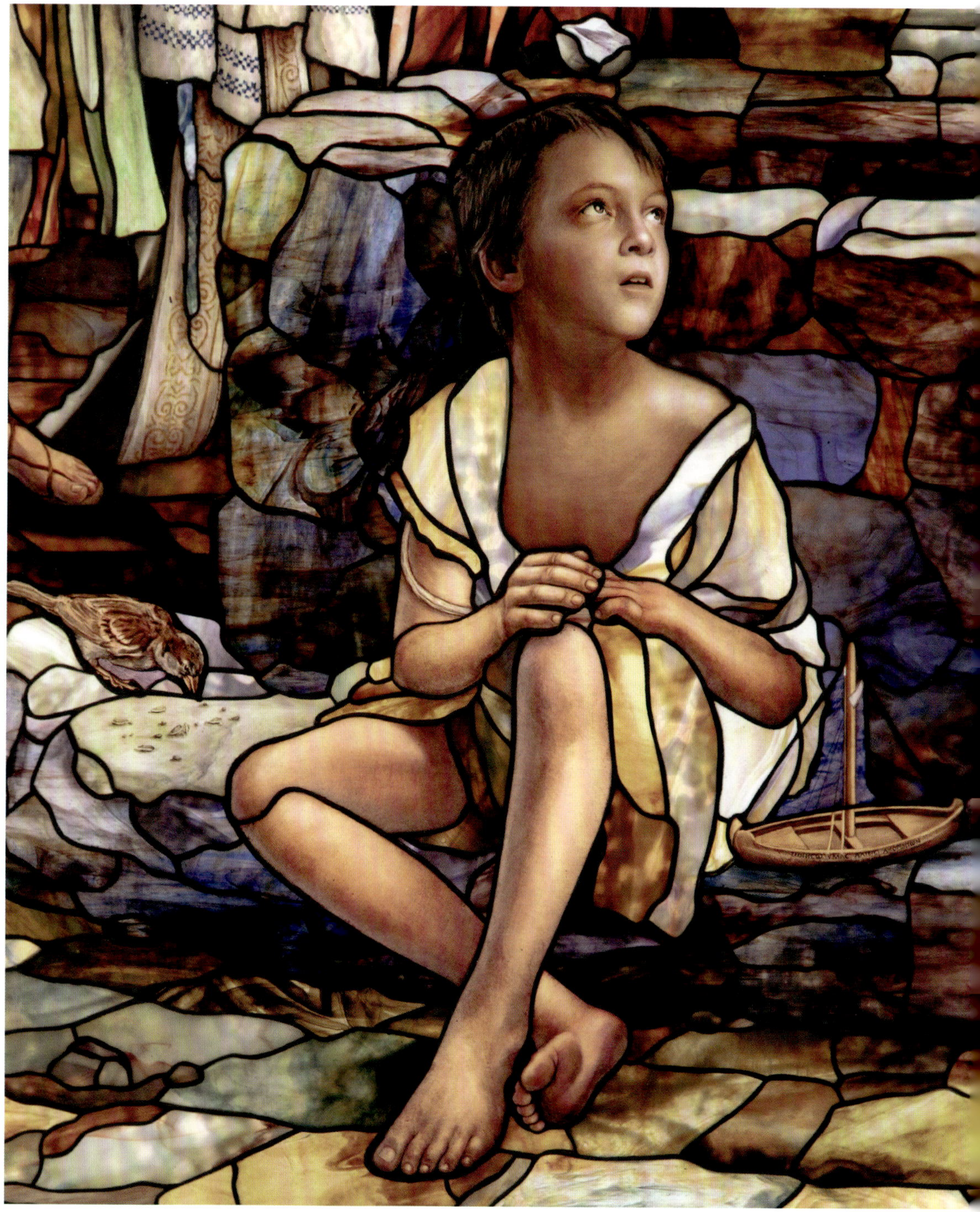

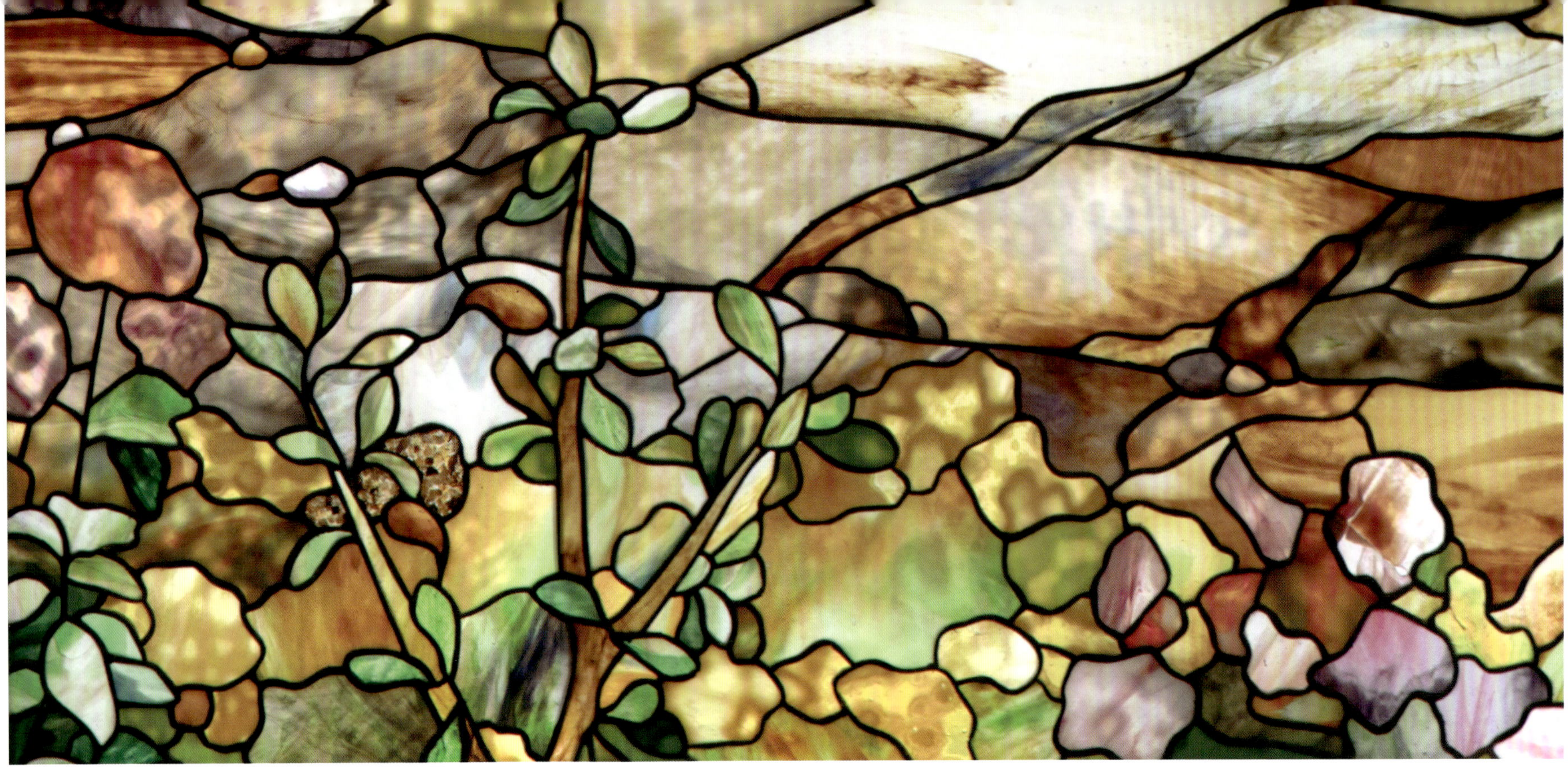

SYMBOLS FROM NATURE

21. OLD TESTAMENT HYSSOP PLANTS

"Take a bunch of hyssop [pink flowers and mint-like leaves], dip it into the blood in the basin and put some of the blood on the top and on both sides of the doorframe. None of you shall go out of the door of your house until morning. When the Lord goes through the land to strike down the Egyptians, he will see the blood on the top and sides of the doorframe and will pass over that doorway, and he will not permit the destroyer to enter your houses and strike you down" (Exodus 12:22–23). This is the ancient promise that Jews celebrate each year as Passover. It was at a dinner commemorating the Passover that Jesus instituted Communion. Now Christians partake of Communion to remember Christ's sacrifice and how, because of His blood, all will live after we die.

22. MYRRH

Myrrh was used anciently in temples to anoint and consecrate the high priests (see Exodus 30:23–25). It was also used to prepare the dead for burial because it acted as a preservative. This made the gift presented by the wise men very meaningful: "On coming to the house, they saw the child with his mother Mary, and they bowed down and worshiped him. Then they opened their treasures and presented him with gifts of gold, frankincense and myrrh" (Matthew 2:11). The myrrh showed that the Magi recognized that Christ—which means "the Anointed One" was born to die for us: "The Son of Man did not come to be served, but to serve, and to give his life as a ransom for many" (Matthew 20:28).

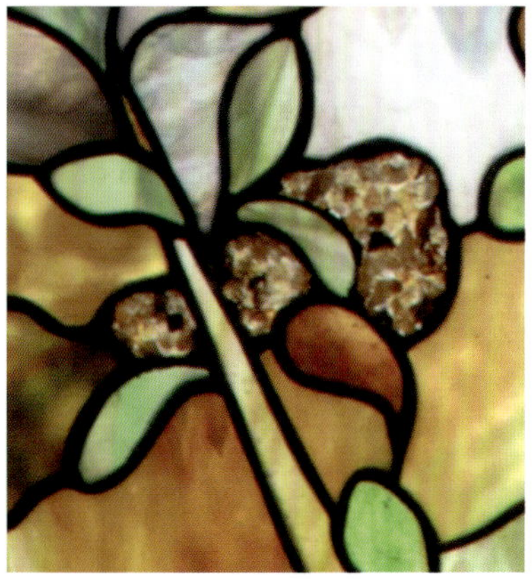

23. ACTUAL BITS OF FRANKINCENSE

Scriptural accounts show that frankincense was used in temple worship (see Exodus 30:34, Leviticus 2:1, 16; 24:7, and Psalm 141:2). As such, it was a symbol of reverence, devotion, and of the divine. The smoke rising from burning incense was reminiscent of prayers ascending to heaven. By presenting this as a gift to the Savior at His birth, the wise men were acknowledging that Christ was holy. The artists chose to preserve actual fragments of frankincense within the window to acknowledge the valuable gift presented to the Christ Child.

24. ALMOND BLOSSOM SYMBOLIZING AARONIC PRIESTHOOD

When the Israelites wandered in the wilderness, there was a disagreement about which tribe should have the responsibility for the priesthood and temple rites. "So Moses spoke to the Israelites, and their leaders gave him twelve staffs, one for the leader of each of their ancestral tribes, and Aaron's staff was among them. Moses placed the staffs before the Lord in the tent of the covenant law. The next day Moses entered the tent and saw that Aaron's staff, which represented the tribe of Levi, had not only sprouted but had budded, blossomed and produced almonds" (Numbers 17:6–8). That same Aaronic priesthood authority would ultimately be held by John the Baptist as he prepared the way for the coming Messiah. Christ Himself recognized John's authority: "Truly I tell you, among those born of women there has not risen anyone greater than John the Baptist" (Matthew 11:11). Christ knew He needed to be baptized by John—who had God's authority—unlike the Sadducees whose authority came only from Rome: "Then Jesus came from Galilee to the Jordan to be baptized by John. But John tried to deter him, saying, 'I need to be baptized by you, and do you come to me?' Jesus replied, 'Let it be so now; it is proper for us to do this to fulfill all righteousness'" (Matthew 3:13–15).

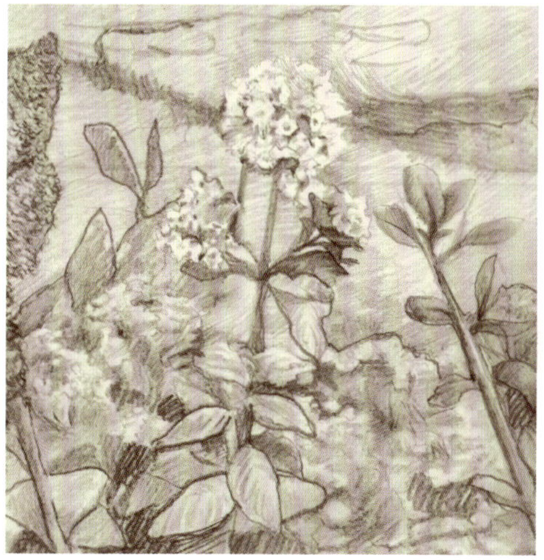

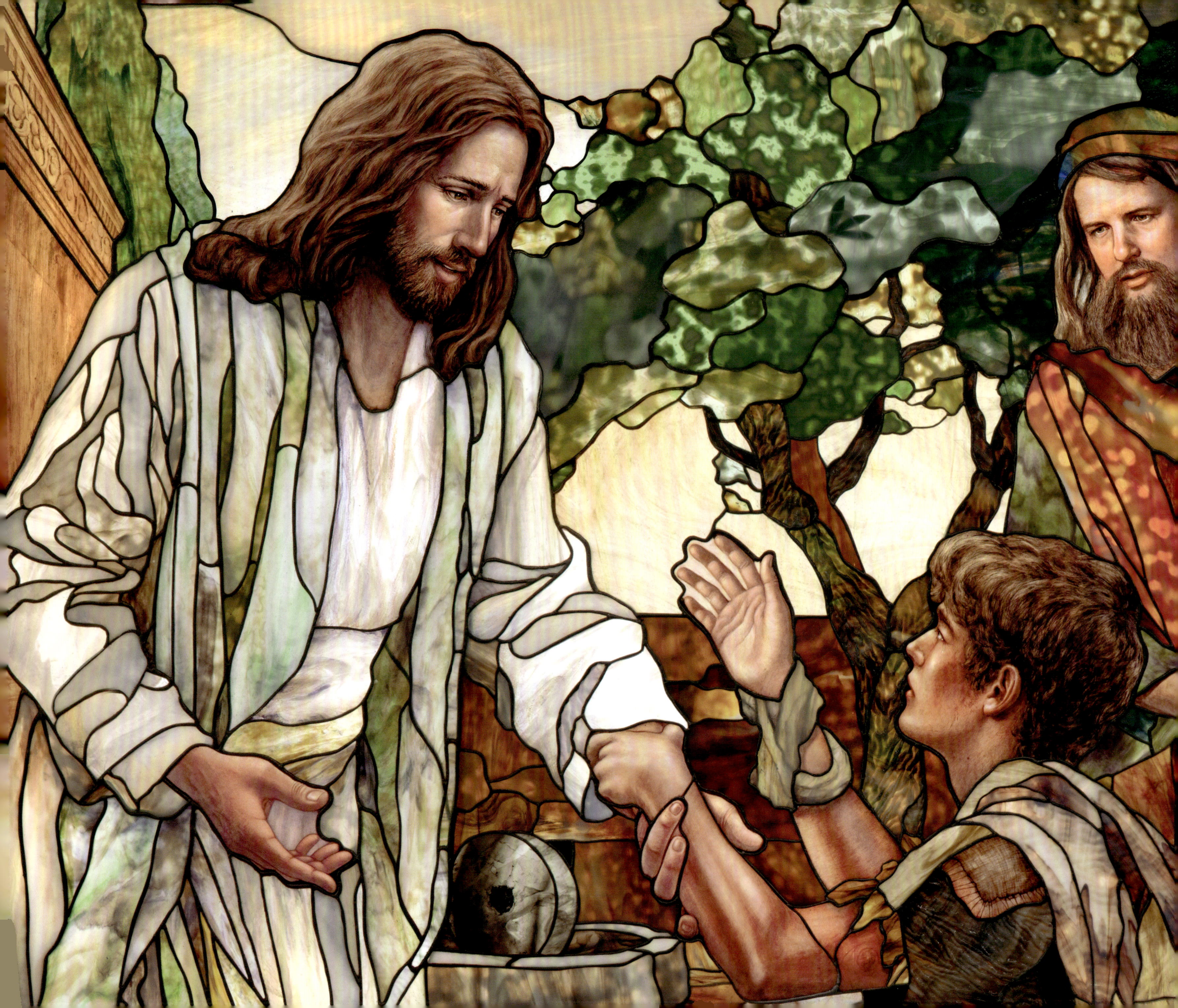

Panel E

Featuring Christ and the Beggar

CHRIST AND HIS COMPASSION | 54

1. Palm branches on capitals recalling Christ's triumphal entry
2. Mausoleum
3. Olive tree representing Gethsemane
4. Christ, who did the Father's will
5. Grasp symbolizing grace
6. Olive press
7. Sparrows

THOSE BLESSED BY CHRIST | 58

8. James with a red shawl recalling his martyrdom
9. Peter holding the keys of the kingdom
10. New fabric on an old garment
11. Young beggar representing all healings
12. Crutch tossed aside
13. Actual coins from the Holy Land

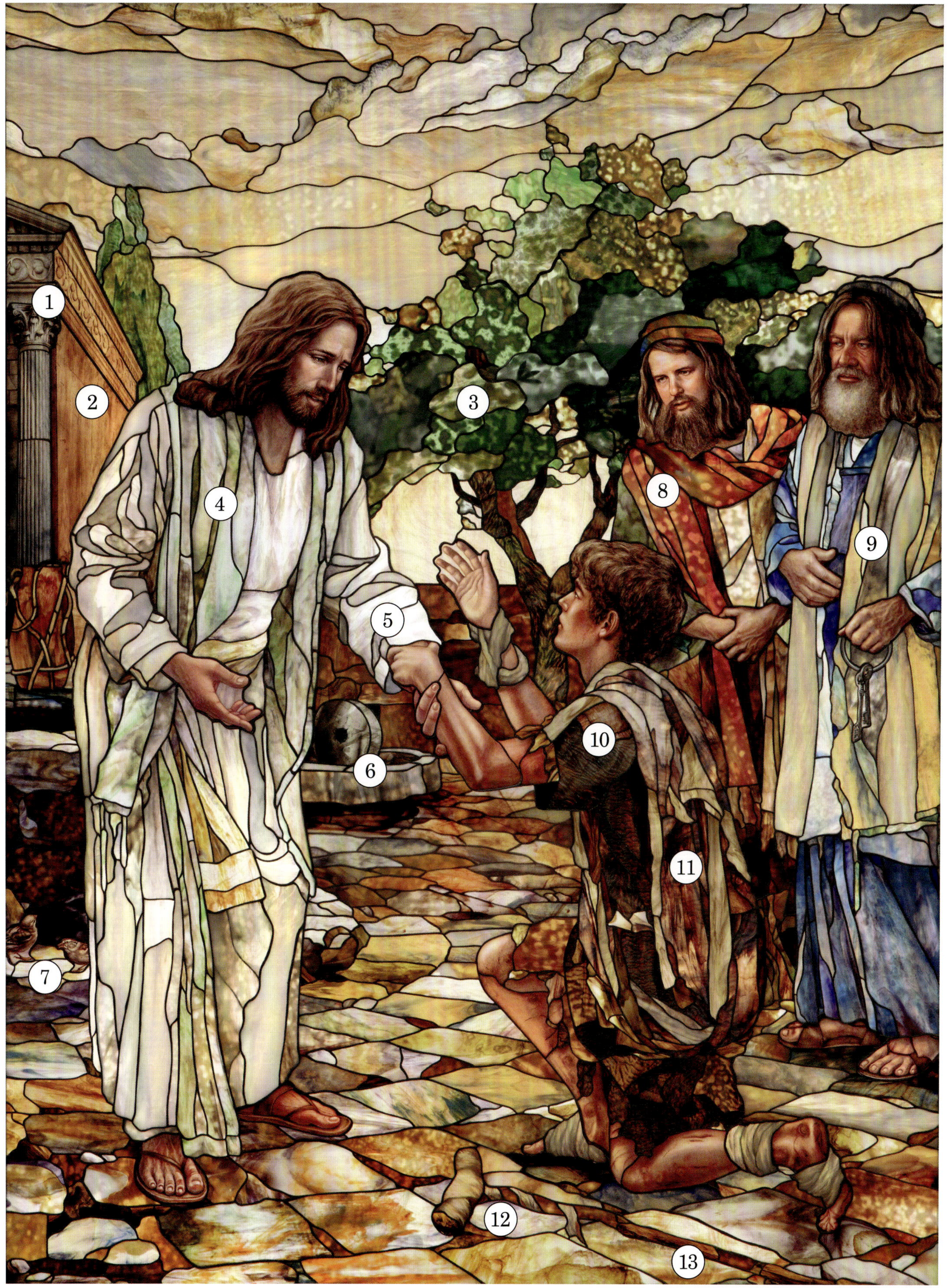

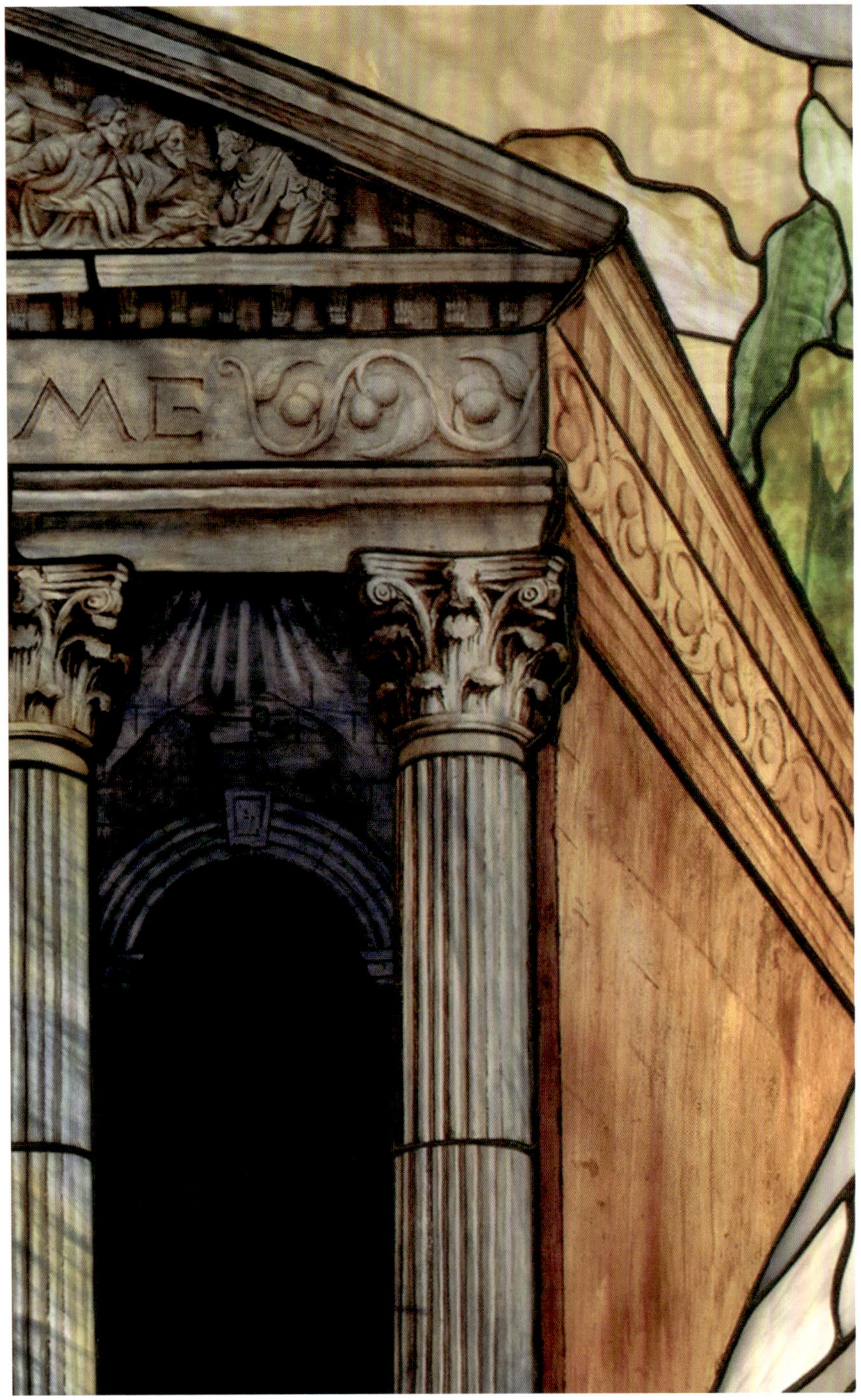

CHRIST AND HIS COMPASSION

1. PALM BRANCHES ON CAPITALS RECALLING CHRIST'S TRIUMPHAL ENTRY

Columns in architecture serve both a structural and decorative purpose. They hold up parts of the building and make it more beautiful. The top portions of columns are called capitals, and various types convey messages, with more elaborate capitals adorning more expensive and important buildings. Palm columns were commonly used in Egypt on temples and tombs. Their imagery of a cluster of palm leaves represented fertility and abundance along with victory and triumph. On the mausoleum in the artwork, these capitals can reflect the Savior's abundant blessings and His victory and triumph over death and hell. They remind us of the palm leaves waved at His triumphal entry into Jerusalem (see John 12:12–15). As the columns support the structure, Christ's Atonement supports us. Without Christ there is no hope. With Christ, "we have this hope as an anchor for the soul, firm and secure" (Hebrews 6:19).

2. MAUSOLEUM

Christ's strongest rebukes were for hypocrites—those who outwardly appeared humble and obedient to God while inwardly were proud and disobedient: "'Woe to you, teachers of the law and Pharisees, you hypocrites! You are like whitewashed tombs, which look beautiful on the outside but on the inside are full of the bones of the dead and everything unclean. In the same way, on the outside you appear to people as righteous but on the inside you are full of hypocrisy and wickedness'" (Matthew 23:27–28). Christ valued living with integrity—the way He and His Father do: "'If you really know me, you will know my Father as well'" (John 14:6–7). On another occasion, Jesus said, "'Now this is eternal life: that they know you, the only true God, and Jesus Christ, whom you have sent'" (John 17:3). The white and clean mausoleum in the art is a symbol of hypocrisy, death, and apostasy. The Savior's back is to this building, because He has overcome all of that and can free us from it as well.

3. OLIVE TREE REPRESENTING GETHSEMANE

After the Last Supper, Jesus walked with His apostles to the ravine between the Temple Mount and the Mount of Olives: "Then Jesus went with his disciples to a place called Gethsemane, and he said to them, 'Sit here while I go over there and pray.' He took Peter and the two sons of Zebedee along with him, and he began to be sorrowful and troubled. Then he said to them, 'My soul is overwhelmed with sorrow to the point of death. Stay here and keep watch with me.' Going a little farther, he fell with his face to the ground and prayed, 'My Father, if it is possible, may this cup be taken from me. Yet not as I will, but as you will'" (Matthew 26:36–39). In all of Christ's recorded life and ministry, nothing was as significant for mankind's salvation than the Atonement, which began in the olive tree grove called Gethsemane. In this sacred place we see one of the few instances in which Christ asked for support from His disciples, and even from His Father, because what He faced was so daunting. His friends were unable to stay awake, but God sent what help He could: "An angel from heaven appeared to him and strengthened him" (Luke 22:43). Still, God could not remove the bitter cup for Jesus without causing bitter consequences for all of us. Because of God's love for us, He willed Christ to continue. Because of Christ's love for us, He said to His Father, "Not my will, but yours be done" (Luke 22:42). That is where the true selflessness and majesty of the gift lies. Christ, who was sinless, voluntarily paid the excruciating cost of our sin. He understood that "wrongdoers will not inherit the kingdom of God" (1 Corinthians 6:9). Jesus was the only one who could meet the demands of justice *and* preserve our freedom by honoring both the justice and mercy of God.

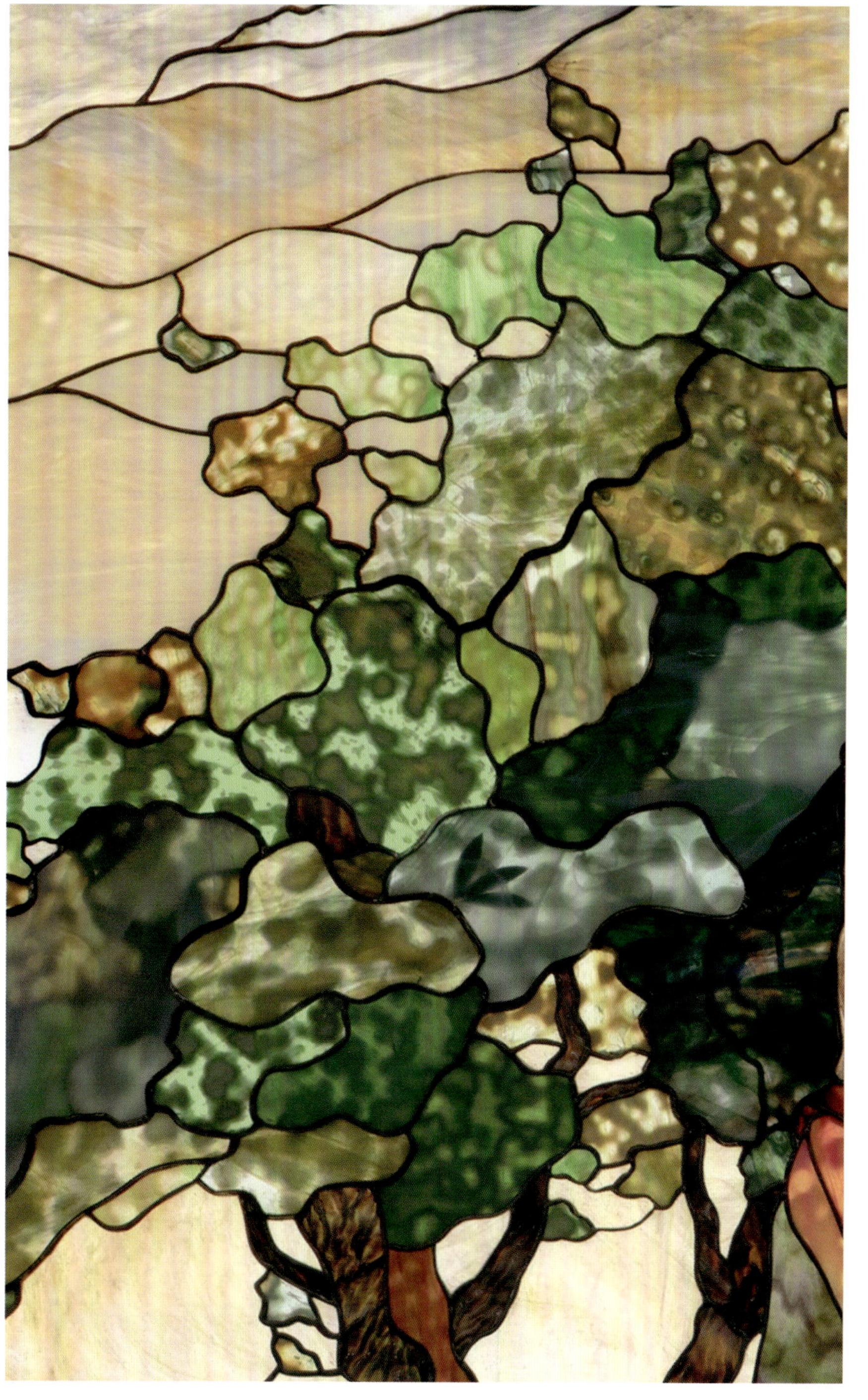

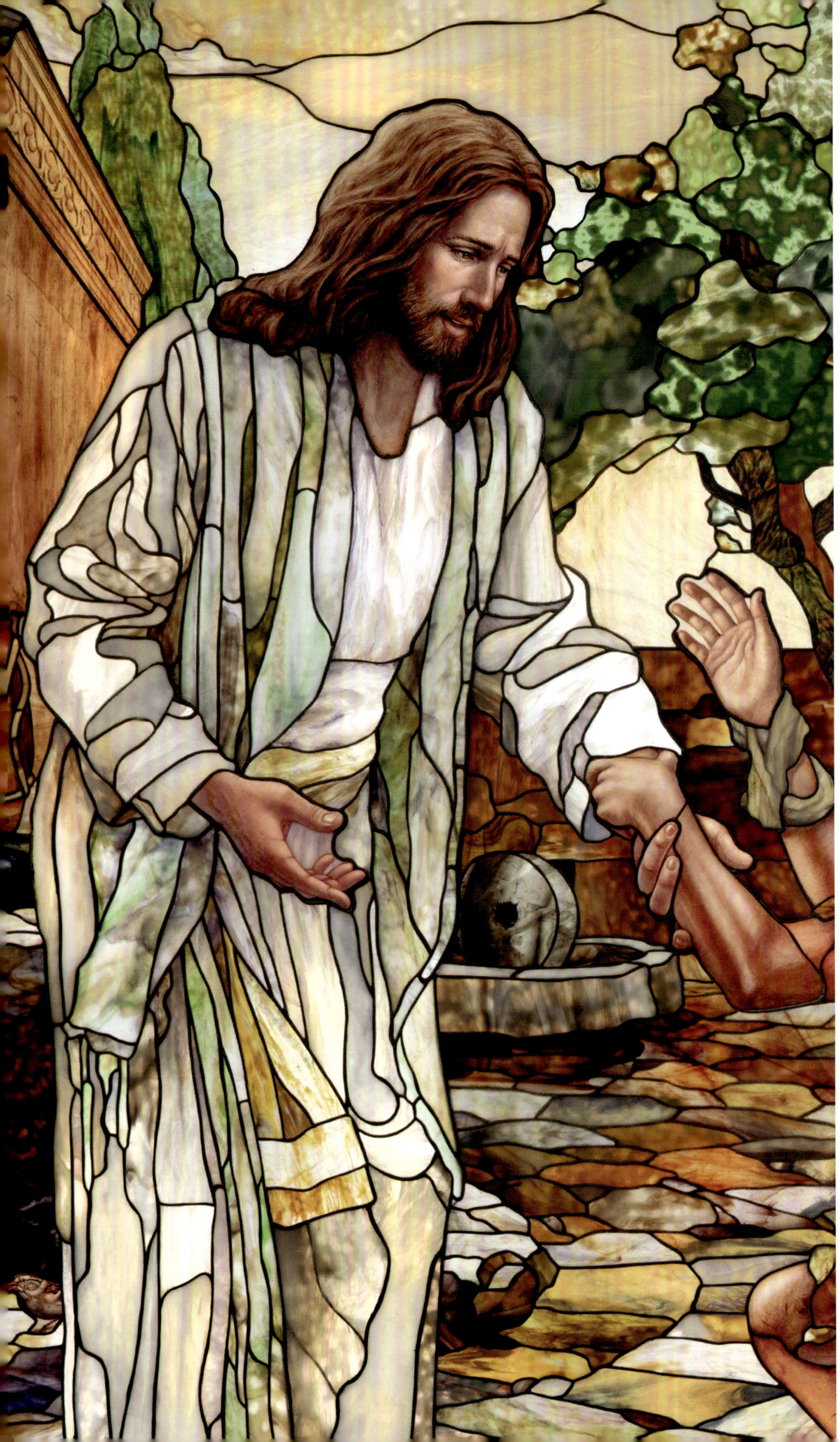

4. CHRIST, WHO DID THE FATHER'S WILL

The central figure in this magnificent window is none other than Jesus Christ, the central figure in the salvation of humankind. He selflessly laid His will aside and instead did only the will of His Father. As the promised Messiah from the foundations of the world, Christ is our Advocate (see 1 John 2:1), Mediator (see 1 Timothy 2:5), Savior (see Luke 2:11), Redeemer (see Job 19:25), and Deliverer (see Romans 11:26). As the Light of the World, Christ illuminates us. Whoever follows Him "will never walk in darkness, but will have the light of life" (John 8:12). "No one comes to the Father except through [Him]" (John 14:6). Without sin, He was the only one who could intercede on our behalf (see Hebrews 7:25). "Therefore God exalted him to the highest place and gave him the name that is above every name, that at the name of Jesus every knee should bow, in heaven and on earth and under the earth, and every tongue acknowledge that Jesus Christ is Lord, to the glory of God the Father" (Philippians 2:9–11). We were not with Him personally during His mortal ministry, yet we can know Him and trust His promises. If we allow Him, He will heal, lift, sustain, and comfort us through every challenge of life. He brings peace beyond our understanding (see John 14:27), and love that is perfect and eternal. He lived for us, died for us, and He lives again. He is the Good Shepherd, and His words from so long ago apply to us still: "My sheep listen to my voice; I know them, and they follow me. I give them eternal life, and they shall never perish; no one will snatch them out of my hand" (John 10:27–28).

5. GRASP SYMBOLIZING GRACE

We have only to extend our hand and reach Christ's reaching. He is there, ready and waiting to enjoy a relationship with us. "Come near to God and he will come near to you. . . . Humble yourselves before the Lord, and he will lift you up" (James 4:8, 10). Christ does not worry about how long it has been since we last thought of Him. His Grace is infinite and eternal. "God is our refuge and strength, an ever-present help in trouble" (Psalm 46:1). There is nothing too small and insignificant, or too big and overwhelming. He is prepared to carry us through it all. In the artwork, Christ is bending forward and holding the young beggar's arm in a tight grasp. That grasp symbolizes the grace offered and received in a relationship with Christ, who has power to lift, cleanse, help, and heal. The artists' positioning created an open space between Christ and the beggar—an invitation for each viewer to step in toward the Lord, look up into His eyes, and grasp His extended arm ourselves.

6. OLIVE PRESS

Gleaning olive oil from olives is a long process. Anciently, the olives were crushed under a large, heavy stone as it was rolled over them. Next, workers would gather the crushed olives in baskets and press them again. The immense pressure finally forced the oil from the olives. Understanding that process gives added meaning to Christ's experience in Gethsemane, which means "olive press." There, the weight of the world's wickedness was experienced by the Lord and Savior: "And being in anguish, he prayed more earnestly, and his sweat was like drops of blood falling to the ground" (Luke 22:44). Think of a time of your own personal suffering and magnify it over and over to even begin to understand what was felt by the Savior as He, innocent and pure of any wrongdoing, suffered for all. It is truly incomprehensible, but because Christ was fully human *and* fully divine, it was possible. He pleaded that the cup be taken from Him, but there was no other way (see Luke 22:42). He was the only being authorized, capable, and qualified to surrender His will out of love. The suffering in Gethsemane and on the cross, followed by His Resurrection from the grave constitute Christ's Atonement. Pondering each sacred moment fills us with humility, gratitude, and overwhelming love and joy. In the artwork, the stone represents not only Gethsemane but also the stone that covered Christ's tomb. Notice the small hint of an open doorway just behind it and remember the words from scripture: "An angel of the Lord came down from heaven and, going to the tomb, rolled back the stone and sat on it" (Matthew 28:2). From that tomb would come the resurrected Lord, and the world—and all eternity—would never be the same.

7. SPARROWS

It is remarkable, humbling, and inspiring to consider that the creator of the universe knows each one of us intimately and loves us personally. Christ is not bound by time. He who cares for the sparrows—small birds that were sold for pennies—cares even more for us: "Indeed, the very hairs of your head are all numbered. Don't be afraid; you are worth more than many sparrows" (Luke 12:6–7). We look at ourselves and struggle to see our worth, but God and Jesus have a much larger perspective. They see the inestimable value and worth of each soul: "For God so loved the world that he gave his one and only Son, that whoever believes in him shall not perish but have eternal life. For God did not send his Son into the world to condemn the world, but to save the world through him" (John 3:16–17). The salvation of God's children is Their greatest focus, and helping us reach our potential is Their greatest joy. Notice the sparrows by the Savior's feet in the art. One sparrow is looking up directly at Him, as if aware of Christ's presence and love. We have only to look, and we will see evidence on all sides testifying that we are known and cherished.

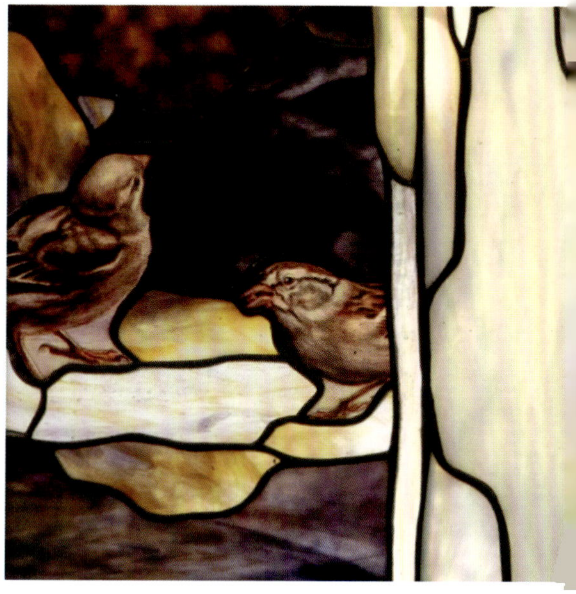

THOSE BLESSED BY CHRIST

8. JAMES WITH A RED SHAWL RECALLING HIS MARTYRDOM

James was one of the first apostles called. Along with his brother John, he immediately left the family fishing business to follow Christ. Jesus once called these two the "sons of thunder" (Mark 3:17). They were witnesses to the Savior's ministry and present on the Mount of Transfiguration. James was the first of the apostles to be martyred for his faith: "It was about this time that King Herod arrested some who belonged to the church, intending to persecute them. He had James, the brother of John, put to death with the sword" (Acts 12:1–2). The artists show James wearing a red scarf across his neck in recognition of the death he suffered for his testimony.

9. PETER HOLDING THE KEYS OF THE KINGDOM

By all scriptural accounts, the apostle Peter had a strong personality. He was rash, as evidenced when he jumped out of the boat and walked on water toward the Savior (see Matthew 14:22–33), and when he cut off the ear of one who came to arrest Jesus (see John 18:10). He was courageous, as seen in his willingness to boldly testify of Christ (see Matthew 16:16) in the face of persecution, even death, and he was vehement when he denied Christ three times (see Luke 22:55–60). Whatever he did, Peter did it with passion and boldness. His commitment made him a formidable leader. His weakness makes him a relatable friend, for aren't Christ's words to him applicable to all of us? "Simon, Simon, Satan has asked to sift all of you as wheat. But I have prayed for you, Simon, that your faith may not fail. And when you have turned back, strengthen your brothers" (Luke 22:31–32). Jesus knew that Peter would "turn back" and be fully converted. Like the Savior, Peter, the greatest of apostles, would be the servant of all (see 2 Peter 1:1). In this artwork Peter stands—as he does traditionally in art—with the keys of the kingdom in his hands. The artists have dressed him in blue so viewers can imagine him enveloped in water, reaching for the Lord's saving hand. Although Peter's eyes are focused on the miracle taking place before him, his thoughts could be turned inward, pondering all that Christ had seen in him. Just as the Savior knows Peter's heart and capabilities, He knows ours.

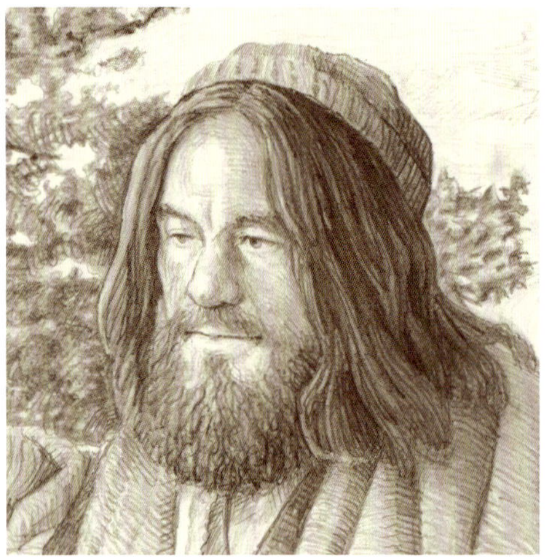

10. NEW FABRIC ON AN OLD GARMENT

"No one sews a patch of unshrunk cloth on an old garment, for the patch will pull away from the garment, making the tear worse" (Matthew 9:16). Christ spoke this truth at the same time He warned of putting old wine into new bottles. The message of both analogies is clear: New life will not be found amid the false traditions and apostasy of the past. Rather, it will be found in Christ and His higher and holier ways. During Christ's ministry, the most common fabrics used would have been natural fibers such as linen and wool, both of which shrank when washed. If, to repair a torn hole, one sewed new fabric that had yet to shrink onto fabric that has already gone through all the shrinking it would do, then when the garment was next washed, that new fabric would shrink disproportionately and put significant strain on the fibers of the old fabric. Instead of repairing the hole, it would increase the damage. Christ taught listeners, then and now, to recognize how old beliefs and cultural habits can keep us from recognizing and benefiting from truth. As we keep our hearts open, asking and seeking regularly (see Luke 11:9–10), then we will be able to discern and embrace Christ's new covenant; this also represents the parable of the Householder (see Matthew 13:51–53) about the householder who brings out his treasure—things new and things old.

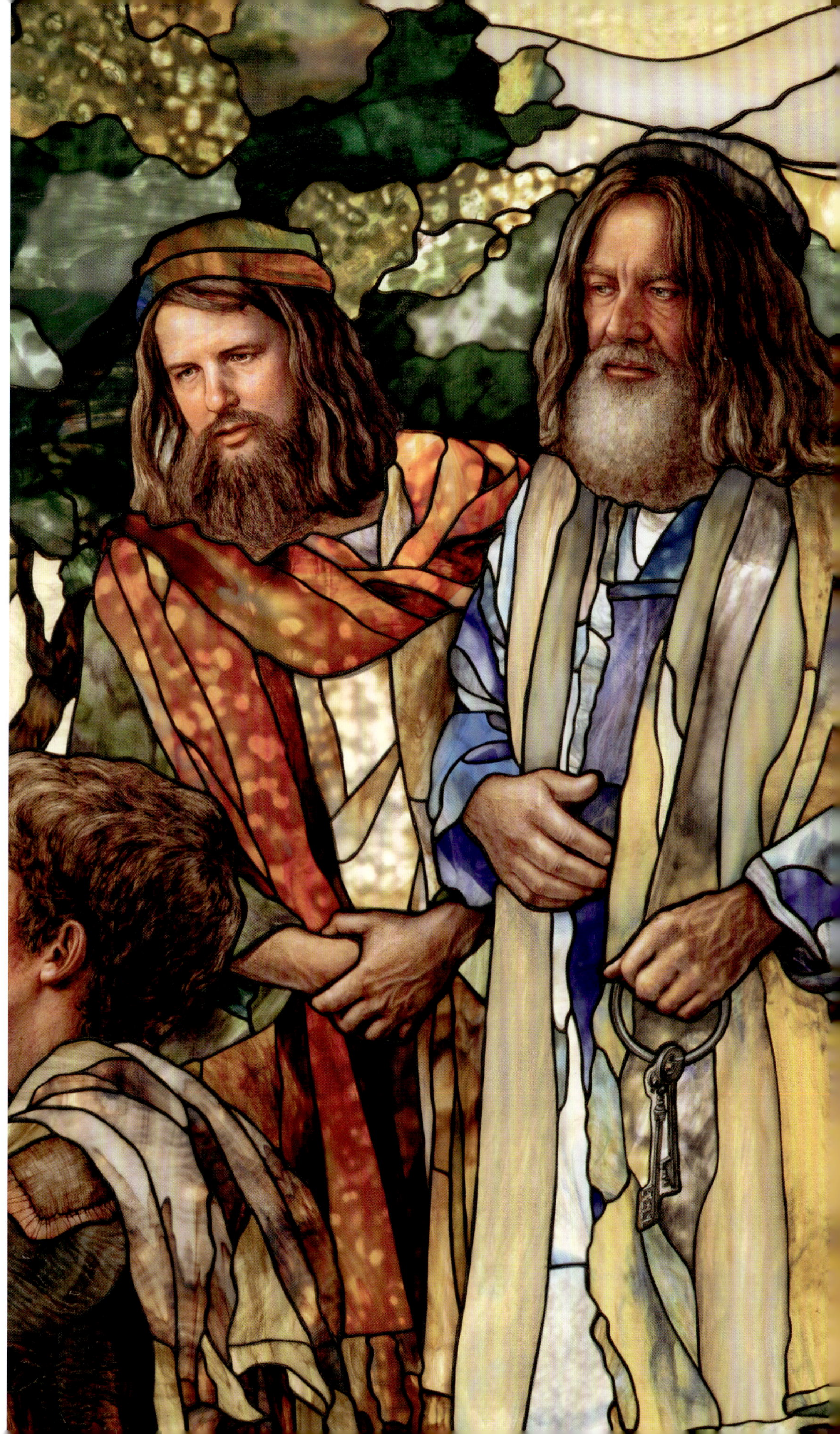

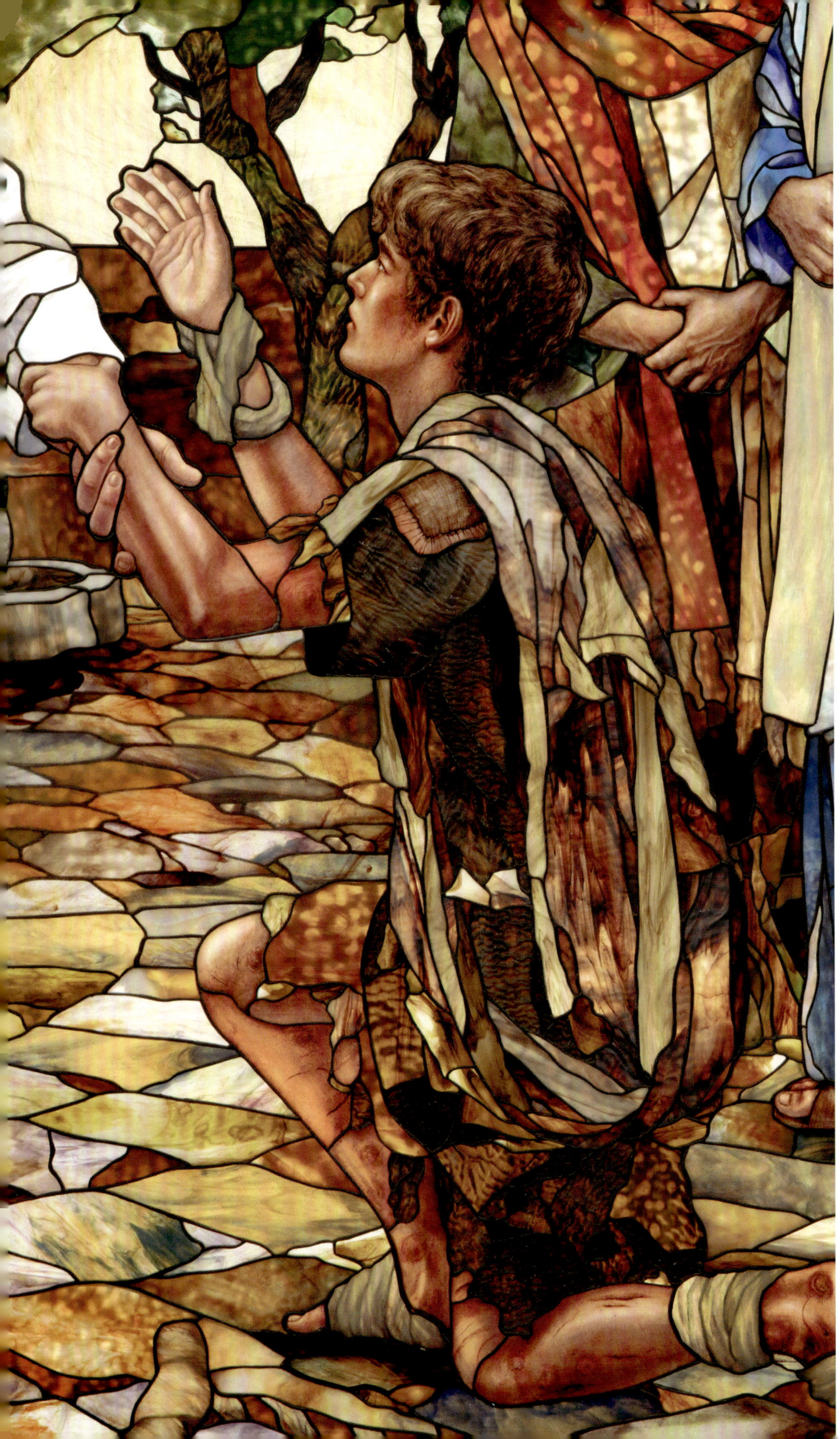

11. YOUNG BEGGAR REPRESENTING ALL HEALINGS

Christ's many healings are represented in the window by one filthy young beggar in the center of this marketplace. The scriptures do not speak of this young man or this place. However, they do speak clearly of Jesus and His divine power: "Jesus went through all the towns and villages, teaching in their synagogues, proclaiming the good news of the kingdom and healing every disease and sickness" (Matthew 9:35). "The blind and the lame came to him . . . , and he healed them" (Matthew 21:14). The fictional moment portrayed in the window is a composite of many actual events. Imagine with the artists the Savior focusing on the needs of this one individual. The beggar is blind, lame, and covered in sores, but as his hand finds and grasps Christ's arm, viewers see healing immediately spreading through the boy's entire body. His sicknesses, like his bandages, fall away. A single tear-drop falls down his cheek as his eyes are opened and his first sight is the face of his loving and compassionate Redeemer.

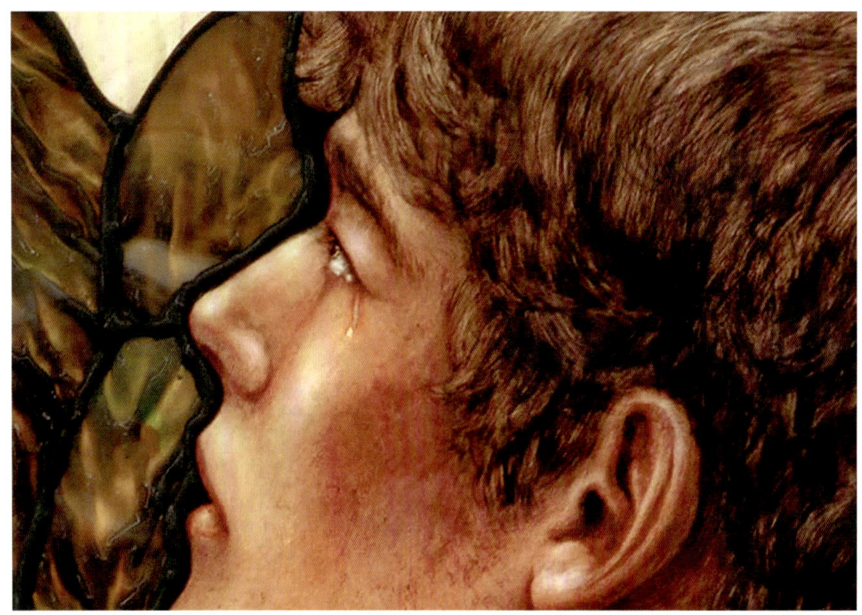

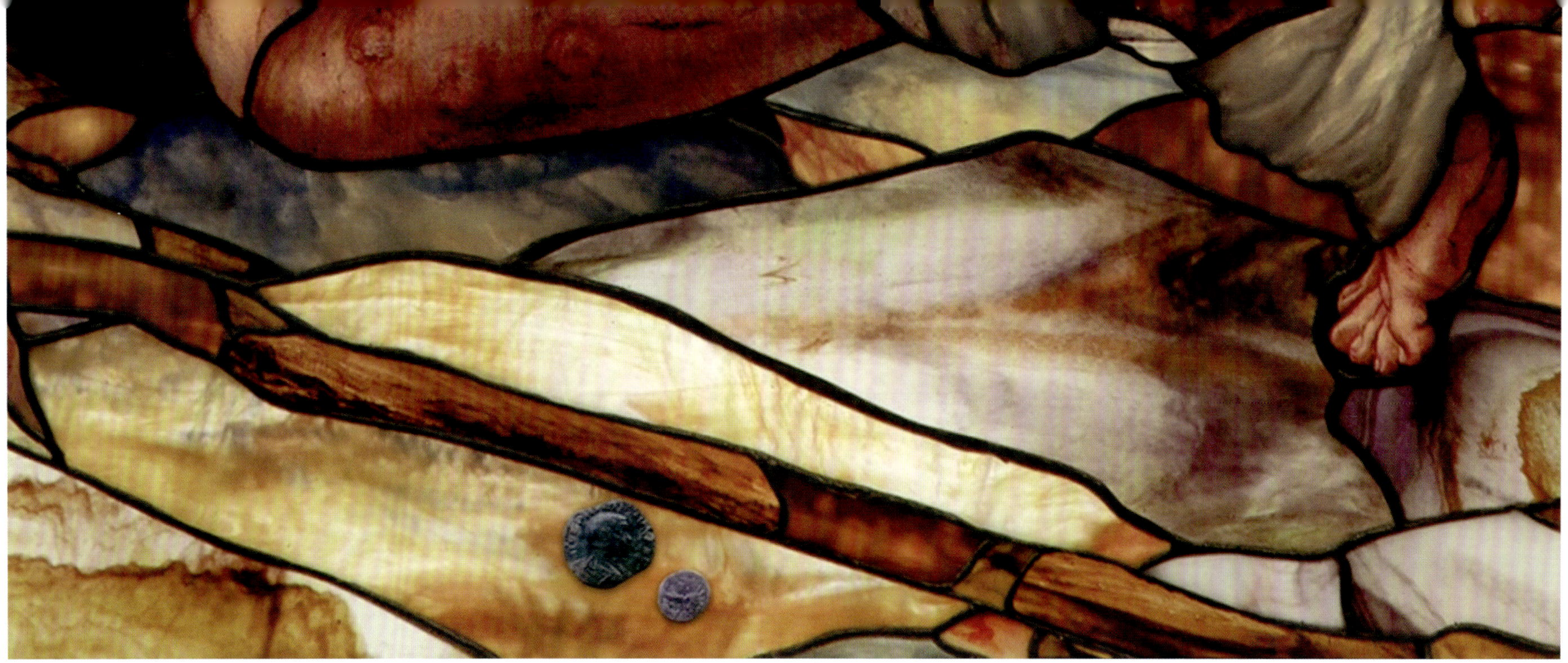

12. CRUTCH TOSSED ASIDE

Christ is shown to be healing a young man who was lame and blind. He, like many in like circumstances, had to beg for his sustenance. One of his few possessions was his crutch. It supported the weight his crippled legs could not. However, to reach the Savior, he had to let go of that crutch—something on which he had leaned and depended his entire life. He had to turn instead to Christ in complete weakness and total vulnerability. As he did, he found Christ's perfect grace and healing. "Therefore, . . . let us throw off everything that hinders and the sin that so easily entangles. And let us run with perseverance the race marked out for us, fixing our eyes on Jesus, the pioneer and perfecter of faith" (Hebrews 12:1–2). The amount of faith that it took for the young man to let go of his crutch would have been immense. He had no guarantee that the person commanding him to arise and be healed was trustworthy. But he hoped: "Now faith is confidence in what we hope for and assurance about what we do not see" (Hebrews 11:1). Like the young man in the window, we must have the humility to let go of anything that keeps us from reaching out to the Savior.

13. ACTUAL COINS FROM THE HOLY LAND

Sacrifice is giving up something good for something better. The coins that the beggar had gathered that day were good, but he freely dropped them to grasp the arm of the Savior and receive His healing and embrace. The coins (genuine coins from Christ's time) encased in the window also remind us of a parable: "Suppose a woman has ten silver coins and loses one. Doesn't she light a lamp, sweep the house and search carefully until she finds it? And when she finds it, she calls her friends and neighbors together and says, 'Rejoice with me; I have found my lost coin.' In the same way, I tell you, there is rejoicing in the presence of the angels of God over one sinner who repents" (Luke 15:8–10). In the window we see the boy sacrifice to find the Savior, and the Savior rejoices as His "lost coin" is found. The authentic coins in the window have both monetary and historic value, yet they are nothing in comparison to the worth of a human soul.

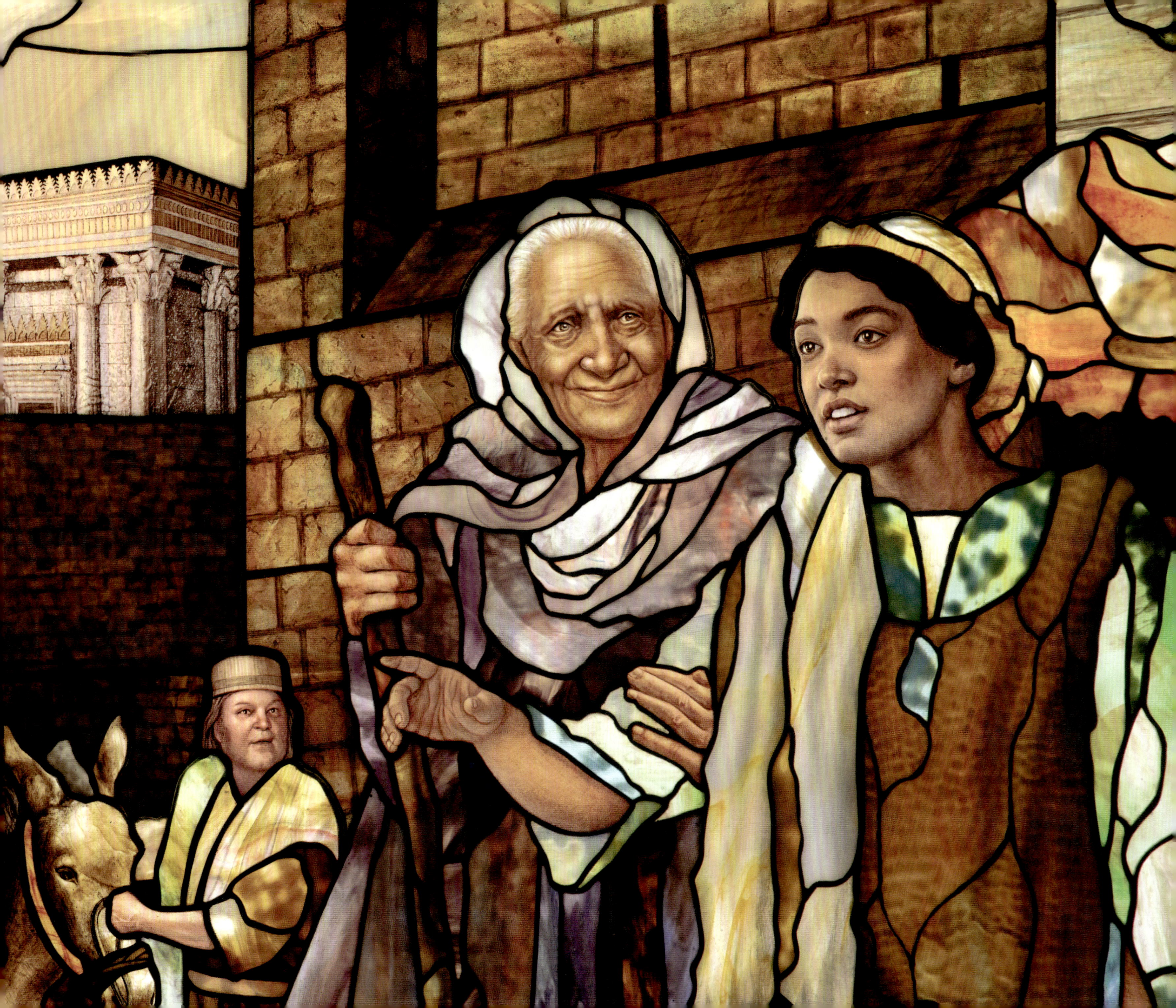

Panel F

Featuring the Widow

TEMPLE, PEACE, AND HEALING | 64

1. Darkening sky representing the storms calmed by Jesus
2. Dove representing the Holy Ghost
3. Trumpeter with ram's horn
4. Smoke from sacrifice
5. The Holy of Holies
6. Leper approaching Christ

FAITH AND SACRIFICE | 68

7. Widow and her mite
8. The good Samaritan
9. The Gentile woman's daughter who was healed
10. Donkey
11. Sheep

PARABLES AND OTHER SYMBOLS | 70

12. Golden coin reminiscent of the wise men and parable of the talents
13. Parable of the wheat and tares
14. Parable of the mustard seed
15. Magenta poppies

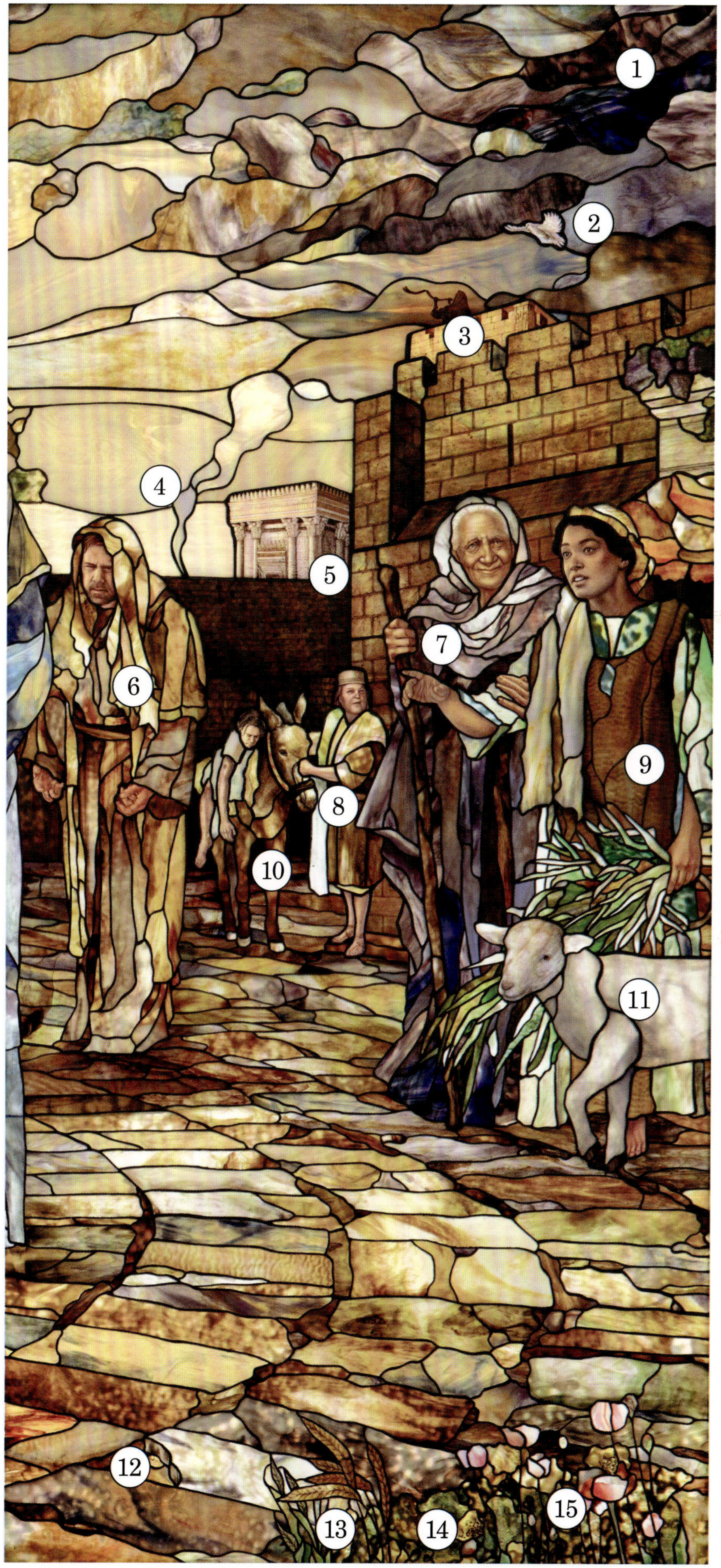

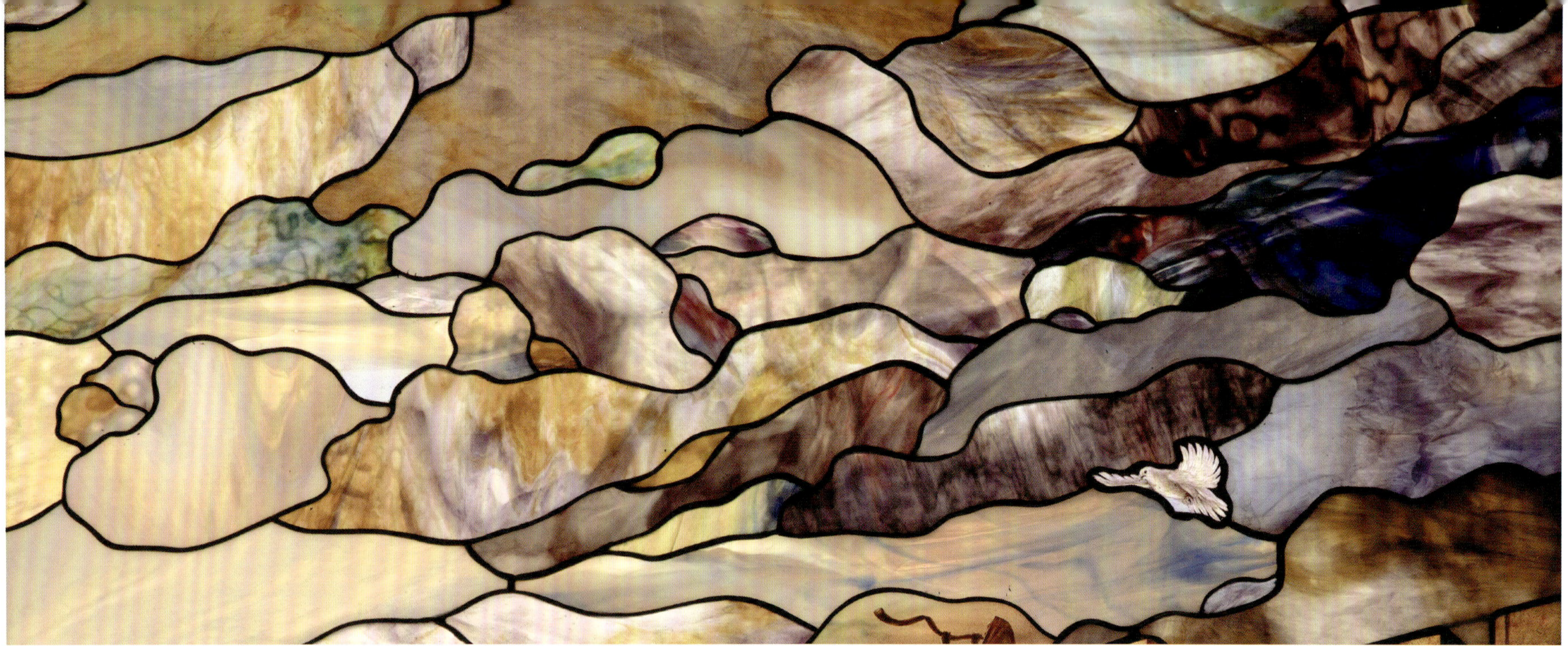

TEMPLE, PEACE, AND HEALING

1. DARKENING SKY REPRESENTING THE STORMS CALMED BY JESUS

What we call the Sea of Galilee is really an inland lake. However, it is deep and can be dangerous because it is below sea level and surrounded by mountains. As hot air rises and cool air rushes in to take its place, violent storms can arise. Matthew recorded one such storm: "Suddenly a furious storm came up on the lake, so that the waves swept over the boat. But Jesus was sleeping. The disciples went and woke him, saying, 'Lord, save us! We're going to drown!'" (Matthew 8:24–25). Mark wrote, "A furious squall came up, and the waves broke over the boat, so that it was nearly swamped. Jesus was in the stern, sleeping on a cushion. The disciples woke him and said to him, 'Teacher, don't you care if we drown?'" (Mark 4:37–38). Then Jesus "got up, rebuked the wind and said to the waves, 'Quiet! Be still!' Then the wind died down and it was completely calm" (Mark 4:39). "The men were amazed and asked, 'What kind of man is this? Even the winds and the waves obey him!'" (Matthew 8:27). Storms are a part of life. Christ did not come to always prevent storms from happening, but to help us when they happen. The disciples were impressed that Jesus could command the elements, but perhaps they should have also marveled that Christ could sleep during storms. It is an example of the internal stillness and peace He offers us amid any storm. In the window artists have reminded us of storms with the darkened sky in panels C and F. However, notice that above Christ, the sky is clear.

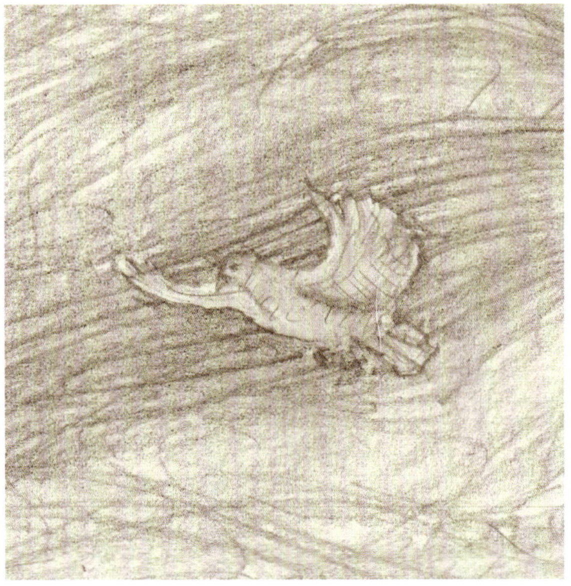

2. DOVE REPRESENTING THE HOLY GHOST

In the Old Testament, Noah sent out a dove from the ark. "When the dove returned to him . . . , there in its beak was a freshly plucked olive leaf! Then Noah knew that the water had receded from the earth" (Genesis 8:10–11). Since then, the dove has come to represent peace and truth. We read of another dove at the baptism of Jesus: "As soon as Jesus was baptized, he went up out of the water. At that moment heaven was opened, and he saw the Spirit of God descending like a dove and alighting on him. And a voice from heaven said, 'This is my Son, whom I love; with him I am well pleased'" (Matthew 3:16–17). On that special day the dove was a sign of the presence of the Holy Spirit testifying of peace and truth. In the window, the dove—like the Spirit—guides people through their personal storms and toward the Savior.

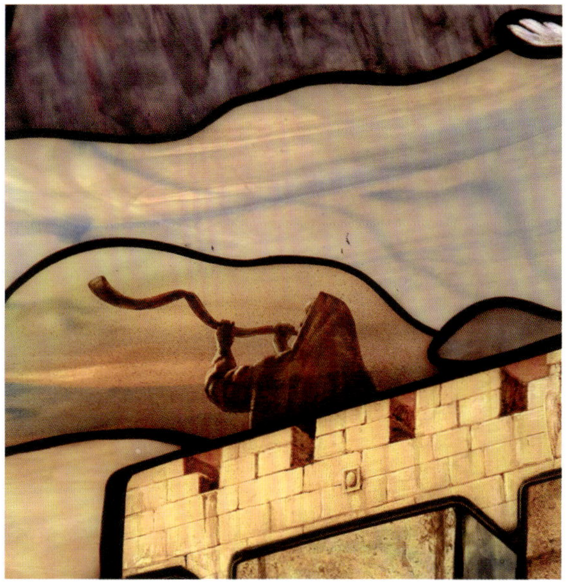

3. TRUMPETER WITH RAM'S HORN

The ram's horn, called a *shofar* in Hebrew, was a common instrument in ancient times. Trumpeters blew it to sound an alarm and warn of danger (see Judges 3:27), but most often it was used to gather the people together at the tabernacle or temple (see Numbers 10:2–10) to worship and pray. The simple sound was clear and unmistakable. Matthew told us that when Satan was tempting the Savior, he "took him to the holy city and had him stand on the highest point of the temple" (Matthew 4:5). This may have been the corner where the trumpeter would have stood. "'If you are the Son of God,' [Satan] said, 'throw yourself down'" (Matthew 4:6). As angels rushed to save Him, surely people would have been impressed. This would have been an easy and quick way for the Savior to gain followers. However, Jesus was not interested in easy or quick ways and "answered him, 'Do not put the Lord your God to the test'" (Matthew 4:7). Artists who created the window placed a trumpeter on a raised corner of a stone building to call us to worship and to remind us that just as Christ overcame temptations, so can we.

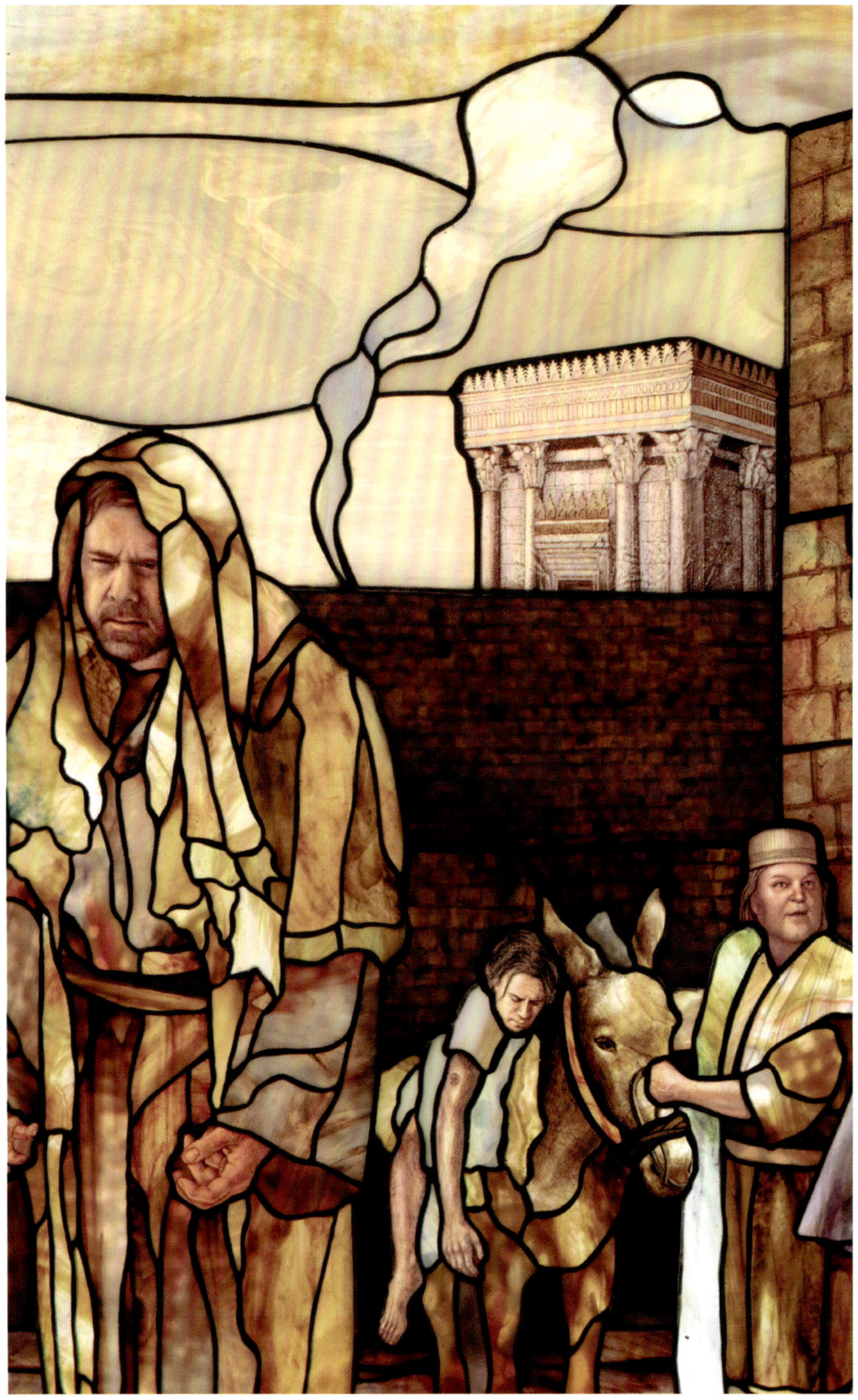

4. SMOKE FROM SACRIFICE

Father Abraham was asked to sacrifice his son Isaac (see Genesis 22). It is hard to comprehend the anguish he must have felt as he faced such a difficult test. Did he love God enough to obey Him even when he asked for the life of his son? Isaac was surely old enough to know what was happening. Did he love and trust his father enough to lay down his life if that was what God asked? Both father and son passed their tests, and gratefully "Abraham looked up and there in a thicket he saw a ram caught by its horns. He went over and took the ram and sacrificed it as a burnt offering instead of his son" (Genesis 22:13). That ram, and all other animals sacrificed through the centuries before the coming of Christ, pointed to the Savior. To fulfill the law of justice, God was willing to sacrifice His son, and Jesus was willing to be sacrificed. He knew this time there would be no ram in the thicket. Still, He was willing to be the great and last sacrifice. In the window we see smoke rising from the altar of the temple—evidence of sacrifice and evidence of love.

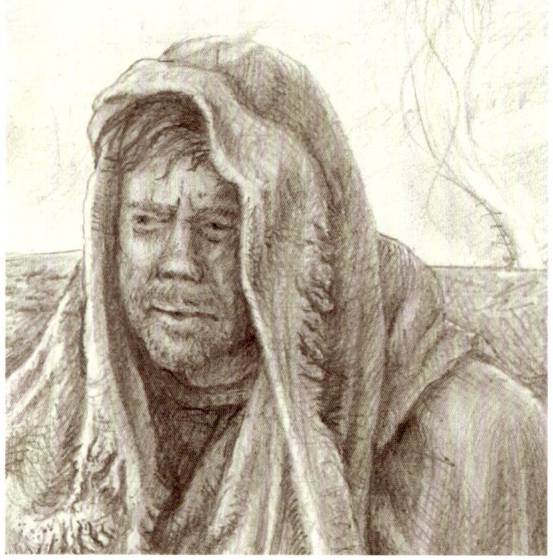

5. THE HOLY OF HOLIES

In the Old Testament we read of the importance of the tabernacle as the children of Israel wandered in the wilderness (see Exodus 25–31 and 35–40). Solomon built a permanent tabernacle—a temple—in Jerusalem. It was destroyed by the Babylonians when they conquered in 586 BC. Later, when Persia overthrew the kingdom of Babylon, Jews who chose to were permitted to return to Jerusalem and rebuild the temple. About 40 years before Christ, Herod rose to power. He expanded the temple mount and doubled the temple's previous dimensions. That was the imposing structure that existed during Christ's time. Although it was built under the direction of wicked Herod, Christ still taught that it was His Father's house (see John 2:16) and claimed it as His own (see Matthew 21:13). Even after Christ's Resurrection, His apostles continued to worship in the temple (see Acts 3:8), and in Malachi 3:1 we read that when Jesus comes again, He "will come to his temple." In the window, we see the sanctuary of the temple that housed the Holy of Holies. Only the high priest could enter the Holy of Holies once a year on the Day of Atonement (Yom Kippur). A large veil blocked the way for all others until the death of Christ when the veil ripped from top to bottom, symbolically announcing that there were no more barriers between God and us. Christ's Atonement made it possible for all to pass through the veil and enter God's presence.

6. LEPER APPROACHING CHRIST

Jesus was in the middle of a multitude when a man with leprosy approached. In Jewish culture, it was inappropriate for this man to be close to people because of his "unclean" condition. Most people in the crowd probably moved away from him, but not Jesus. The man pled, "Lord, if you are willing, you can make me clean" (Matthew 8:2). If the leper emphasized the words *if you are willing*, it would have shown submission. It would have implied he would have still worshipped the Lord even if the cleansing were not granted. If the leper emphasized *you*, it would have shown complete faith in Jesus Christ's power. If he emphasized *me*, it would have demonstrated a sweet acknowledgment that not only was Christ the infinite Atoner but also his intimate Savior. However he said the words, imagine the leper's joy when "Jesus reached out his hand and touched the man. 'I am willing,' he said. 'Be clean!'" (Matthew 8:3). On another occasion, Jesus entered a synagogue on the Sabbath, where a man with a withered hand was present. Knowing that the Pharisees did not consider it lawful to heal on the Sabbath, Jesus first taught, "'It is lawful to do good on the Sabbath.' Then He said to the man, 'Stretch out your hand.' So he stretched it out and it was completely restored, just as sound as the other" (Matthew 12:12–13). Luke told of another healing when Jesus was at the border between Samaria and Galilee. Ten men with leprosy met Him asking for pity. Jesus cleansed all of them and they went their way rejoicing. Only one—a Samaritan—turned to thank Him. Jesus asked, "Where are the other nine?" (Luke 17:17). Then He said to the thankful man, "Rise and go; your faith has made you well" (v. 19). Ten were cleansed that day, but only one was made well and whole. In the artwork, one man represents all these men.

FAITH AND SACRIFICE

7. WIDOW AND HER MITE

A poor widow came to donate money to the temple treasury. She probably had no idea Jesus was nearby in the courtyard observing, or that she was about to become the object of the lesson He taught His disciples: "Truly I tell you, this poor widow has put more into the treasury than all the others. They all gave out of their wealth; but she, out of her poverty, put in everything—all she had to live on" (Mark 12:43–44). The woman in the window represents this widow, and you can see an authentic mite from Christ's time artfully embedded at the top of her staff. It would have been worth 1/64 of a day's working wage—only a few dollars in today's currency. Jesus taught that it is not the *quantity* of our sacrifice, but the *quality* of our hearts that matters to God. This woman also represents the parable of the persistent widow that Christ gave when teaching about prayer (see Luke 18:1–8). In addition, the woman represents the Gentile mother who begged for Jesus to heal her daughter. After feeding the 5,000 and walking on the water, Jesus and His disciples journeyed to the Mediterranean coast. There a Canaanite woman—an outsider, a Gentile—approached the Lord and asked for mercy for her troubled daughter. Some readers are bothered by the Savior's response: "I was sent only to the lost sheep of Israel." When she persisted in asking for a miracle, He said, "It is not right to take the children's bread and toss it to the dogs" (Matthew 15:24, 26). The Lord was not calling this woman a dog. Rather, He was teaching that God's kingdom is one of order. Christ came first to the Israelites. The gospel would go to the Gentiles later. This woman could have been offended, but instead she meekly responded, "Even the dogs eat the crumbs that fall from their master's table." To which the Savior said, "Woman, you have great faith! Your request is granted" (Matthew 15:27–28), and her daughter was healed. Most teachers give the lesson first and then the test. In this case, Jesus tested this woman's faith and then taught the lesson.

8. THE GOOD SAMARITAN

An expert in the law of Moses approached Jesus and asked, "What must I do to inherit eternal life?" (Luke 10:25). The Savior said to love God and to love his neighbor. The expert prodded, "And who is my neighbor?" (v. 29). It was in answer to that question that Christ taught the parable of the good Samaritan. The Jews viewed the Samaritans as second-class citizens because over the centuries they had intermarried with outsiders. Understanding that tension makes the message of the parable even more significant. A man fell among thieves and was beaten and left for dead. Both a Jewish priest and a Levite saw him and passed by. Finally, a Samaritan had compassion on the man and helped him. Then the Savior asked, "Which of these three do you think was a neighbor to the man?" (v. 36) and the expert said, "The one who had mercy on him." Jesus said, "Go and do likewise" (v. 37). Jesus was not asking the expert to do anything He was unwilling to do Himself. Taken from an eternal view, the parable becomes an allegory of the Fall and redemption of mankind. Adam, like the man in the parable, fell. Christ, like the Samaritan—also hated and despised—saved him.

9. THE GENTILE WOMAN'S DAUGHTER WHO WAS HEALED

The elderly woman in panel F not only represents the widow who cast her mite into the temple treasury, but also the Gentile mother who sought healing for her daughter. The young woman next to her represents her daughter. This young woman reaches out to Jesus with one hand and in the other holds palm leaves. In this way, she also represents all the believers who met the Lord when He entered Jerusalem riding on a donkey. Christians across the globe call the Sunday before Easter "Palm Sunday" and remember the day of Christ's triumphal entry. That year Jesus had come to Jerusalem not just to celebrate the Passover but to become the Passover sacrifice for all. People waved branches of palm trees (see John 12:13). The multitudes shouted,

"Hosanna to the Son of David!" (Matthew 21:9; see also Psalm 118:26). *Hosanna* means "save now we pray." Most people in the crowd hoped this new king would save them from earthly oppression. However, Jesus had not come to save the Jews from the Romans, but rather to save all humankind from sin and wickedness. He came as the King to invite all who would to enter the kingdom of heaven.

10. DONKEY

Nowhere in the gospels does it say that Mary did anything but walk to Bethlehem. Maybe tradition has been influenced by artists who have depicted Mary on a donkey. Maybe we all wish there could have been a little help for this young mother who was so close to delivery. One way or the other, we can be certain Christ rode on a donkey during the triumphal entry, as prophesied in Zechariah 9:9. We also know that in the parable of the good Samaritan the injured man is taken to an inn on a donkey. Not only did the Samaritan save the man and bind up his wounds, but he provided for his care. Similarly, Christ's redemption not only restores life but also provides a better quality of life. Jesus said, "I have come that they may have life, and have it to the full" (John 10:10). In Greek mythology, the donkey has many negative connotations, but in the Bible and early Christianity, the animal is often a symbol of service, humility, and peace.

11. SHEEP

At Christmas we read of angels who came to shepherds who were "keeping watch over their flocks at night" (Luke 2:8). Some have suggested that perhaps the reason the shepherds were working at night was because a lamb was being born. Indeed, the Lamb of God was being born. Animal sacrifices through the centuries foreshadowed the sacrifice of Christ. In addition to being the Lamb, Jesus is also the Good Shepherd. In the parable of the lost sheep, the Savior taught, "Suppose one of you has a hundred sheep and loses one of them. Doesn't he leave the ninety-nine in the open country and go after the lost sheep until he finds it? And when he finds it, he joyfully puts it on his shoulders and goes home" (Luke 15:4–6). We are the lost sheep Christ came to find and save. As He atoned for us, He carried our sins, pains, and sorrows so we could go home rejoicing. On another occasion Jesus likened the righteous and unrighteous to sheep and goats. Sheep can be easily led. Goats, on the other hand, buck and fight against authority. We see the sheep in panel F and the goat in panel B. As we choose to be led by our Good Shepherd and learn not to fight against His authority, we will one day hear Him say, "Come, you who are blessed by my Father; take your inheritance, the kingdom prepared for you since the creation of the world" (Matthew 25:34).

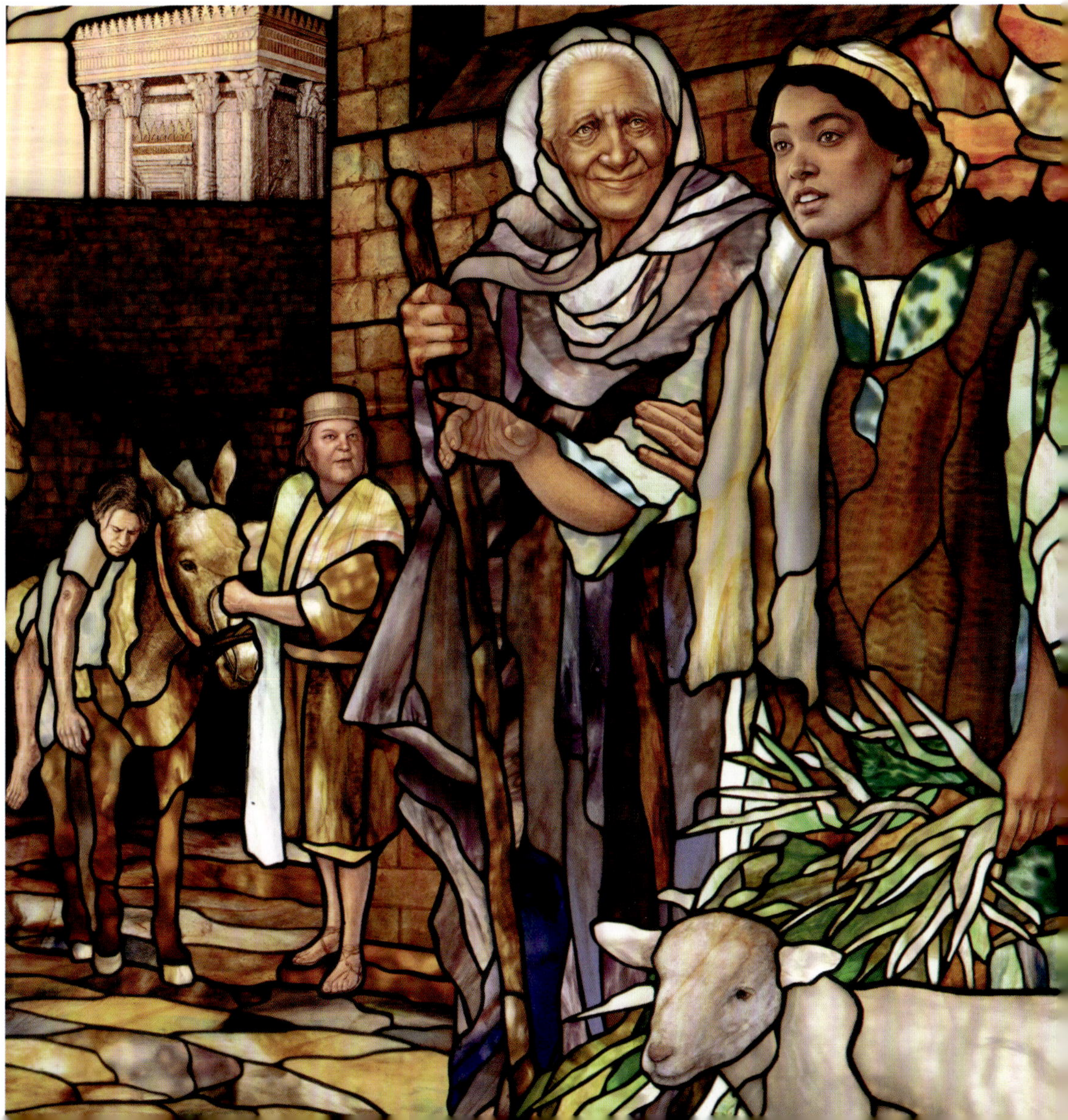

PARABLES AND OTHER SYMBOLS

12. GOLDEN COIN REMINISCENT OF THE WISE MEN AND PARABLE OF THE TALENTS

When the wisemen visited the Christ child, they came bearing gifts. One of those gifts was gold, because they recognized and honored Him as the King of Kings. Later, the grown Christ taught people to not leave the gifts they are given unused (see Matthew 25:14–30). The parable of the talents can be interpreted as having a stewardship over money, preparing for the Second Coming, or developing our God-given abilities. Another way to understand the main idea is to think of talents as books: to one the master gave five books, to another two books, and to another one book. The first two servants read their books and the Lord was pleased. He welcomed them into His library! The third servant did not care enough to read the book, so the Lord took the book away. The Master was not being mean. He simply knew that additional books would have been more burden than blessing until the servant changed his attitude and read what he had already been given. Even if the master had welcomed the third servant into His library, he would have valued nothing there. Grace is a gift from God that too many do not value—and sometimes even bury. The coin in the window can remind us to appreciate, value, and use this amazing gift.

13. PARABLE OF THE WHEAT AND TARES

There is always opposition to the work of the Lord. Jesus knew this personally and taught this truth clearly in the parable of the wheat and the tares. The good seed represents God's kingdom in mortality, and the tares represent the enemy's efforts to confuse and destroy. The tares cannot be burned without harming the wheat as well. This parable has symbolic connections to what is happening in the world as Christ's Second Coming draws closer. The righteous will be gathered and protected, and the unrepentant ultimately consumed (see Matthew 13:24–30, 36–43). In the window, viewers see a small cluster of wheat and tares growing together. They look similar when they first begin to grow. However, as they mature, the head of wheat begins to bow down with the weight of good grain. The tares—which are inconsumable—look like wheat but offer no nourishment. Are we like wheat, bowing down in humility before God and offering sustenance to others, or are we like tares, standing tall and proud but with nothing of value to contribute?

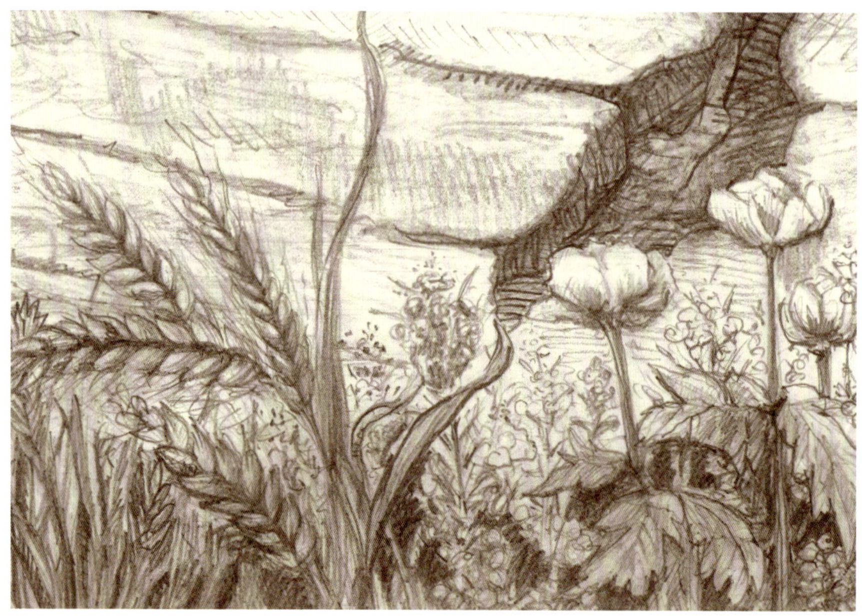

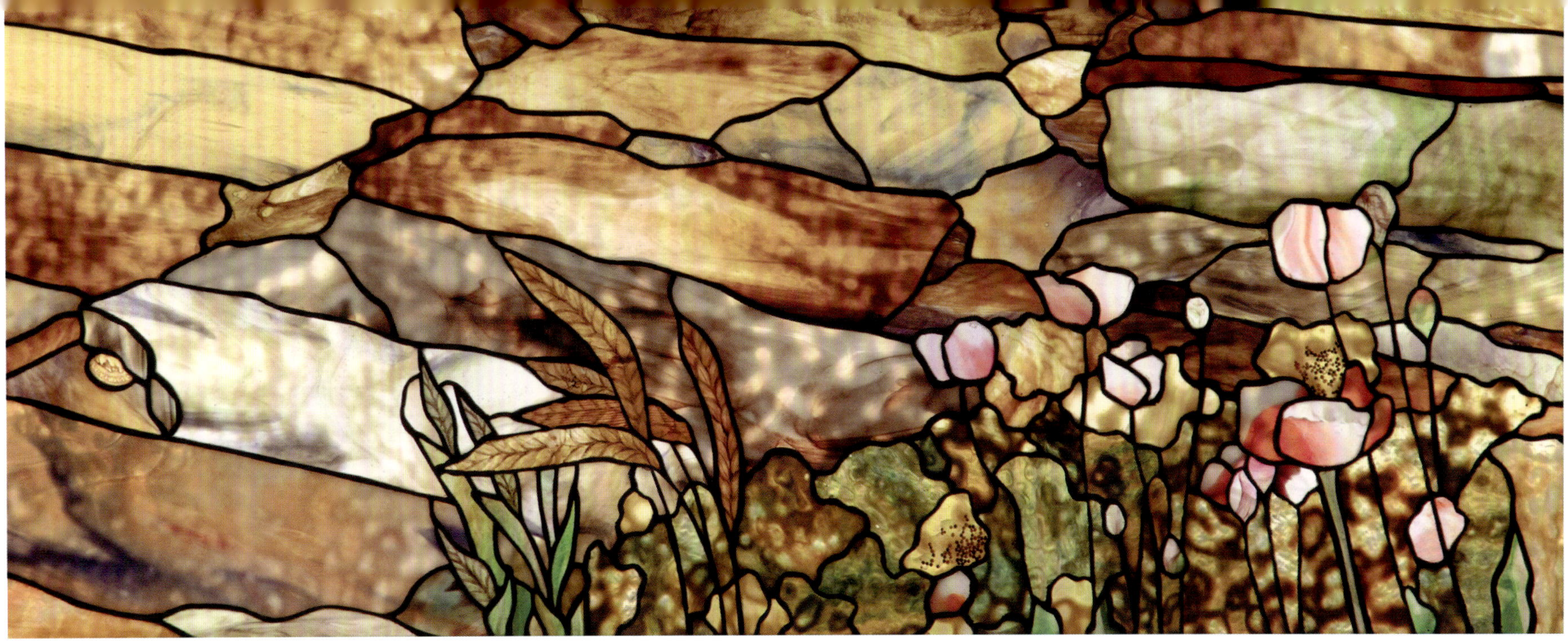

14. PARABLE OF THE MUSTARD SEED

Jesus taught that the kingdom of heaven is like a mustard seed (see Matthew 13:31). Despite its tiny size, the seed can grow into a plant, which can ultimately mature to be a tree with branches strong enough to support the birds who build nests there. Like the kingdom itself, each of us can also grow in knowledge, goodness, and power. Our faith might start out weak and small, but as we continue to nourish it through experience and study, it can become a strong tree offering shade and assistance to others in their own faith journeys. There is no seed in the artwork because it would be too small to be seen. However, artists have included mustard plants, reminding us to nourish our faith and grow ever closer to God.

15. MAGENTA POPPIES

The poppy plant is the source of pain killers. In art, poppies are often used as a symbol of death. In Matthew 27:34, we read that during the crucifixion Christ was offered "wine to drink, mixed with gall." Gall is made from myrrh—the very gift brought by the wise men at Christ's birth. It is meant to dull the senses and ease pain. Were those crucifying Christ truly interested in quenching His thirst or easing His pain? If so, it was probably only to extend His suffering. What could seem at first to be an act of mercy was most likely an act of mockery and ridicule. The wine was sour, and the gall was bitter just like the hardened hearts of Christ's persecutors. How different they were from Jesus Christ who comes to us in our thirst and pain—not with bitter wine and gall, but with living water and true healing.

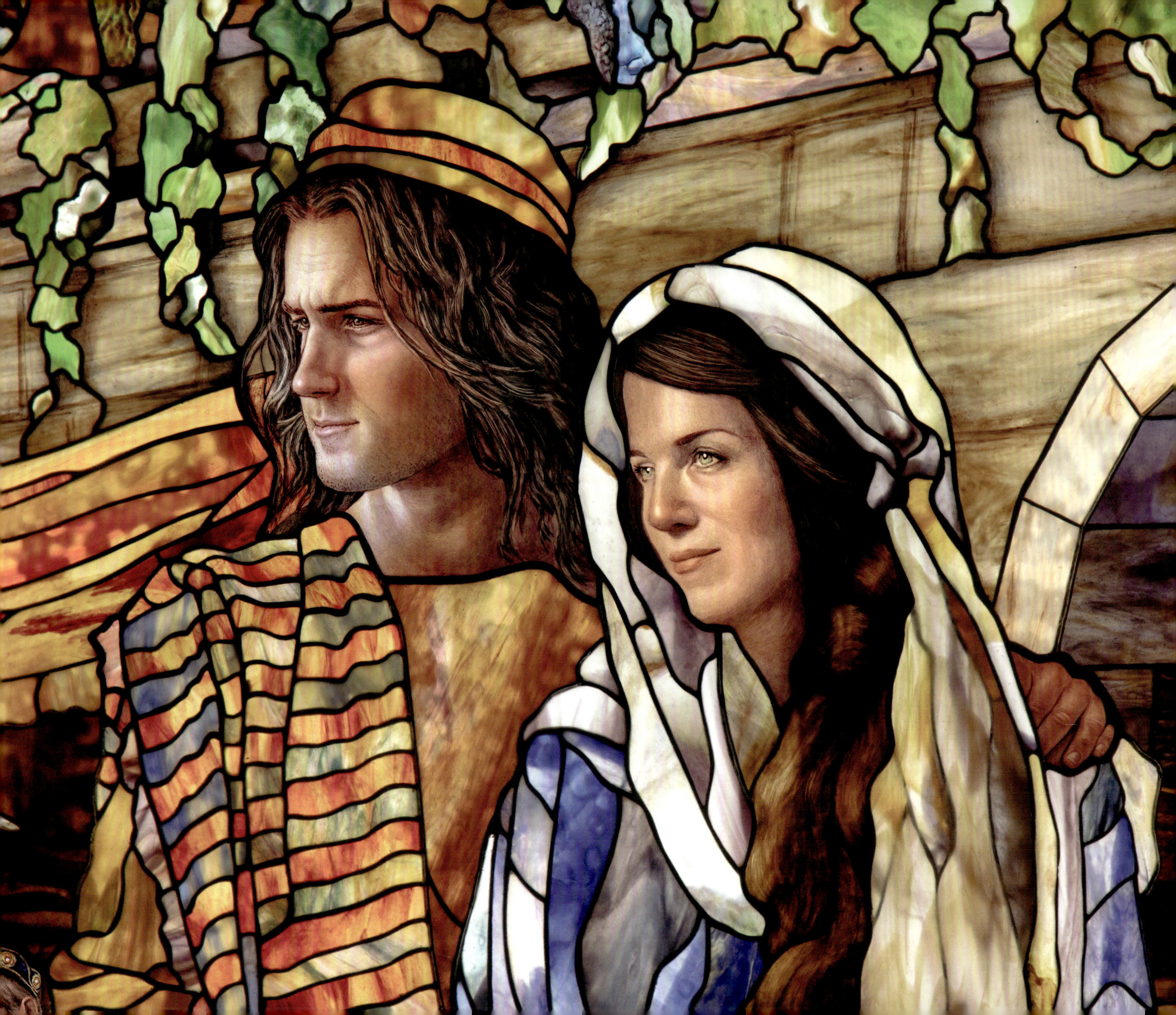

Panel G

Featuring John and Mary

TITLES AND TEACHINGS | 74

1. Thorns on the crown of the building
2. Traditional symbols of the authors of the Gospels
3. Rose of Sharon carved in the pillars' capitals
4. Lamb's blood on doorposts
5. Closed door
6. Laborer in the vineyard; also representing the unprofitable servant
7. Sadducee holding a bag of money, also reminiscent of the parable of the rich fool
8. Parable of the friend at midnight
9. Grapes representing Communion
10. Alpha and Omega
11. A light to the world

MARY AND APOSTLES | 80

12. Two turtle doves like those sacrificed by Mary and Joseph
13. John who was commissioned to care for Mary
14. Mary, Christ's mother
15. Sickles symbolizing gathering
16. Matthew, tax collector turned apostle
17. Lamp representing those held by the wise virgins
18. Scales
19. Christ's temptations, Judas's thirty pieces of silver, and the moneychangers
20. Oil vessel

PRODIGALS AND SERMONS | 84

21. The older brother of the prodigal; also represents the rich man who refused to help Lazarus and the unmerciful servant
22. The prodigal son, also represents the poor man Lazarus and the servant of the unmerciful servant
23. Pig calling to mind the prodigal and the evil spirits cast into swine
24. A Herodian temple stone; also indicates Christ is the chief cornerstone
25. Actual chunks of salt from the Dead Sea
26. Unleavened bread for Communion
27. Rooster representing Peter's denial

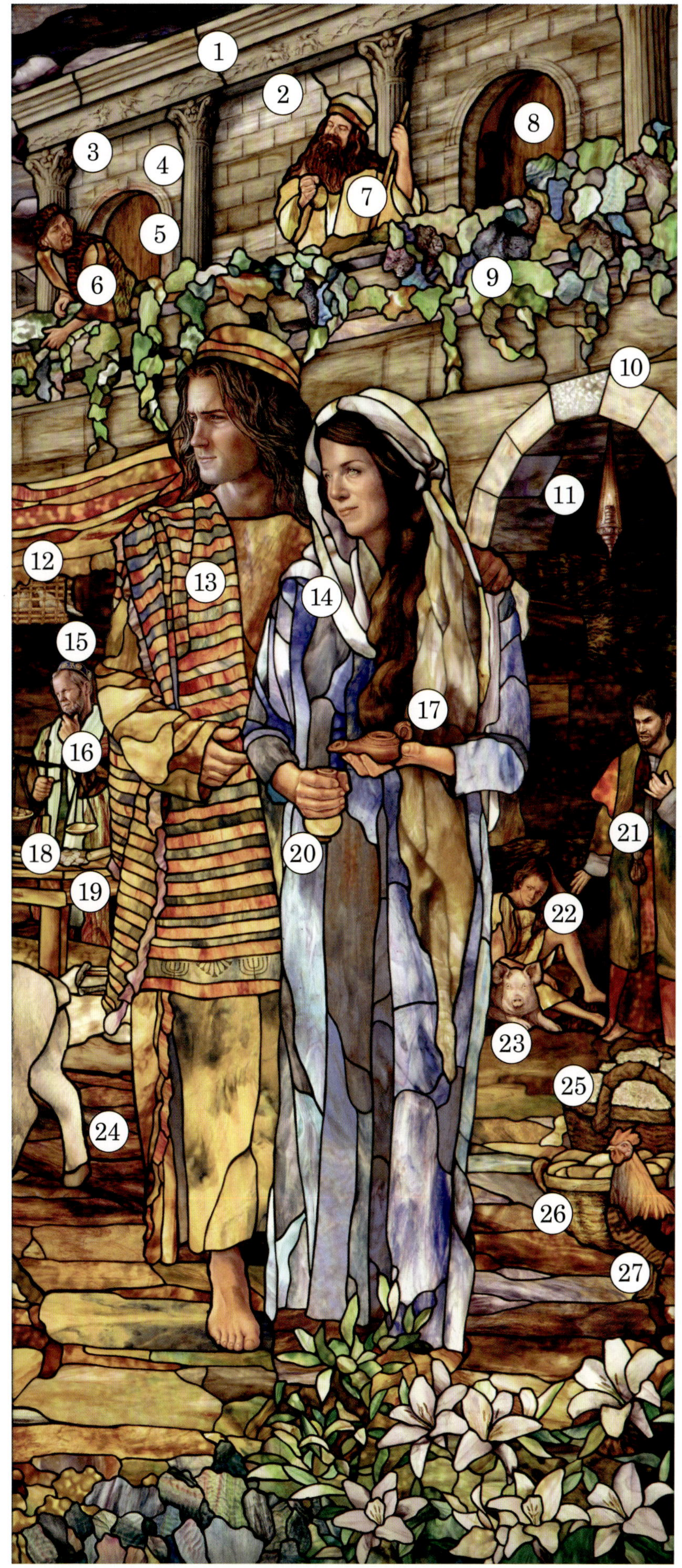

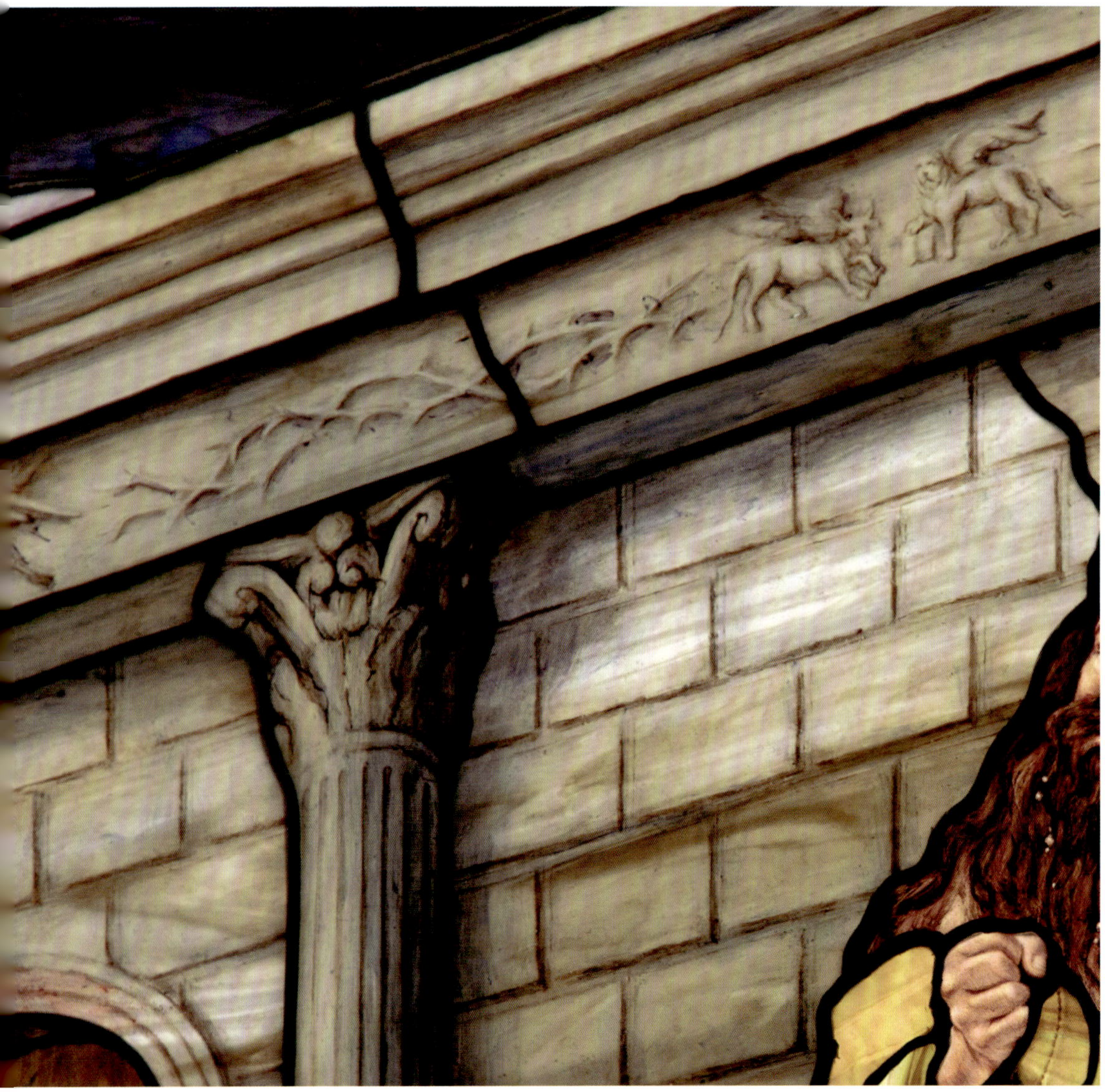

TITLES AND TEACHINGS

1. THORNS ON THE CROWN OF THE BUILDING

Once Jesus was condemned by Pilate to be crucified, the Roman leader turned Him over to soldiers who would carry out the sentence. These ruthless men were not only determined to kill Jesus, but also wanted to ridicule and abuse Him. If this condemned Jew claimed to be the Jewish king, they would make Him a crown. John recorded, "The soldiers twisted together a crown of thorns and put it on his head" and mocked Him by crying, "Hail, king of the Jews!" (John 19:2–3). The sharp thorns caused physical pain and the mocking words and deriding laughter caused emotional pain. The soldiers were blind to the fact that the very man they put to death would be the One to deliver *them* from death; the very man they belittled so mercilessly would one day be the One to offer them mercy. Because of Christ's Atonement, even these cruel soldiers would have the opportunity to repent.

2. TRADITIONAL SYMBOLS OF THE AUTHORS OF THE GOSPELS

Where would we be without the books left by the writers of the gospels? Surely these were not the only records written by early Christians, but they are the ones that survived and could be authenticated. Two are written by apostles: Matthew and John. Two are written under the direction of apostles: Mark writing with authority from Peter, and Luke writing with authority from Paul. According to Christian tradition and early Christian art, it was common to connect the four writers of the gospels with the four beings in Ezekiel's vision recorded in the Old Testament (see Ezekiel 1:10). Similarly, in the book of Revelation, John refers to four creatures (see 4:6–8): a winged human, a lion, a calf, and an eagle. Perhaps Matthew is represented by the angel/man because he emphasized that Jesus was both fully divine and fully human. Mark could be represented as a lion because he taught of Christ's kingship and majesty. Luke may be shown as an ox, an animal used for sacrifices, because his writings focused on Christ's sacrifice. Finally, John might be associated with an eagle because eagles come from above as did Jesus: "The Word became flesh and made his dwelling among us" (John 1:14). The gospels were written for different audiences. Matthew wrote to the Jews, Mark and Luke were written to the Gentiles, and John was written to people who had chosen to be disciples of Christ.

3. ROSE OF SHARON CARVED IN THE PILLARS' CAPITALS

In the book of Revelation, John records a vision he had of the War in Heaven in which Satan was cast out. Michael and those who fought with him "triumphed over [Satan] by the blood of the Lamb" (12:11). No wonder God commanded His children to perform sacrifices—each one foreshadowing Christ's great and last sacrifice. He was teaching all that we must be among those who "have washed their robes and made them white in the blood of the Lamb" (Revelation 7:14). In early Christian art, roses were often used to represent Christ's blood. Because of Christ's Atonement, we can repent of our sins and be completely forgiven and cleansed.

4. LAMB'S BLOOD ON DOORPOSTS

The final plague of Egypt was that the firstborn in each family would die (see Exodus 11:1–10). To protect the children of Israel, the Lord commanded that each household sacrifice a male lamb without blemish and place the blood on the door posts of the house (see Exodus 12:1–7). The Lord promised the plague would pass over the houses marked with the blood of the sacrifice (see v. 13). He was teaching the Israelites that Christ would be the Lamb of God without blemish (see John 1:29) who would offer Himself as the great and last sacrifice for all. Through His blood we can all be saved (see 1 Peter 1:18–20).

5. CLOSED DOOR

The Lord has said, "Here I am! I stand at the door and knock. If anyone hears my voice and opens the door, I will come in and eat with that person, and they with me" (Revelation 3:20). In other scriptures we are told to do the knocking (see Matthew 7:7), but in Revelation it is Jesus who is knocking and hoping we will let Him in. In this metaphor, He does not stand afar off calling us to reach out for Him. He stands close to the doors of our hearts. It is as if He is reaching out to us. He will not and cannot enter our lives without permission, but this image assures us that His desire is to come in and dine together.

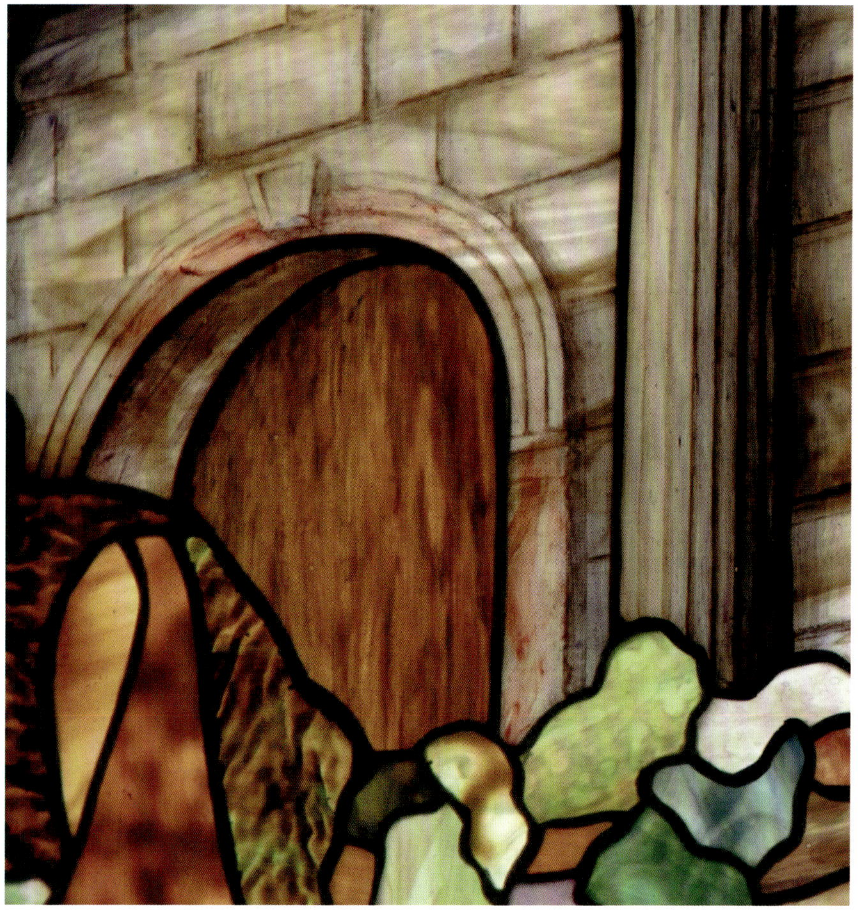

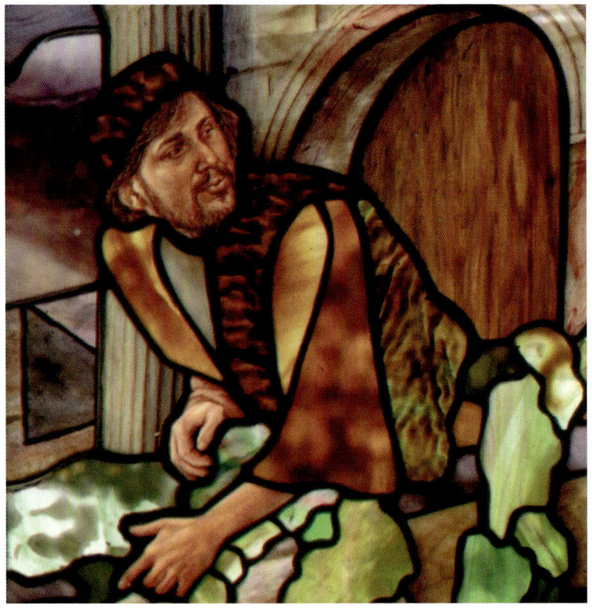

6. LABORER IN THE VINEYARD; ALSO REPRESENTING THE UNPROFITABLE SERVANT

Peter once expressed concern over what kind of reward he and the other Apostles would receive for their service to the Lord. In response, Jesus told a story about various laborers who gathered at the marketplace to seek employment as day laborers. In the first hour, a householder contracted with some of them to work in his vineyard for a penny—enough to feed a family for one day. The householder then needed more help and returned to the marketplace to hire others for the same amount in the third, sixth, ninth, and even eleventh hours. As the workday ended, he paid each worker a penny as promised. Those who worked the longest felt slighted even though they received what they had agreed to. We quickly sympathize with these men until we remember that working in the Lord's vineyard is not a drudgery, but rather a privilege. Instead of comparing our efforts to those of others, let us remember that regardless of the hour in which we enter the Lord's service, we can be assured that He will give us all we need. Service in the kingdom of God is not just about what we get. It is about how God teaches us to love others and become more like Him. To that end, we need the vineyard as much as the vineyard needs us (see Matthew 19:27–30; 20:1–16). In a related parable, we read of the lord of the house who expected to be served dinner before his servant ate (see Luke 17:7–10). The lord, who paid the servant, was not being unfair by asking the servant to do what he agreed to do when he was hired. This is often called the parable of the unprofitable servant. When we consider what a privilege it is to labor for and with the Lord and the abundant blessings we enjoy as we do so, we are and will forever be unprofitable servants.

7. SADDUCEE HOLDING A BAG OF MONEY; ALSO REMINISCENT OF THE PARABLE OF THE RICH FOOL

Sadducees were the social elite of the Jews in Christ's day. Roman leaders put them in charge of the temple, and they shamelessly enriched themselves through unjust fees and exchange rates demanded from those who came to worship. Christ often had strong words to say about them and all those who cared more about money than the riches of heaven. On one occasion when Jesus was teaching a large crowd of people, a man requested that the Lord tell his brother to split the inheritance with him (see Luke 12:13). How sad to think that in the very moment when he had the Savior's full attention, he chose to talk about money! Jesus responded, "Watch out! Be on your guard against all kinds of greed; life does not consist in an abundance of possessions" (Luke 12:15). To illustrate the point, He taught this parable: "The ground of a certain rich man yielded an abundant harvest" so he built a bigger barn to hold everything, and then he took it easy. He ate, drank, and was merry because he had "plenty of grain laid up for many years. . . . But God said to him, 'You fool! This very night your

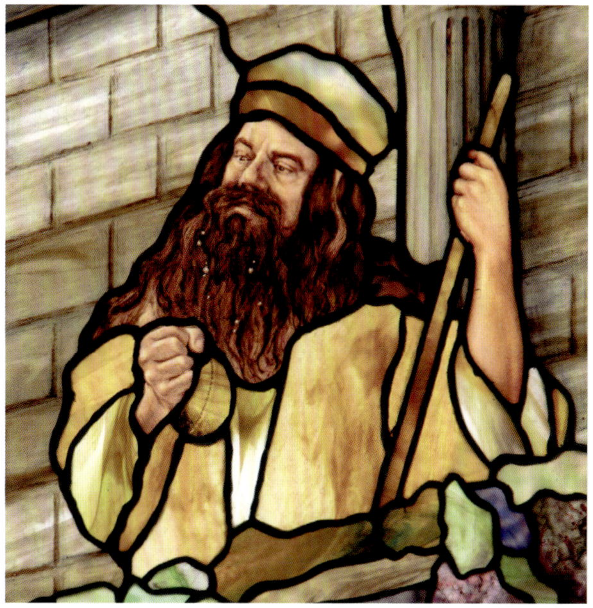

life will be demanded from you. Then who will get what you have prepared for yourself?' This is how it will be with whoever stores up things for themselves but is not rich toward God" (vv. 16–21). Notice how the Sadducee in the window clutches his gold close to his heart, foolishly trusting his wealth to save him. All his riches will be lost when he dies. In an eternal perspective they mean so little and yet they keep him from coming closer to the One who offers the riches of heaven.

8. PARABLE OF THE FRIEND AT MIDNIGHT

On the second story of the building in this panel are two doors. The one on the left is closed, reminding us that we must open the door when the Savior knocks. The one on the right shows a man doing just that—opening his heart to welcome the Lord. This image also calls to mind the parable of the friend at midnight that was given as the Lord taught about prayer. "Suppose you have a friend, and you go to him at midnight and say, 'Friend, lend me three loaves of bread; a friend of

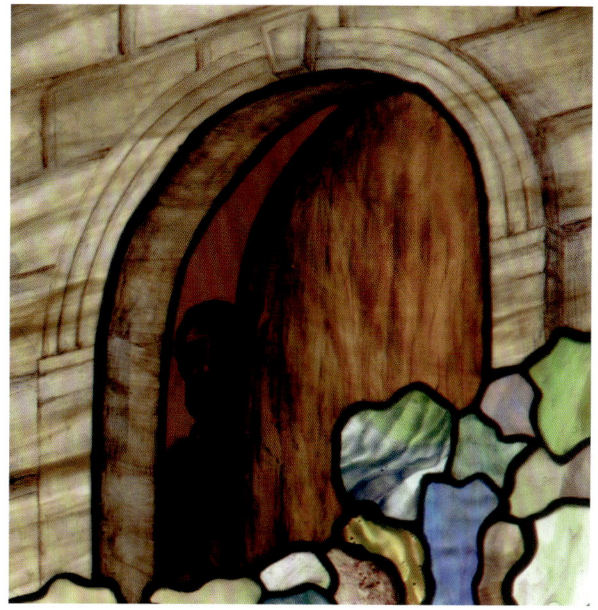

mine on a journey has come to me, and I have no food to offer him.' And suppose the one inside answers, 'Don't bother me. The door is already locked, and my children and I are in bed. I can't get up and give you anything'" (Luke 11:5–7). The Savior knew that is not how a true friend would respond. He continued to explain that, despite the audacity and the late hour, a real friend "will surely get up and give you as much as you need" (v. 8). That's what friends do! To make the application of the parable to prayer clear, Jesus said, "So I say to you: Ask and it will be given to you; seek and you will find; knock and the door will be opened to you. For everyone who asks receives; the one who seeks finds; and to the one who knocks, the door will be opened" (vv. 9–10). God will always open the door when we knock. God is our friend at midnight.

9. GRAPES REPRESENTING COMMUNION

On the evening before His Atonement, Jesus took His apostles to an upper room to celebrate the Passover. The supper they ate was a sacred meal instituted through Moses to remember and celebrate the delivery of Israel from Egyptian slavery. However, this time would be different. Jesus changed the symbolic nature of the bread and wine. Instead of symbolizing delivery from slavery, they would now represent the body and blood of Christ, which deliver us from the slavery of death and sin. As the group left the upper room and walked to Gethsemane, Jesus taught His apostles that He is the True Vine, and His disciples are the branches. "Remain in me, as I also remain in you. No branch can bear fruit by itself; it must remain in the vine. Neither can you bear fruit unless you remain in me. I am the vine; you are the branches. If you remain in me and I in you, you will bear much fruit; apart from me you can do nothing" (John 15:4–5). This is the sacred connection we remember when we partake of the emblems of Communion.

10. ALPHA AND OMEGA

In the book of Revelation, Jesus described Himself as "the Alpha and Omega . . . who is, and who was, and who is to come, the Almighty" (Revelation 1:8). Alpha is the first letter, the beginning, of the Greek alphabet, and Omega is the last letter, the end. Christ was the creator of the world and will be there at the end of the world. In the artwork, these letters are seen carved into the top of the keystone arch reminding us that none of us can pass through the gate of heaven without Jesus. Without His Atonement we, like an arch without a keystone, would crumble and fall to death and sin. Jesus is central to our worship—the keystone of our faith, hope, and trust.

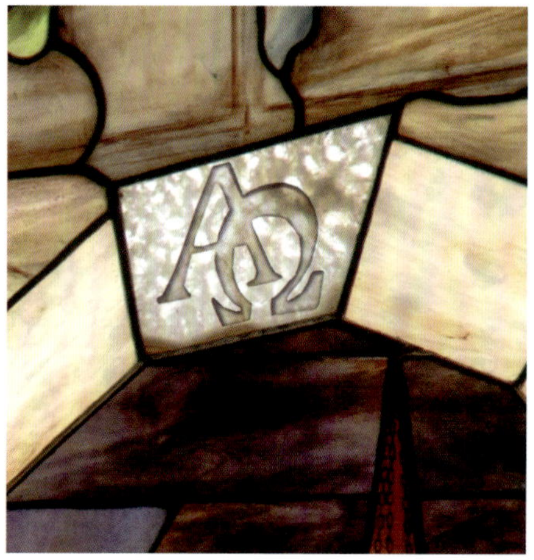

11. A LIGHT TO THE WORLD

The lamp depicted in the window is in an elevated position allowing its light to spread and illuminate the way. Jesus Christ declared, "I am the light of the world" (John 9:5). He also told His disciples to be lights to the world (see Matthew 5:14). He taught, "A town built on a hill cannot be hidden. Neither do people light a lamp and put it under a bowl. Instead they put it on its stand, and it gives light to everyone in the house. In the same way, let your light shine before others" (vv. 14–16). How do we reconcile this teaching with Christ's command to "be careful not to practice your righteousness in front of others to be seen by them" and to "not let your left hand know what your right hand is doing" (Matthew 6:1, 3)? Perhaps the key is to remember it is His light we are to hold up and not our own. Our motive must be to not glorify ourselves but to "glorify [our] Father in heaven" (Matthew 5:16).

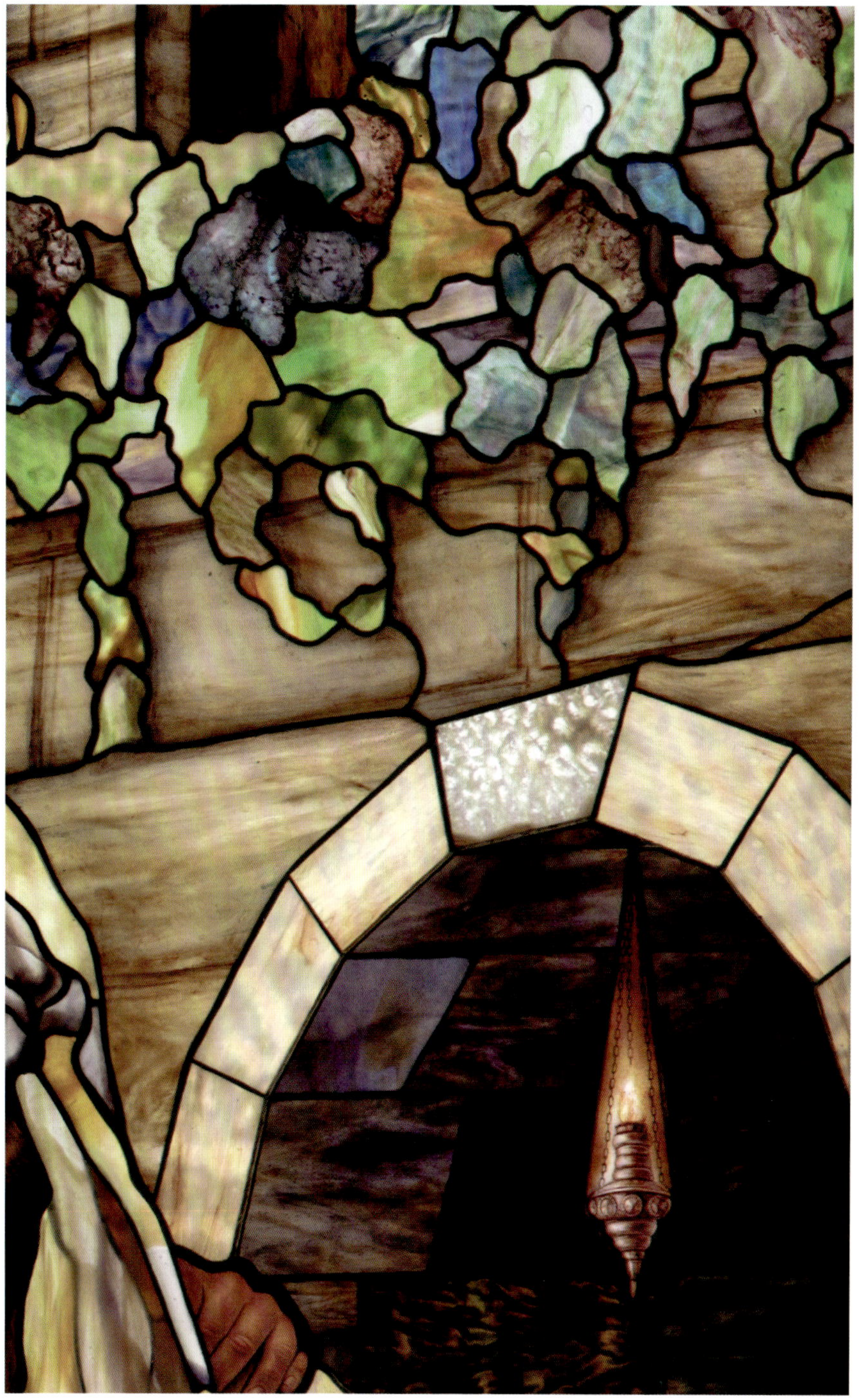

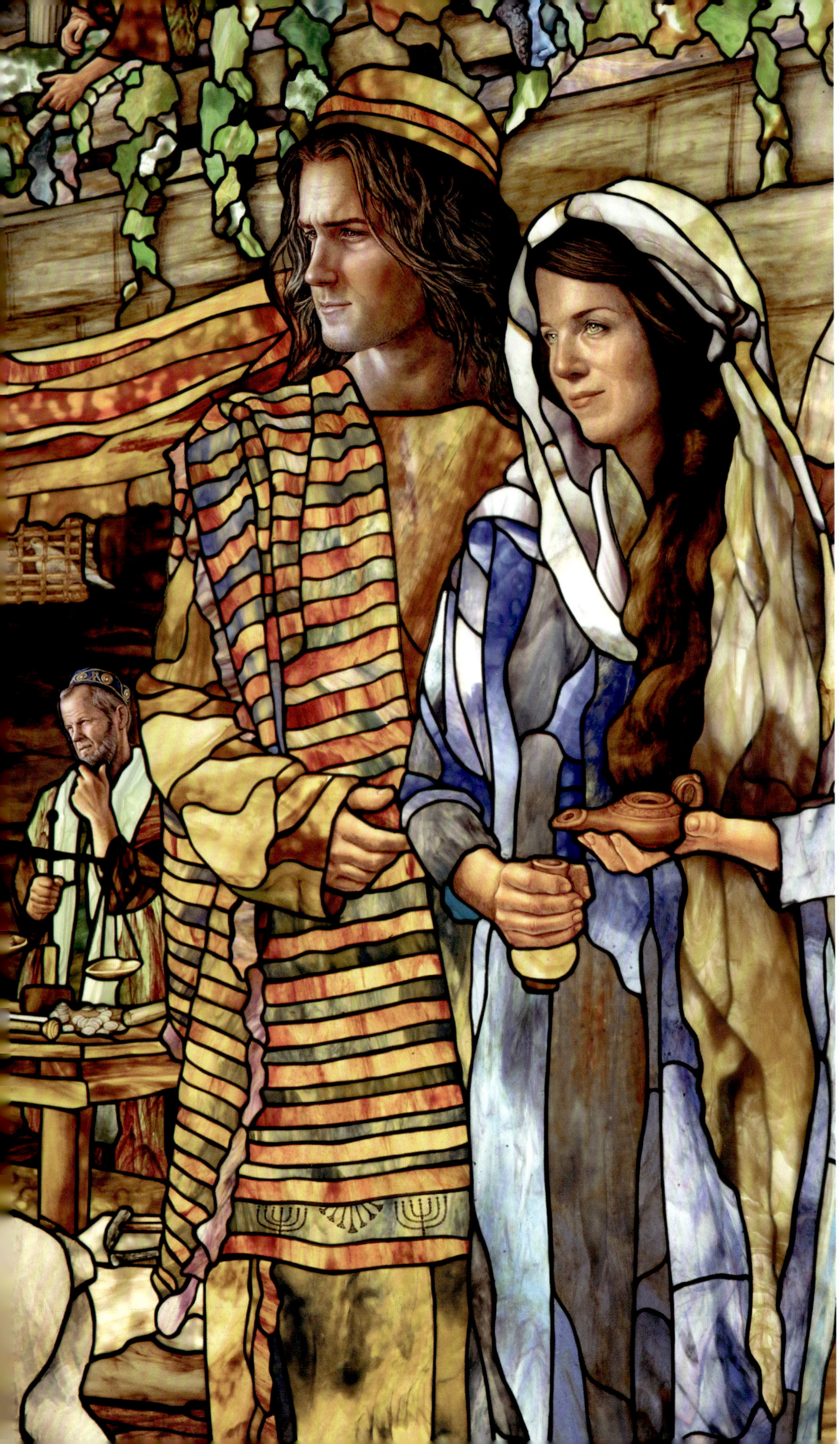

MARY AND APOSTLES

12. TWO TURTLEDOVES LIKE THOSE SACRIFICED BY MARY AND JOSEPH

The two turtledoves in the canopy-covered shop portrayed in the window remind us how poor Joseph and Mary were as to the things of this world. They could not afford the customary sacrifice when baby Jesus was presented at the temple. The law of Moses made allowance for the poor to offer two doves instead of a lamb. God knew that Mary's "Lamb" would be offered as a sacrifice for everyone thirty-three years later. For now, doves would do. Doves are traditionally symbols of peace and truth. Early Christian tradition also speaks of two turtledoves as reminders of the Old and New Testaments.

13. JOHN WHO WAS COMMISSIONED TO CARE FOR MARY

From the cross Jesus told John that Mary was to be his mother and "from that time on, this disciple took her into his home" (John 19:27). What a demonstration of love Christ showed in that moment of extreme suffering—He was concerned with the welfare of His beloved mother. What a demonstration of trust Christ showed in that moment when John knew He could depend on him. Notice the pattern of seven trumpets and seven candlesticks woven into the end of John's shawl. It reminds us of John's revelation recorded in the final book of the New Testament. John is purposely shown barefoot. In Christ's day, servants did not typically have sandals or shoes, so being seen barefoot is a statement of John's willingness to be Christ's servant. During the last supper, Jesus "got up from the meal, took off his outer clothing, and wrapped a towel around his waist. After that, he poured water into a basin and began to wash his disciples' feet, drying them with the towel that was wrapped around him" (John 13:4–5). Thus He showed them with His own example that "the greatest among you will be your servant" (Matthew 23:11).

14. MARY, CHRIST'S MOTHER

The scriptures tell us relatively little about Mary, the mother of Jesus. However, what is recorded speaks volumes about her greatness. She was young when an angel announced she would be the mother of the Son of God. Surely the pronouncement brought many questions and concerns. Nevertheless, instead of responding with doubt and fear, she showed faith. In one of the humblest replies ever spoken, Mary meekly stated, "I am the Lord's servant. . . . May your word to me be fulfilled" (Luke 1:38). With that statement and how she lived her entire life, she demonstrated one of the attributes we can all strive to develop: meekness.

15. SICKLES SYMBOLIZING GATHERING

Jesus taught, "The kingdom of heaven is like a net that was let down into the lake and caught all kinds of fish" (Matthew 13:47). The net reminds us of the call of the Apostles to be fishers of men, but also the responsibility of all disciples to be engaged in gathering. On another occasion, Jesus compared the gathering of souls to planting and harvesting a field. Notice the sickles hanging in a shop next to the turtledoves. These are instruments used to reap and gather. Jesus said, "Open your eyes and look at the fields! They are ripe for harvest. Even now the one who reaps draws a wage and harvests a crop for eternal life, so that the sower and the reaper may be glad together" (John 4:35–36).

16. MATTHEW, TAX COLLECTOR TURNED APOSTLE

The Savior did not call His Apostles from the elite of society or the ruling class of the people. On the contrary, He called common men in whom others may not have seen potential. Matthew was a publican, or tax collector. He was hated and seen by most Jews as a traitor because he served Rome by collecting taxes and whatever he chose to charge in addition. People in the world would have thought it foolish for Jesus to call such a man as an Apostle. They would have seen Matthew as weak. Little did they know that Jesus meant to call the "foolish" and "weak things of the world" to confound the wise and strong (1 Corinthians 1:27).

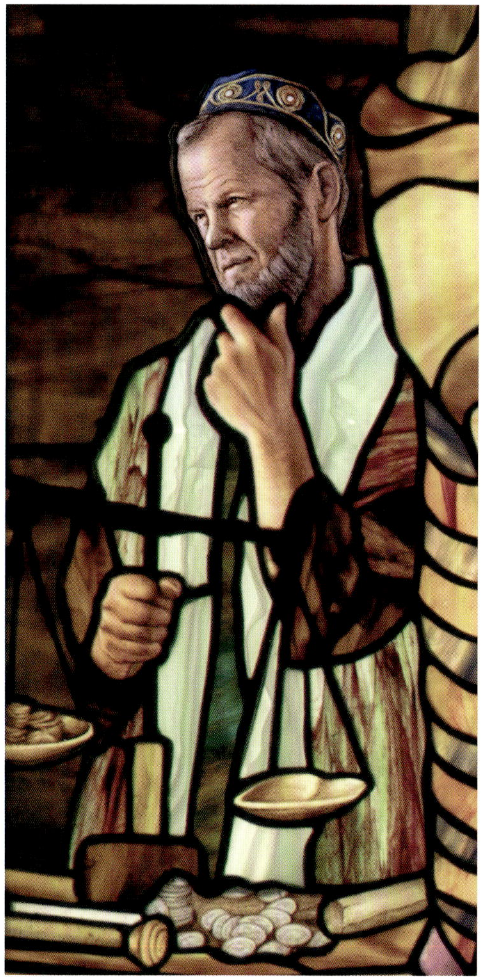

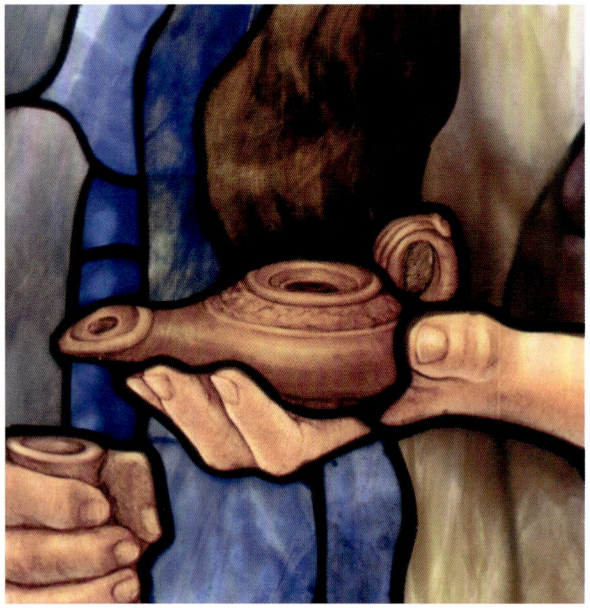

17. LAMP REPRESENTING THOSE HELD BY THE WISE VIRGINS

The woman in the window representing the virgin Mary also represents the wise virgins in the parable of the ten virgins (see Matthew 25:1–13). In her hands, she holds a lamp. In Christ's day, it was customary for a bride to wait with her bridesmaids for her groom. When the groom arrived later in the evening, the maids went out to meet him and his companions with lamps to light the way. With that context in mind, Jesus taught about His Second Coming with these words: "At that time the kingdom of heaven will be like ten virgins who took their lamps and went out to meet the bridegroom" (Matthew 25:1). Five were wise and took oil with them, and five were foolish and did not. At midnight there was a cry that the bridegroom was coming, so all the virgins began to trim their lamps. The foolish had run out of oil and were sent by the wise to buy. While they were gone, the bridegroom came and the foolish missed the wedding because they were unprepared.

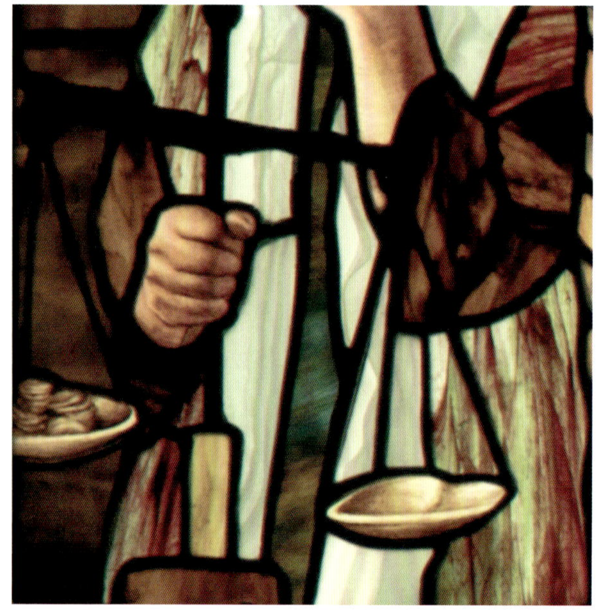

18. SCALES

Scriptures teach that Jesus will be the judge of all mankind: "The Father judges no one, but has entrusted all judgment to the Son" (John 5:22). Notice the scale portrayed in the window—a symbol of judgment. Tax collectors like Matthew used scales to determine if the full amount due had been paid. Considering eternal judgment, Jesus will not measure our good deeds against our bad deeds, but whether we have chosen Him and accepted His Atonement and, through our faith, welcomed Him into our lives. In Hebrew, the basic word that was translated as *atonement* is *kaphar*, a verb that means "to cover." At the Judgment, we will either stand covered with Christ's Atonement, or we will stand naked—covered in His mercy or exposed to the full demands of justice. In the artwork, one side of the scale is shaped as a heart, for Jesus said, "For where your treasure is, there your heart will be also" (Matthew 6:21). Notice a pure heart outweighs whatever riches fill the other side of the scale.

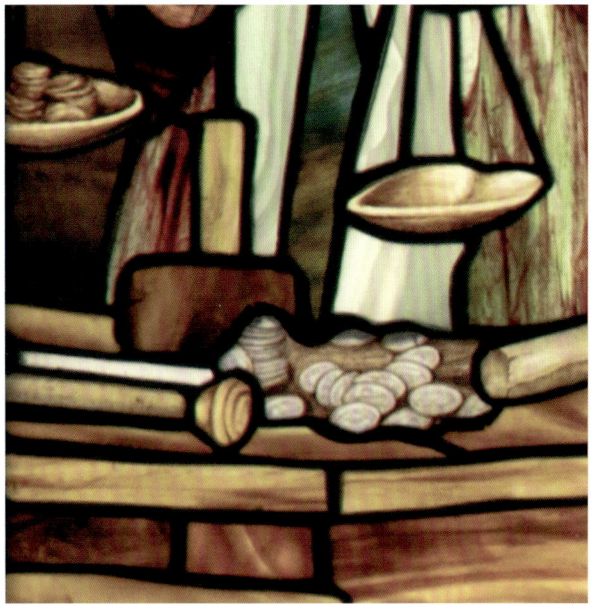

19. CHRIST'S TEMPTATIONS, JUDAS'S THIRTY PIECES OF SILVER, AND THE MONEYCHANGERS

After Jesus was baptized, Satan tempted Him. The last temptation was that if the Lord would worship Satan, he would give Jesus all the things of this world (see Matthew 4:9). The coins in the window can remind us of the worldly temptations we all face. May we, like Jesus, remember to "worship the Lord your God, and serve him only" (v. 10). The coins in the window also represent the money Judas received for betraying the Savior (see Matthew 26:15). It is interesting to note that thirty pieces of silver was the price of a slave at that time. Finally, the coins on the table remind us of the moneychangers who exchanged regular currency into temple money for exorbitant fees. Jesus called out and punished the moneychangers for gouging worshipers who had no other choice but to pay whatever was asked (see Matthew 21:12–13).

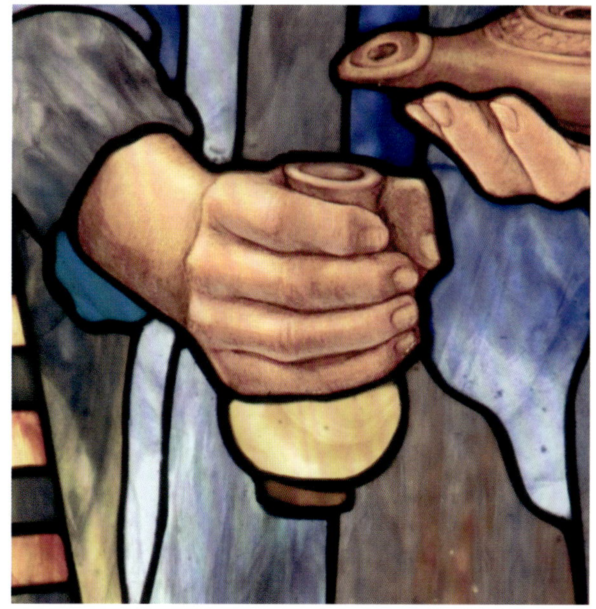

All three of these examples remind us money should never take the place of God as being most important in our lives and the focus of our devotion and worship. Jesus said, "You cannot serve both God and money" (Matthew 6:24).

20. OIL VESSEL

No one can read the parable of the ten virgins (see Matthew 25:1–13) without wondering why the wise would not share their oil with the foolish. Remember that the oil represents personal righteousness, which cannot be shared. It is accumulated drop by drop by the choices we make day after day and week after week throughout our lives. We cannot choose to be chaste for someone else. We cannot choose faith and repentance for someone else. As the Second Coming of Christ draws closer, we must choose for ourselves to be prepared like the wise virgins.

PRODIGALS AND SERMONS

21. THE OLDER BROTHER OF THE PRODIGAL; ALSO REPRESENTS THE RICH MAN WHO REFUSED TO HELP LAZARUS AND THE UNMERCIFUL SERVANT

In the parable of the prodigal (or "lost") son (see Luke 15:11–32) some relate to the prodigal and others to the older brother who is faithfully serving his father while his younger brother wastes his inheritance in a distant land. It seems unfair that the repentant son gets a party, and the faithful son doesn't. What we must remember is that the point of the parable is not about what we will receive for our choices, but rather on whom we will become. The point isn't which son gets the most, but that both sons have a long way to go to become like the good father. Similarly, in Luke 16:19–31 we read about the rich man who completely rejected poor Lazarus when the beggar needed his help. In the next life, the tables are turned, and it is the rich man who finds himself in need and asking for compassion from Lazarus, who is in a much better place. Once again, we all find ourselves at different times relating to both men. It is not about rewards or punishments but being true disciples who seek to pattern our lives after Jesus Christ. Finally, the angry man in the window can represent the unmerciful servant (see Matthew 18:21–35), who was forgiven a great debt only to turn around and cast another man who owed him much less into prison. What right do any of us have to withhold forgiveness when we have all been forgiven so much and so freely?

22. THE PRODIGAL SON; ALSO REPRESENTS THE POOR MAN LAZARUS AND THE SERVANT OF THE UNMERCIFUL SERVANT

The prodigal son in the parable of Jesus willingly and knowingly rebelled. He demanded his portion of the inheritance from his father and wasted it in riotous living (see Luke 15:11–32). We don't know if the same is true for Lazarus (see Luke 16:19–31). Were his destitute circumstances a consequence of his own poor choices or simply misfortune? What about the servant who owes little but is punished by the unmerciful servant who owed much and was forgiven? (see Matthew 18:21–35). We don't know the reasons for either of their debts. Whether the struggles in our own lives are consequences of our own choices, the consequences of others' choices, or just a result of living in this world where bad things happen indiscriminately, we all must turn to the Lord. He offers healing, hope, and divine tutoring through it all.

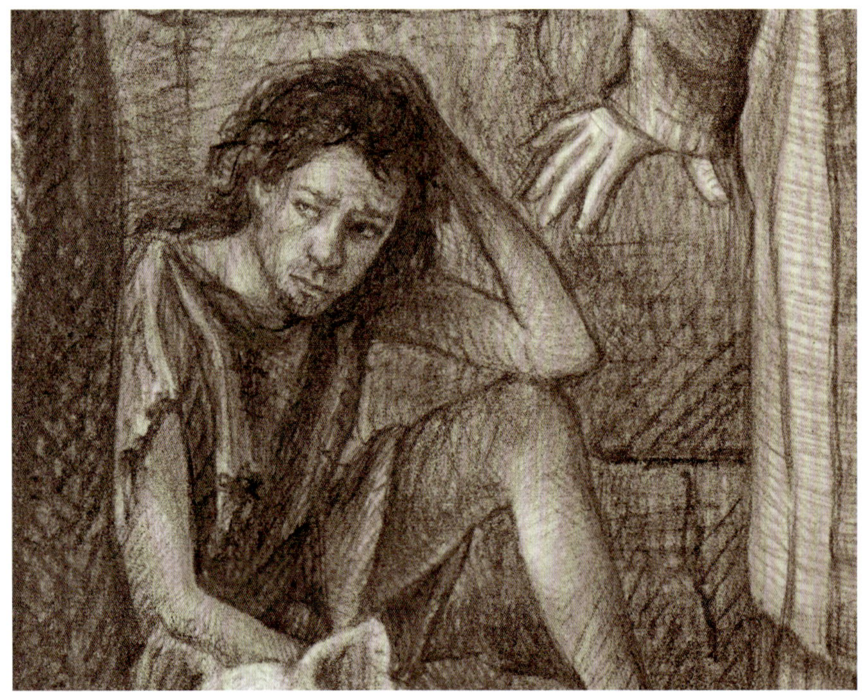

23. PIG CALLING TO MIND THE PRODIGAL AND THE EVIL SPIRITS CAST INTO SWINE

For a young man who grew up in a faithful Jewish family to be feeding pigs shows how completely the prodigal son had rejected his father and his faith. However, it also reminds us of a sacred turning point when this young man came to himself and determined to no longer be held captive by the poor choices of the past (see Luke 15:17–18). The pig in the window also reminds us of when the Lord cast out evil spirits. Evil spirits knew who Jesus was. One called out, "I know who you are—the Holy One of God!" (Mark 1:24). Later in Christ's ministry, evil spirits begged to be cast into a herd of swine. The experience did not end well for the swine, but it did for "the man from whom the demons had gone out, sitting at Jesus' feet, dressed and in his right mind" (Luke 8:35). Additionally, the pig portrayed is a symbol of Christ's teaching to "not throw your pearls to pigs" (Matthew 7:6). As we follow Christ's teachings, let it be with hope for change. We never know when the current "pig" from whom we guard pearls can, like the prodigal son, come to himself, make better choices, and welcome the pearls we can then gladly share.

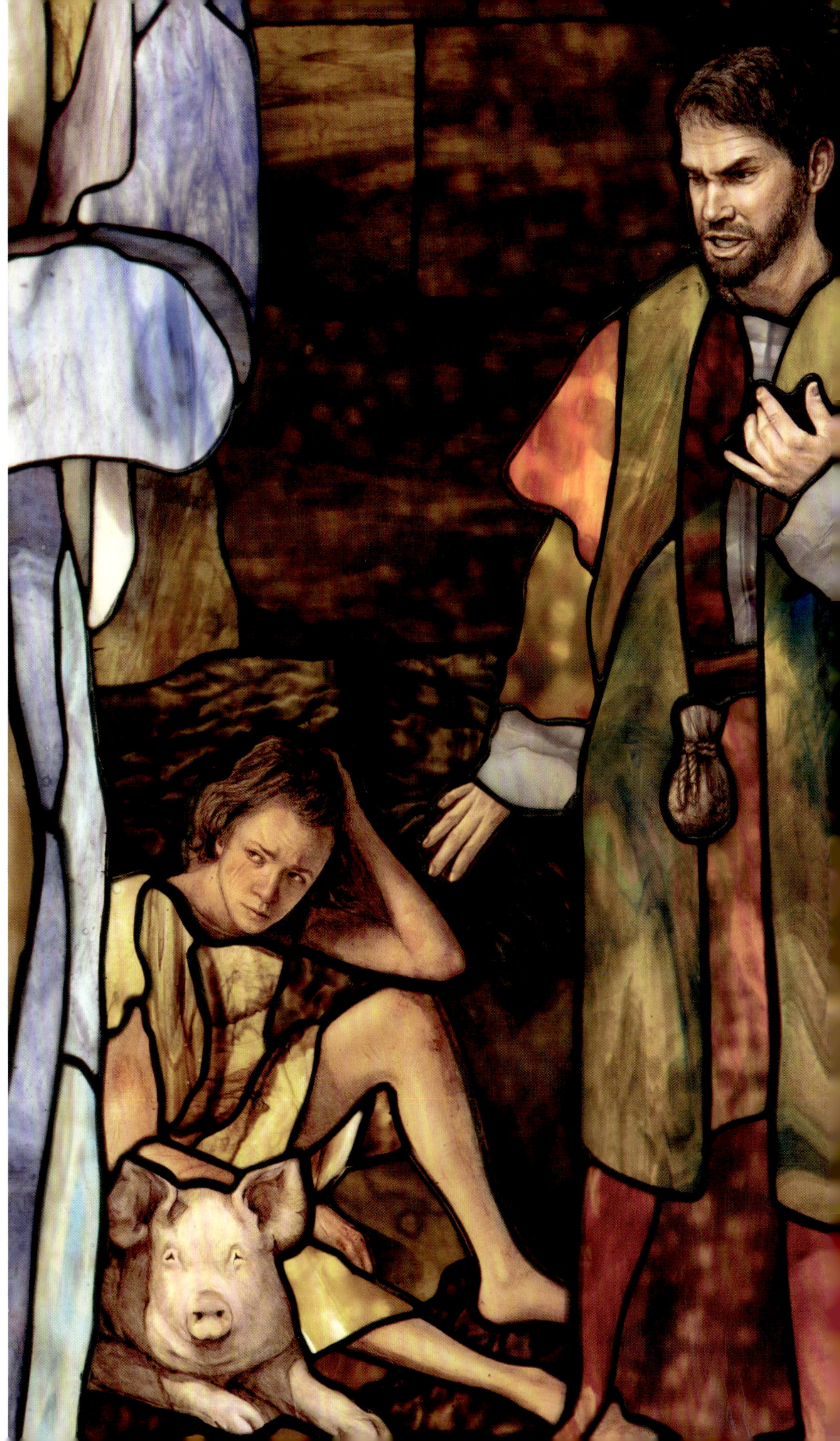

24. A HERODIAN TEMPLE STONE; ALSO INDICATES CHRIST IS THE CHIEF CORNERSTONE

The stone portrayed in the window is similar to the carved stones used to build the temple during the time of Herod. It also reminds us of Ephesians 2:20, where we read that Christ's Church is "built on the foundation of the apostles and prophets, with Christ Jesus himself as the chief cornerstone." The meaning is extended by the abandoned hammer and chisel, showing how the chief priests rejected the firm foundation upon which they could have built.

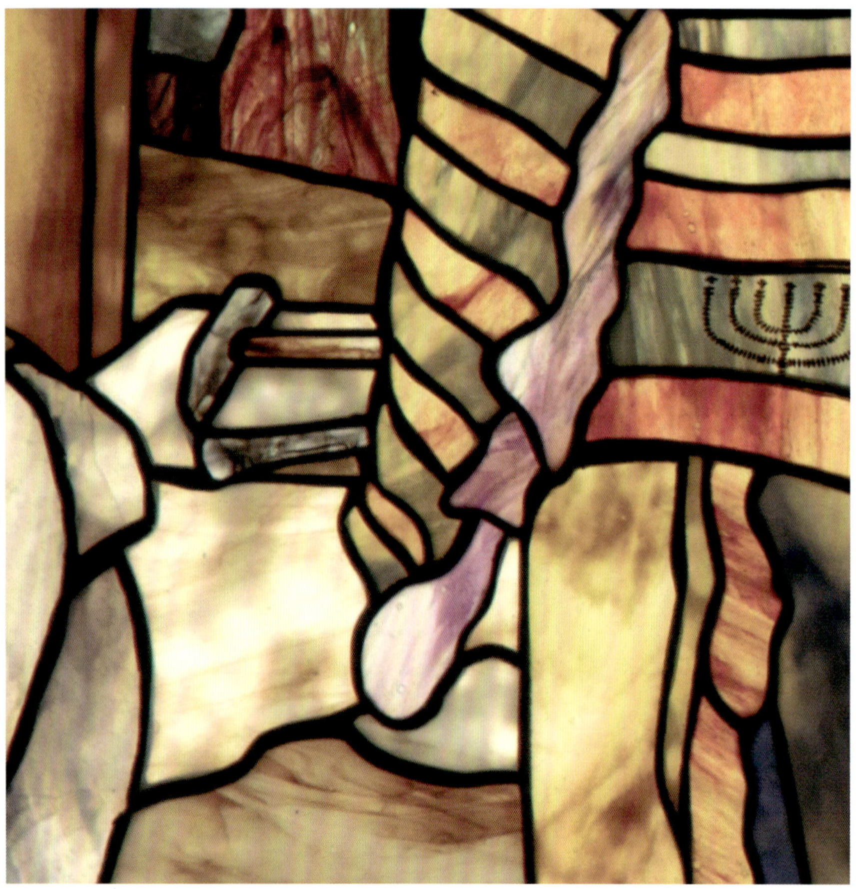

25. ACTUAL CHUNKS OF SALT FROM THE DEAD SEA

Jesus told His followers, "You are the salt of the earth" (Matthew 5:13). Along with giving flavor, salt was a preservative, which made it valuable. Disciples, like salt, must remain pure. Salt only loses its effectiveness when it becomes contaminated. In the artwork, artists have not only portrayed salt, but have included actual salt from the Dead Sea.

26. UNLEAVENED BREAD FOR COMMUNION

Jesus and His apostles were celebrating the Passover in what we now call the Last Supper. The bread would have been unleavened. Jews use unleavened bread to remind them that when the Israelites left Egypt, they did so in such a hurry that there was not time for bread to rise. Now Jesus used the bread as part of Communion: "While they were eating, Jesus took bread, and when he had given thanks, he broke it and gave it to his disciples, saying, 'Take and eat; this is my body'" (Matthew 26:26). The unleavened bread portrayed in the window can also remind us how, earlier in His ministry, the Savior compared the kingdom of God to yeast that a woman mixed into the flour so that the dough would rise (see Luke 13:20–21). Disciples, like yeast, can uplift everyone around them and help the world be better.

27. ROOSTER REPRESENTING PETER'S DENIAL

In Matthew 26 we read that after being arrested in Gethsemane, Jesus was unjustly tried and cruelly persecuted at Caiaphas's palace. Peter stood outside watching and waiting. A woman approached him and asked if he was a follower of Jesus. Peter denied. A little later, another woman identified him as having been with Jesus (see v. 71). Peter again denied. Finally, a man said he had seen him in Gethsemane with Jesus (see John 18:26), and Peter "began to call down curses, and he swore to them, 'I don't know the man!'" (Matthew 26:74). Then, as Christ had foretold, a rooster crowed. We don't know the motivation of Peter on that day. Perhaps he was feeling weak and afraid. Perhaps he was doing what Jesus had previously asked him to do so he could continue to lead the flock. Whatever the reason, Peter denied and "wept bitterly" (v. 75). Those bitter tears were turned to joy when the resurrected Christ gave Peter three opportunities to reaffirm his love and devotion (see John 21:15–17).

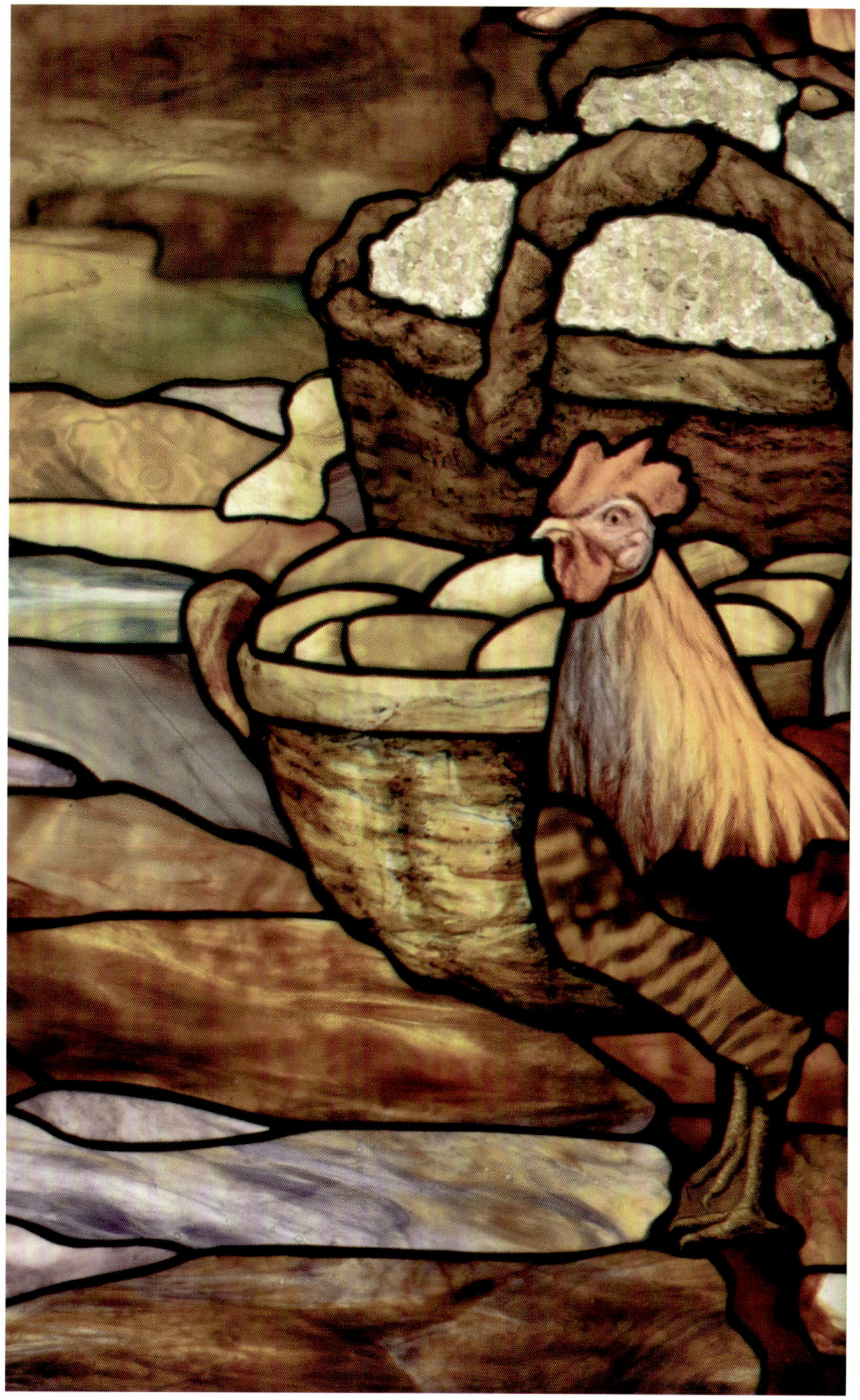

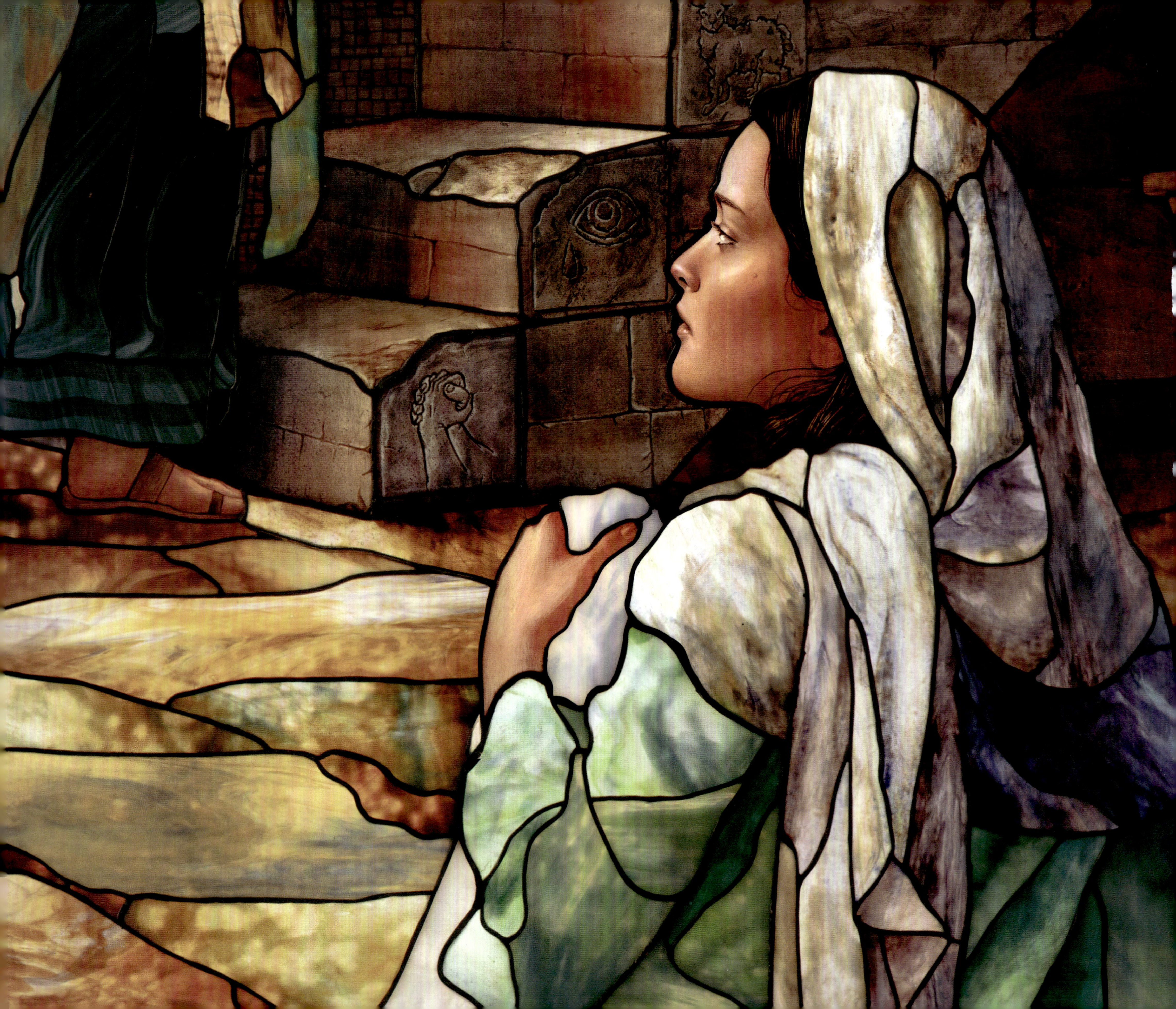

Panel H

Featuring Mary Magdalene

JUDGMENTS AND REVELATION | 90

1. Joseph of Arimathea
2. Pontius Pilate
3. Caiaphas, the high priest
4. Symbols of judgment
5. Madaba map of the Holy Land
6. Seven churches in Revelation
7. Serpent with seven heads
8. Four horses

PATH TO CHRIST | 94

9. Broken vessel
10. "Help me overcome my unbelief"
11. Path of the Beatitudes
12. Mary Magdalene
13. Lilies and wormwood

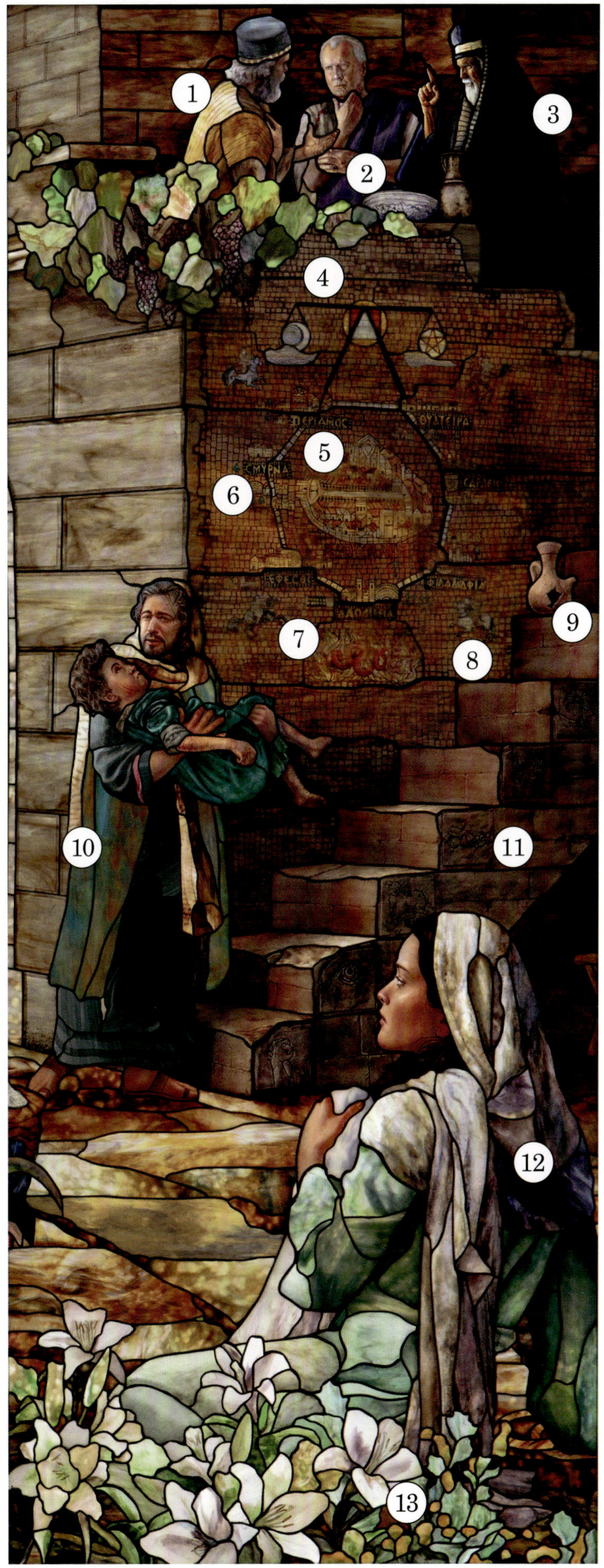

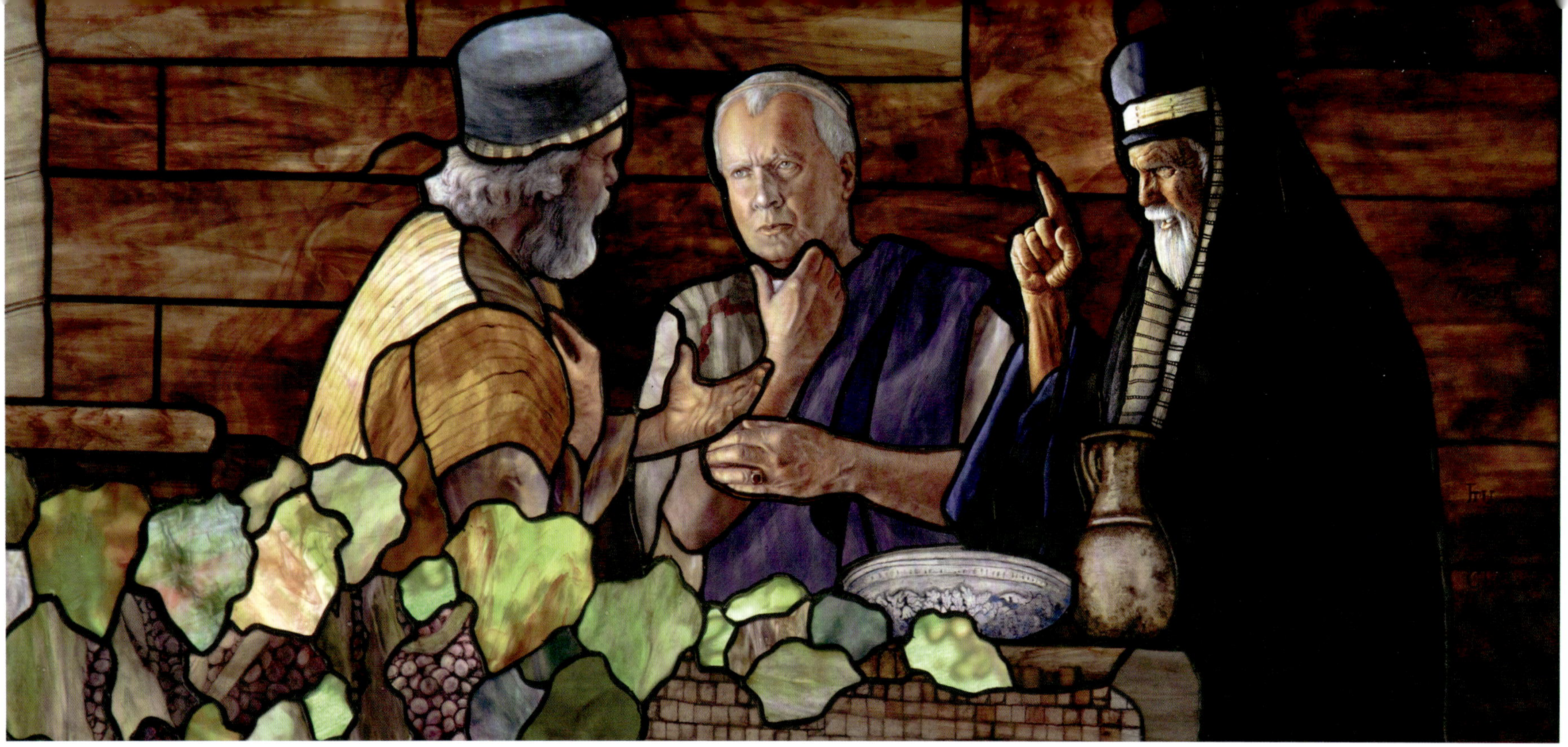

JUDGMENTS AND REVELATION

1. JOSEPH OF ARIMATHEA

Arimathea was a local Jewish town, and Joseph was a wealthy man who came from there (Matthew 27:57). He was a member of the governing Jewish council, called the Sanhedrin (see Mark 15:43; Luke 23:50). He was "a good and upright man" (Luke 23:50), someone who was "waiting for the kingdom of God" (Mark 15:43). He was also "a disciple of Jesus, but secretly" (John 19:38) and went against the Sanhedrin's decision to condemn the Lord (Luke 23:51). After Jesus's death, Joseph of Arimathea went to Pontius Pilate and "asked for Christ's body" (Matthew 27:58). The depiction in the window shows this request as Joseph of Arimathea meets with Pilate, who considers and grants it. Joseph of Arimathea had a new tomb in a garden where no one had ever been buried. In Christ's time, tombs were family-centric. When a family member died, the body was often prepared and laid to rest on a burial bench inside a natural cave or stone-cut tomb, sealed by a blocking stone. After the body decomposed, the tomb was reopened, and the bones were collected and placed permanently in a smaller box, called an ossuary. That box was buried in smaller alcoves in the family tomb. Joseph along with Nicodemus went to help prepare Christ's body with spices and linen for burial, and help His body be laid to rest inside the newly cut tomb. Although he was not public about his devotion to Jesus when He was alive, Joseph of Arimathea showed his devotion "boldly" (Mark 15:43) after His death. He provided a powerful example of generosity with financial means and acting upon spiritual directives.

2. PONTIUS PILATE

Pontius Pilate was the Roman governor, or prefect, who ruled Judea around AD 26–36. The ruling Jews delivered Jesus to Pilate to be judged by Roman authority to answer their accusations against Him for blasphemy and sedition, both worthy of death (John 18:31). Pilate interviewed and saw Jesus's innocence, perceiving the chief priests had only delivered up Jesus to be condemned "for envy" (KJV, Matthew 27:18). He told them: "I find no basis for a charge against him" (John 18:38), saying this three times (see also John 19:4, 6). Although Pilate found Jesus to be innocent and had power to release the Lord, he tried to appease the growing tumult of the thronging crowd by appealing to a Passover custom of releasing a prisoner. He gave innocent Jesus as one option or the robber/murderer Barabbas as the other. Bewilderingly, the people chose Barabbas, preferring a murderer in their midst to a Messiah—a fitting metaphor of a sinner going free at the expense of the blood of the innocent Son of God. Pilate's own wife, based on a divine dream, begged her husband to have nothing to do with the case against Jesus (see Matthew 27:19). Despite his wife's counsel, and his own knowledge of Jesus's innocence, Pilate gave in to the pressures of the crowd. In cowardice of conscience, he condemned the Christ to be crucified. He tried to clear himself of his part in Jesus's death through a ritual action: "He took water and washed his hands in front of the crowd. 'I am innocent of this man's blood,' he said. 'It is your responsibility!'" (Matthew 27:24). Pilate's name is now forever had in infamy, a name to remind us that when courage is needed, compromise is insufficient. In the stained-glass artwork, Pilate talks with Caiaphas the high priest and Joseph of Arimathea. A basin and pitcher of water for hand washing sit on the ledge below him, with grapes on the vessel indicating that his only hope of true cleansing for his sins is through the atoning blood of Christ.

3. CAIAPHAS, THE HIGH PRIEST

Since Moses's time, the sons of Aaron had been chosen to be the priests and high priests in the Levitical priesthood. They offered the sacrifices and conducted the work of the tabernacle/temple. Among all the descendants of Aaron, there was one chosen to be the presiding high priest. At the time of Christ's public ministry, a man named Caiaphas filled that position. He was the head of the Sanhedrin, the ruling Jewish council of around seventy men that acted as a judicial court on Jewish matters in Palestine. After Jesus was arrested, He was taken to Caiaphas's palace to be judged "where the teachers of the law and the elders had assembled" (Matthew 26:57). Caiaphas and the others had long "plotted to take [Christ's] life" (John 11:53), and when He was finally before Caiaphas, the high priest "questioned Jesus about his disciples and his teaching" (John 18:19). Jesus responded, "Why question me? Ask those who heard me," causing one of the officers who stood nearby to strike Jesus and condescendingly question, "Is this the way you answer the high priest?" (John 18:21–22). At this mockery of a trial, the Sanhedrin "were looking for false evidence against Jesus so that they could put him to death" (Matthew 26:59). After various accusations, Caiaphas asked Jesus, "Are you not going to answer?" Jesus simply remained silent. Caiaphas demanded, "Tell us if you are the Messiah, the Son of God." Jesus responded, "You have said so" and then prophesied that they would see the Son of Man coming in the clouds of heaven. "Then the high priest tore his clothes and said, 'He has spoken blasphemy! Why do we need any more witnesses? Look, now you have heard the blasphemy. What do you think?'" The council responded, "He is worthy of death" (Matthew 26:62–66). In the window, Caiaphas is depicted raising a finger to Pilate in wicked and judgmental accusation against Jesus, who is the only "righteous Judge" (2 Timothy 4:8) before whom all mankind will one day stand (see 2 Corinthians 5:10).

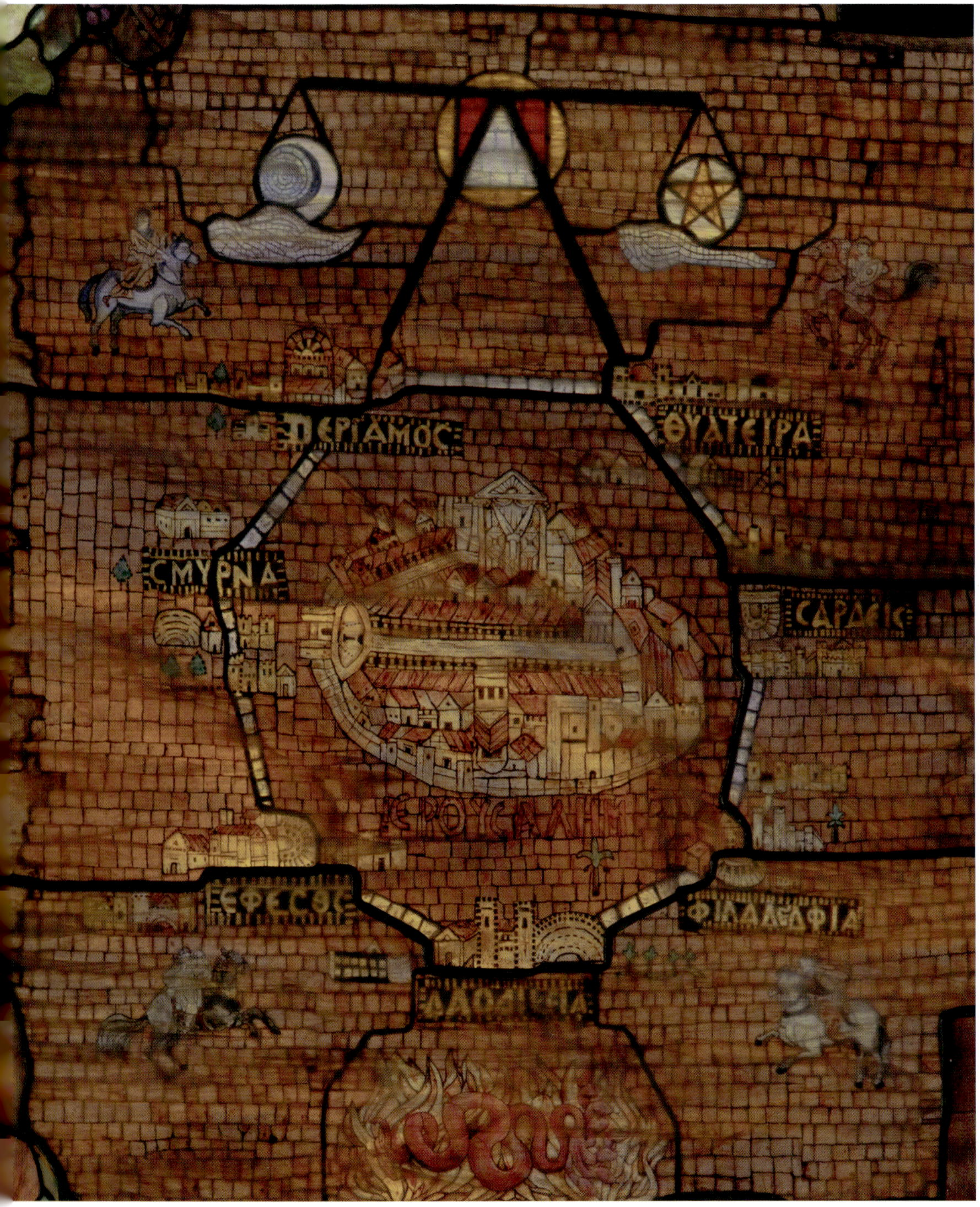

4. SYMBOLS OF JUDGMENT

On the wall below Joseph of Arimathea, Pilate, and Caiaphas is a mosaic of tiles with imagery of symbols representing sacred scriptural concepts. There is a scale representing the Second Coming of Jesus Christ when He returns to judge all mankind, living and dead (John 5:26–29). Below the scales are clouds signifying His coming from the clouds in glory. On one scale is a moon and on the other a star, representing resurrected bodies and their splendor as described by Paul in 1 Corinthians 15:40–42. The center yellow circle represents heaven, the red square a symbol of Jesus's saving blood reaching all four corners of the earth. The center triangle in white represents God the Father, Jesus the Son, and the Holy Spirit.

5. MADABA MAP OF THE HOLY LAND

The Madaba map is the oldest known surviving map of Jerusalem. With its locations rendered in Greek, the original mosaic map was made between AD 542 and 570 and likely served to orient Christian travelers as they journeyed to the Holy Land. In modern times, it was rediscovered in 1884 in the Byzantine church of Saint George in Madaba, Jordan. The map covers a broad area, including the Nile delta, Mount Sinai, the Moab desert, the Dead Sea, the Jordan River, Jericho, Bethlehem, and other sacred Biblical sites. A prominent feature of the map is the detailed depiction of the Old City of Jerusalem (with "Jerusalem" written in Greek underneath), including the Lion's Gate, Golden Gate, Damascus Gate, Zion's Gate, and the Church of the Holy Sepulcher, which marks the traditional spot of the crucifixion and Jesus's tomb.

6. SEVEN CHURCHES IN REVELATION

The cities surrounding Jerusalem in the Madaba map are associated with seven cities in the book of Revelation, written in Greek. Just below the sixth is Ἔφεσος (Ephesus), the first Church to whom John wrote (see Revelation 2:1). The other cities are the churches in Asia (modern Türkiye): Smyrna, Pergamum, Thyatira, Sardis, Philadelphia, and Laodicea, all of which are mentioned in Revelation 1:11. These seven churches are the focus of the first three chapters of Revelation. To each of these seven churches John wrote prophecies, rebukes for their sins, and testimony of the victory of Jesus Christ. There are different interpretations, of course, of the significance of the number seven (sometimes associated with completion or wholeness) and of these seven congregations (perhaps representing all Christian churches). Whatever the interpretation, it is clear from John's revelation that disciples of Jesus Christ are to repent and wash their sins in the blood of the Lamb so they can "eat from the tree of life" (Revelation 2:7), overcome the spiritual "second death" (v. 11), be given the "hidden manna" and a "new name" (v. 17), have "authority over the nations" (v. 26), "be dressed in white" and acknowledged by Jesus "before my Father and his angels" in "the book of life" (Revelation 3:5), have written on "them the name of my God and the name of the city of my God, the new Jerusalem, which is coming down out of heaven from my God; and I will also write on them my new name" (Revelation 3:12), and they are "to sit with me on my throne" (v. 21), signifying salvation in the kingdom of heaven.

7. SERPENT WITH SEVEN HEADS

This image represents Satan, whom John saw and described in the book of Revelation in figurative language as "an enormous red dragon with seven heads" (Revelation 12:3). This serpent, reminiscent of the serpent who deceived Adam and Eve in the Garden of Eden, was a terrible dragon that wanted to destroy the Son of God. The archangel Michael fought back against "that ancient serpent called the devil, or Satan, who leads the whole world astray" (Revelation 12:9), conquering him (see vv. 7–8). John heard a voice say: "Now have come the salvation and the power and the kingdom of our God, and the authority of his Messiah. For the accuser of our brothers and sisters, who accuses them before our God day and night, has been hurled down. They triumphed over him by the blood of the Lamb and by the word of their testimony; they did not love their lives so much as to shrink from death" (Revelation 12:10–11). John warned, however, that the serpent now waged war against "those who keep God's commands and hold fast their testimony about Jesus" (Revelation 12:17). While it sounds ominous, remember that all those who are valiant in the faith of Jesus can triumph over the seven-headed serpent of Satan "by the blood of the Lamb and by the word of their testimony" (Revelation 12:11).

8. FOUR HORSES

In the book of Revelation, John wrote that he saw a book or scroll with seven seals, or sections. When the first four seals were opened by the Lord, John saw what are known as the four horsemen of the apocalypse. In order, he saw riders on a white horse, a red horse, a black horse, and a pale horse. Like all of John's visions, the riders of these four horses have various interpretations and applications across different Christian faiths. John told us the rider of the white horse was symbolic of "conquest" (Revelation 6:2), the rider of the red horse had a sword and took "peace from the earth" (v. 4). The rider of the black horse was "holding a pair of scales in his hand" to measure out food and resources in a seeming time of famine (vv. 5–6). The rider of the pale horse "was named Death, and Hades was following close behind him" (v. 8) and they were given power to kill a fourth of the earth. Some see these horsemen as preceding the coming of Christ. Others interpret them as events after Christ's life, such as representing the turbulent prophecies in Matthew 24 prior to the Lord's return. Whatever the timetable, human conquest, contention, famine, death, and hell have been facets of mortal struggle from the beginning of time and will be until the end. They will only be smothered out by the rider of another "white horse, whose rider is called Faithful and True": the "King of Kings and Lord of Lords" (Revelation 19:11, 16).

PATH TO CHRIST

9. BROKEN VESSEL

Broken vessels or pottery are common in the Bible to symbolize spiritual principles. A good pot or vessel is useful, but one that leaks or is broken is usually cast aside. However, in the Lord's eyes, broken things can be mended and made useful again. As the Lord told Jeremiah, we are clay in the potter's hands (see Jeremiah 18:6). All of us, to one degree or another, are "marred" by rebellion and sin (v. 4). "So the potter formed it into another pot, shaping it as seemed best to him" (v. 4). Each of us must be born again by the Spirit of God (see John 3:1–8), made whole by the grace of Christ. Yes, we are broken, but the Lord asks us to bring Him "a broken spirit; a broken and contrite heart" (Psalm 51:17). With that brokenness, the Lord can heal and make us whole, remaking us in His holy image. "Can I not do with you, Israel, as this potter does?" the Lord asks (Jeremiah 18:6). Yes, He can.

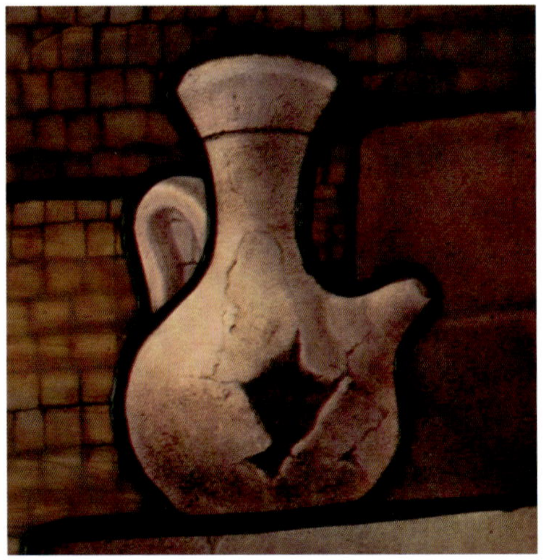

10. "HELP ME OVERCOME MY UNBELIEF"

A father brought his son to Christ's disciples to be healed of being nonverbal and having seizures that caused the boy to go rigid and foam at the mouth. But the disciples couldn't heal him. "'You unbelieving generation,' Jesus replied, . . . 'Bring the boy to me'" (Mark 9:19). The father said to the Master, "If you can do anything, take pity on us and help us" (v. 22). There was dual suffering in his voice—his son's but also his own as an exhausted and distraught father. "Everything is possible for one who believes," the Savior reminded the father (v. 23). Simultaneous suffering between father and son was also coupled with simultaneous faith and doubt within the father. He humbly and honestly responded, "I do believe; help me overcome my unbelief!" (v. 24). Many of us believe, but also carry aspects of unbelief. The shadow of doubt eventually descends on every traveler of the road of faith. Winds and storms cause us to falter. Many doubts result from our own spiritual inability to hear, the cacophony of the popular crowd throwing us into the fire of shaken faith where we convulse and seize. But if we turn to the Lord and plead, "Help me overcome my unbelief!" our spiritual suffering can be cast out and healed, just like the boy's physical seizures and the father's doubts. In the window, the father turns resolutely toward the stairs representing the Beatitudes—the path to following Christ and accessing His power.

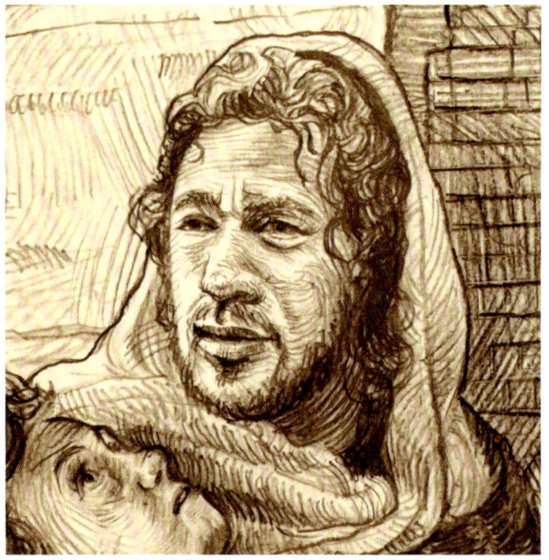

11. PATH OF THE BEATITUDES

The Lord's Sermon on the Mount is recorded in Matthew 5–7. In it, Christ's gospel is encompassed in powerful teachings that lie at the heart of His message, teaching His disciples how to follow Him. It begins with Jesus teaching us how to live in a state of being "blessed." The statements are known as the Beatitudes. People in the world might teach about being blessed differently: Blessed are the educated! Blessed are the wealthy! Blessed are the beautiful, famous, and powerful! However, Christ taught: "Blessed are the poor in spirit, . . . those who mourn, . . . the meek, [and] the merciful" (Matthew 5:3–5, 7). These states of spiritual blessedness, however, don't appear to be random. He isn't just calling out arbitrary qualities. There appears to be an order to His declarations. Each of the Beatitudes represents a specific step in our progress toward Christlike living. We begin by recognizing our soul is inherently "poor" in sin, we begin to "mourn" for our shortcomings, becoming "meek" and submissive. We then begin to "hunger and thirst for righteousness," and become filled with God's Spirit, which causes us to turn more outward toward others and become "merciful." Our hearts become "pure" and we become "peacemakers" who are willing and able to suffer persecution like the "prophets who were before you" (see Matthew 5:3–12). The artists represented these eight states of spiritual blessedness in Christ as stairs, including a visual symbol for each, such as a tear for mourning and a lamb for meekness.

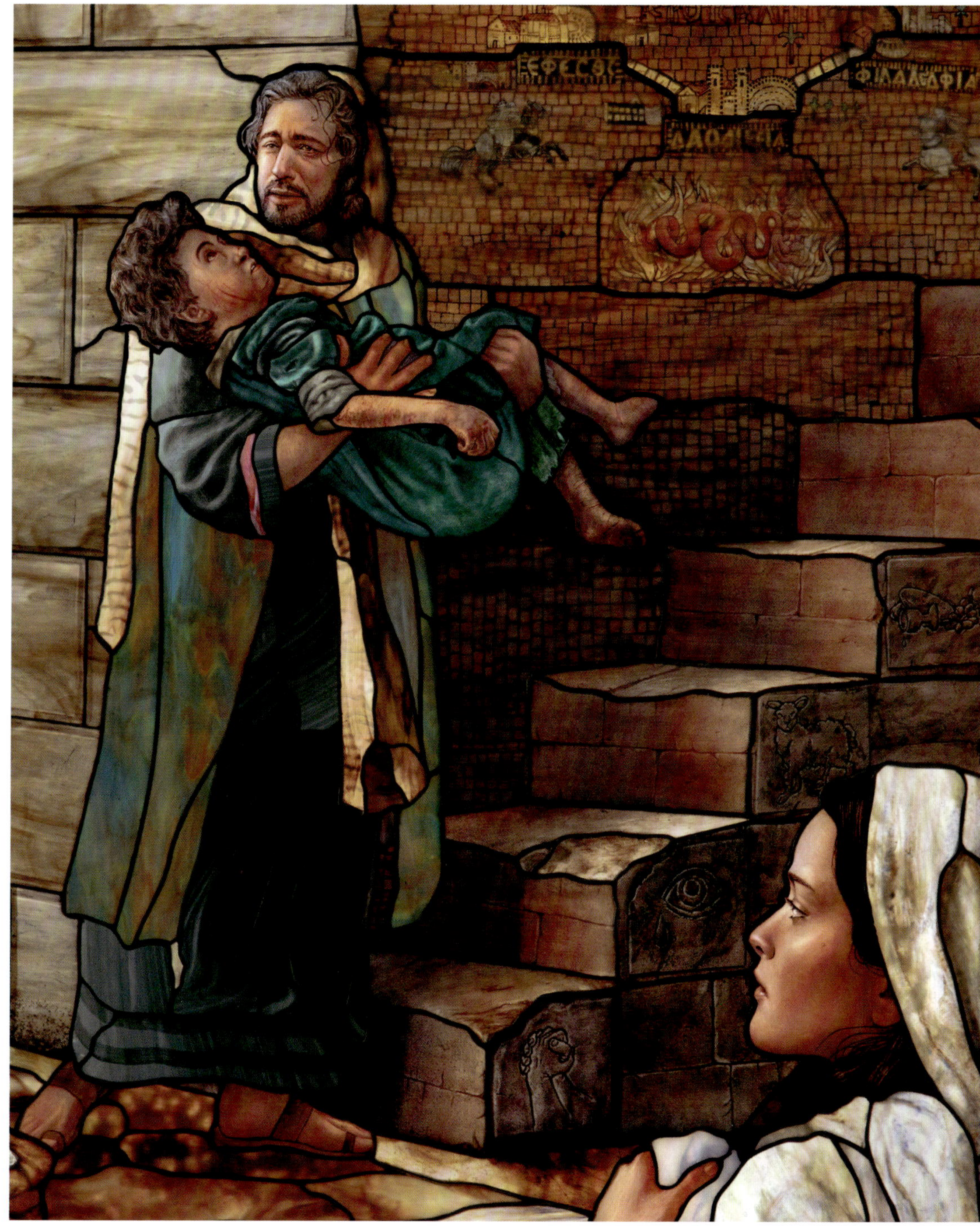

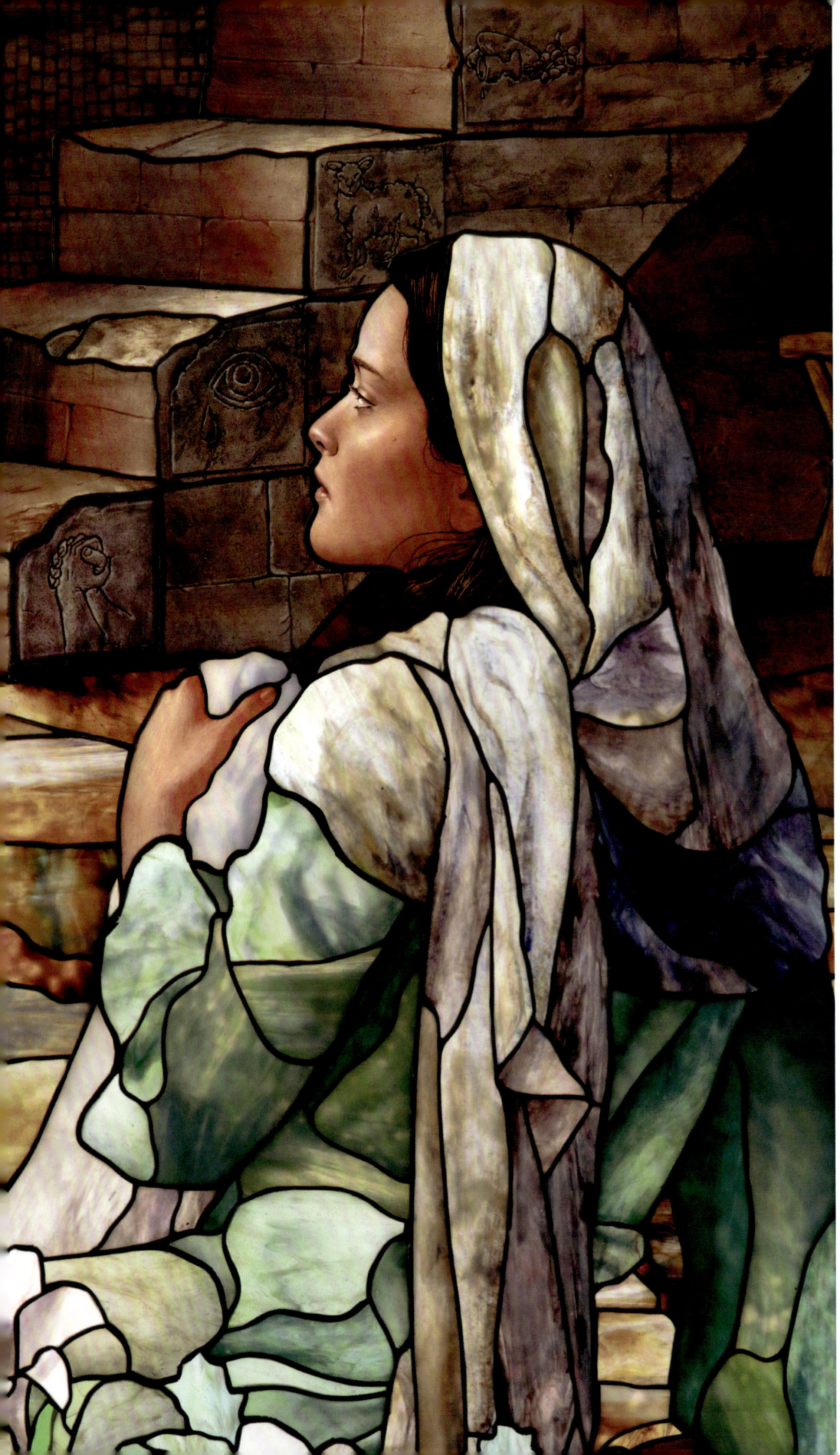

12. MARY MAGDALENE

Mary Magdalene is shown in the window as holding Christ's burial shroud near her heart. This great disciple was from a town next to the Sea of Galilee called Magdala. Just as Jesus was known as Jesus of Nazareth, Mary was known as Mary of Magdala, or Mary Madgalene. Since women of the day were usually known by a name that linked them to a husband, father, brother, or son, it is possible that Mary Magdalene was unattached. Magdala was known for processing fish. Luke spoke of "some women" like Joanna, Mary Magdalene, and many other women who "were helping to support [Jesus and the apostles] out of their own means" (Luke 8:2–3). Mary Magdalene had "been cured" of "seven demons" who "had come out" of her (Luke 8:2). We don't know what those demons were, but the claim that Mary had been a prostitute is not stated in the Bible. Mary's devotion to Jesus was deep and loyal. All four gospel writers place Mary Magdalene as a crucial figure in events surrounding the Crucifixion, burial, and Resurrection of the Lord. Both Mark and John place Mary Magdalene as the first person to ever see the resurrected Lord. After seeing the risen Christ, "Mary Magdalene went to the disciples with the news: 'I have seen the Lord!'" (John 20:18), becoming the first of many to testify of the reality of the Resurrection of Jesus Christ.

13. LILIES AND WORMWOOD

Lilies are a beautiful flower referred to many times in the Bible. The Savior famously used lilies to teach us not to worry so much about things like our clothing or physical welfare (see KJV, Matthew 6:28 and KJV, Luke 12:27). Over time, lilies have become a symbol of rebirth, renewal, and in Christianity, resurrection. Here in the artwork, lilies spring beneath Mary Magdalene, the first witness of the resurrected Lord, symbolic of Jesus's conquering death and giving spiritual and physical rebirth. Contrasting with the beautiful lilies is a plant called wormwood, which is often associated with pain and anguish. Wormwood as a name is found in the book of Revelation, where John described future calamities: "A great star, blazing like a torch, fell from the sky on a third of the rivers and on the springs of water—the name of the star is Wormwood. A third of the waters turned bitter, and many people died from the waters that had become bitter" (Revelation 8:10–11). Wormwood as a plant is from the herb *Artemisia*. Moses mentioned it as emblematic of someone "whose heart turneth away this day from the Lord our God, to go and serve the gods of these nations; lest there should be among you a root that beareth gall and wormwood" (KJV, Deuteronomy 29:18). In the *Screwtape Letters*, C. S. Lewis named Screwtape's nephew, a novice devil who is trying to learn how to spiritually corrupt followers of the Lord, "Wormwood." As opposed to the lily of life, wormwood is emblematic of bitter spiritual death.

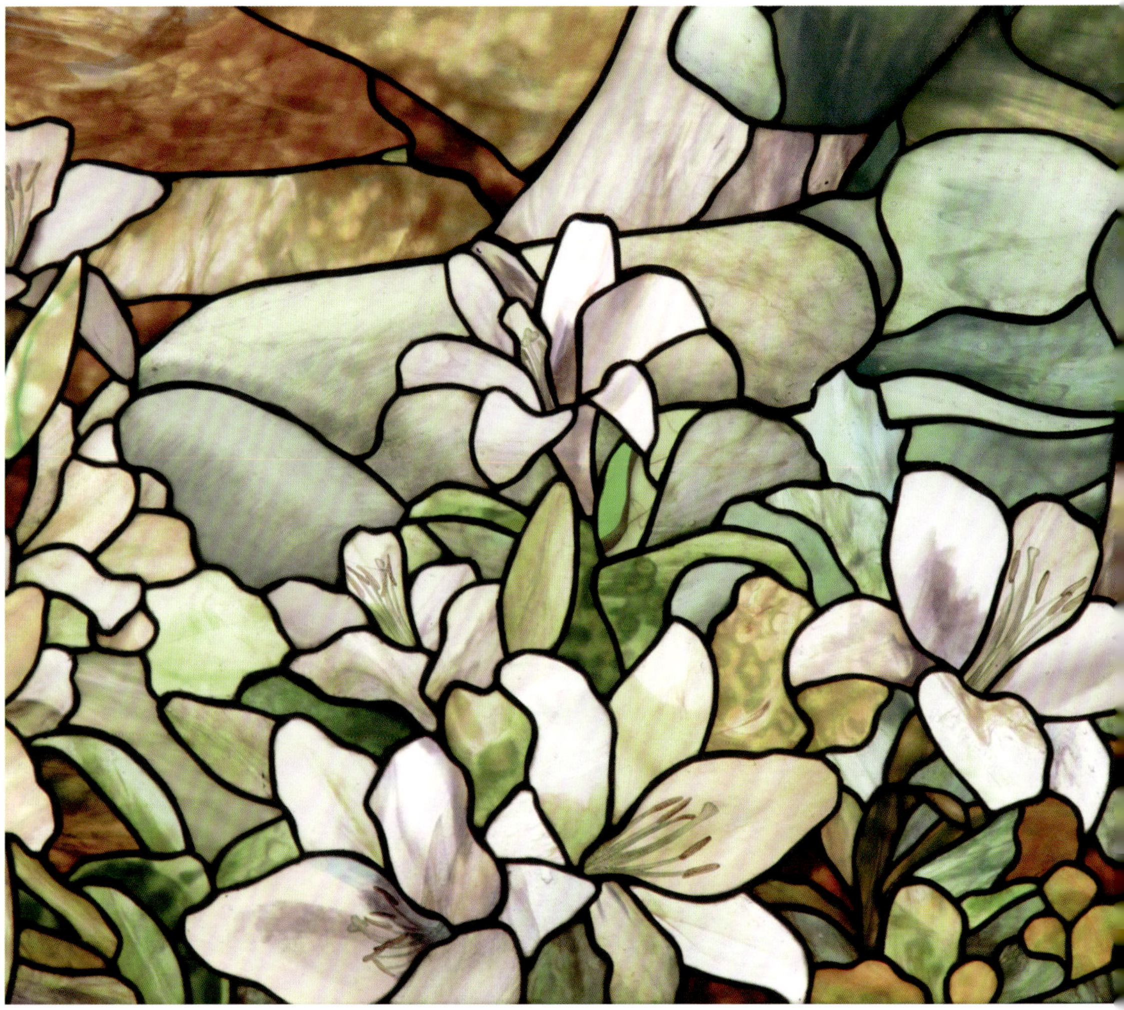

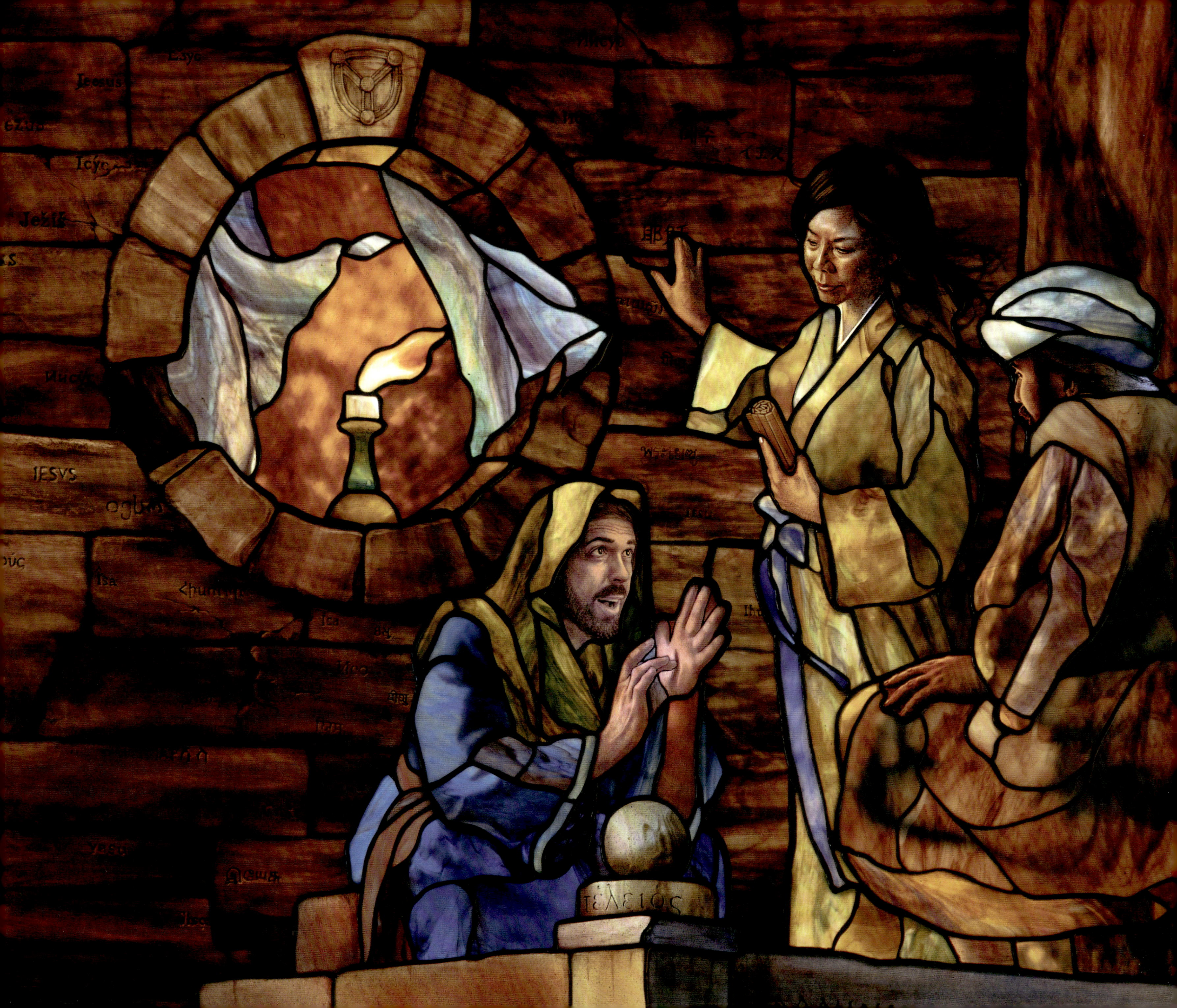
Jesus
IESVS
Isa

Panel I

Featuring the Flame in the Window

ALL PEOPLE AND LANGUAGES | 100

1. Shield of the Trinity
2. Twelve apostles
3. Day of Pentecost and gift of tongues
4. Gospel going to all nations
5. Name of Jesus in many languages
6. Believing Thomas
7. Perfect sphere
8. Everything in common
9. "Do you love me more than these?"

LIFE AND DEATH | 106

10–12, 14. Spiritual prison
13. Roman guard with sword
15. Become as a child
16. Anointing jar and tear bottle

FALSE GODS AND WORLDLINESS | 108

17. False goddess Diana
18. Laurel wreath of victory
19. Golden calf
20. The *Omphalos* of Delphi
21. Altar to the unknown god
22. Rusting sword and symbolic pot
23. Lemons of luxury
24. Roman vase
25. Basket of spices

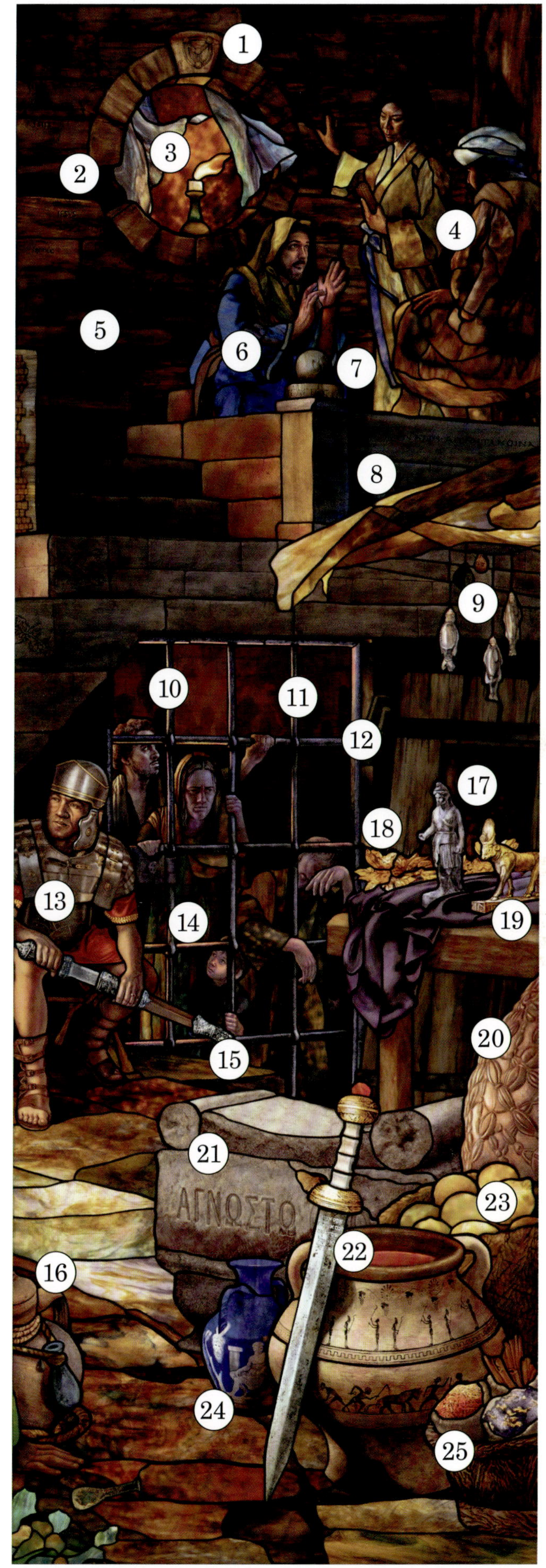

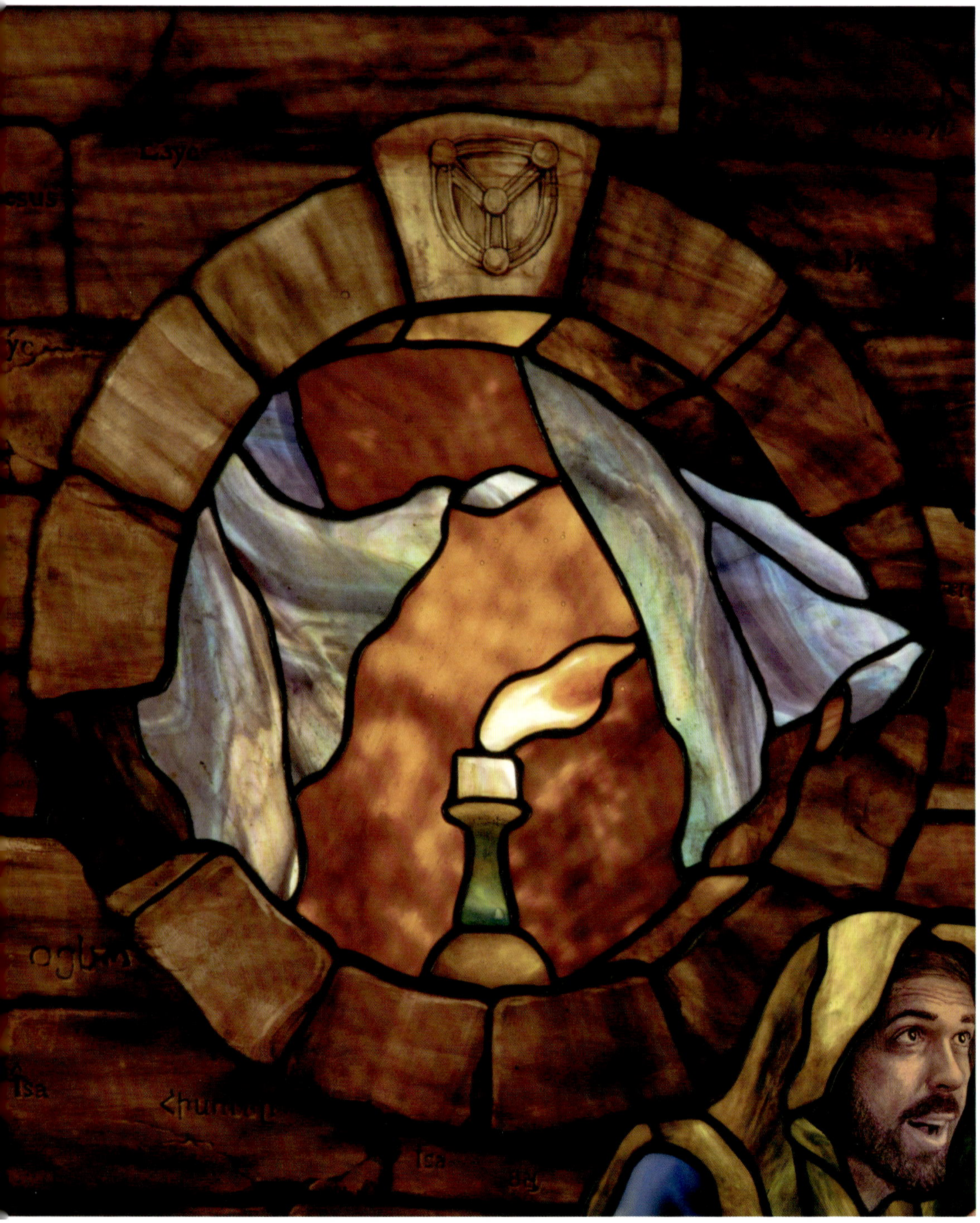

ALL PEOPLE AND LANGUAGES

1. SHIELD OF THE TRINITY

Above the circular window with the rushing mighty wind of the Pentecostal Holy Spirit is a traditional symbol of the Father, Son, and Holy Spirit known as the Shield of the Trinity. This symbol dates to the twelfth century and represents concepts of the nature of the Father, Son, and Spirit articulated in traditional Christian creeds, particularly the Athanasian Creed. The three outer circles of the diamond each represent God. On the top left is the Father, the top right is the Son, and the bottom is the Holy Spirit. The center circle is also God. The lines from each circle to the center circle traditionally say the word *is.* So, connecting the circles and lines, it says, "the Father is God," "the Son is God," and "the Holy Spirit is God." The outer lines connecting the circles traditionally say the words *is not.* So it teaches, "the Father is not the Son," "the Son is not the Holy Spirit," and "the Holy Spirit is not the Father."

2. TWELVE APOSTLES

There are twelve stones that comprise the circular window, not counting the Shield of the Trinity keystone. These twelve stones represent the twelve apostles of Christ. The apostle Paul, in his letter to the Saints in Ephesus, wrote that the global Saints of God should all be united in one faith, "built on the foundation of the apostles and prophets, with Christ Jesus himself as the chief cornerstone" (Ephesians 2:20). Viewers of the window will notice, however, that one stone is missing. This represents Judas Iscariot, who betrayed Jesus to the conspiring chief priests for thirty pieces of silver (see Matthew 26:14–16). Convicted to the core by his conscience for betraying the innocent Lamb of God, Judas hanged himself (see Matthew 27:3–5). After Jesus's resurrection, this left only eleven apostles. The disciples met, and Peter commented on the void in the twelve, saying, "It is necessary to choose one of the men who have been with us the whole time the Lord Jesus was living among us, beginning from John's baptism to the time when Jesus was taken up from us. For one of these must become a witness with us of his resurrection" (Acts 1:21). They nominated two potential replacements for Judas: Justus and Matthias. Luke records: "Then they prayed, 'Lord, you know everyone's heart. Show us which of these two you have chosen to take over this apostolic ministry, which Judas left'" (Acts 1:24), and Matthias was chosen. The missing stone in this circle represents this event recorded in Acts.

3. DAY OF PENTECOST AND GIFT OF TONGUES

After Jesus's resurrection, He appeared to His disciples at Jerusalem. He then instructed them about a promise He had made to them at the last supper, the night before He was killed—the promise to send "the Spirit of truth" or "the Advocate, the Holy Spirit, whom the Father will send in my name." This Holy Spirit cannot be seen, but "lives with you and will be in you" (John 14:17, 26, 17). Before the Lord ascended into heaven, He promised them "you will receive power when the Holy Spirit comes on you" (Acts 1:8), commanding them to "stay in the city [of Jerusalem] until you have been clothed with power from on high" (Luke 24:49). The apostles did as they were told. The outpouring of power from the Holy Spirit came on the day of Pentecost (see Acts 2:1). Luke recorded: "Suddenly a sound like the blowing of a violent wind came from heaven and filled the whole house where they were sitting. They saw what seemed to be tongues of fire that separated and came to rest on each of them. All of them were filled with the Holy Spirit and began to speak in other tongues as the Spirit enabled them" (Acts 2:2–4). The diverse crowd of Jews who had gathered for Passover in Jerusalem and heard them speak in other tongues were amazed. To illustrate this miraculous event, the artists painted the name of Jesus in over forty languages. Thomas is shown using American Sign Language (ASL) as he testifies to have seen the marks in the palms of the Risen Lord (see John 20:28). It is as if the Spirit was so strong in the room that it could not be contained. The message of Christ is depicted as seeping through the walls. When some mocked the gift of tongues that was on display, Peter testified to the crowd of the redemption and resurrection of Jesus as the promised Messiah, telling them to "repent and be baptized, every one of you, in the name of Jesus Christ for the forgiveness of your sins. And you will receive the gift of the Holy Spirit" (Acts 2:38). About 3,000 people accepted Christ that day and joined the disciples. The wind blowing through this window represents the Pentecostal power of receiving the Holy Spirit that clothes believers with the promised power and gifts of the Holy Spirit of God (see 1 Corinthians 12–13).

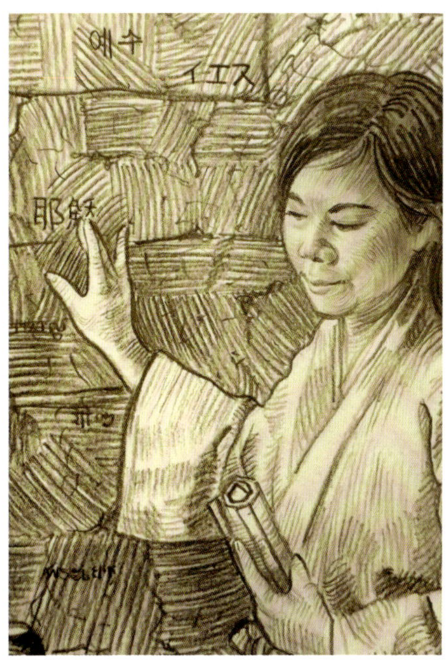

4. GOSPEL GOING TO ALL NATIONS

After Jesus was resurrected but before He ascended to heaven, He gave His eleven apostles who had gathered in Galilee a divine injunction: "Go and make disciples of all nations, baptizing them in the name of the Father and of the Son and of the Holy Spirit, and teaching them to obey everything I have commanded you" (Matthew 28:19). Prior to this great commission, Christ's disciples had only preached to groups of Israelites (see Matthew 10:5–6). But now, the good news of the Lord's gospel was to be taken to the world. While in the coastal port of Joppa, the chief apostle Peter had a vision reminding Him of this commission (see Acts 10:9–16). Peter then baptized a righteous Roman soldier named Cornelius, the first Gentile convert, and opened the way to bring people of all nations into the gospel of Jesus Christ. These figures in the art glass represent this world-changing event, an Indian man and Asian woman touching the name of Jesus in Chinese as they're being instructed by the figure representing the apostle Thomas. Today, believers of Christ are found among all nations, kindreds, tongues, and peoples.

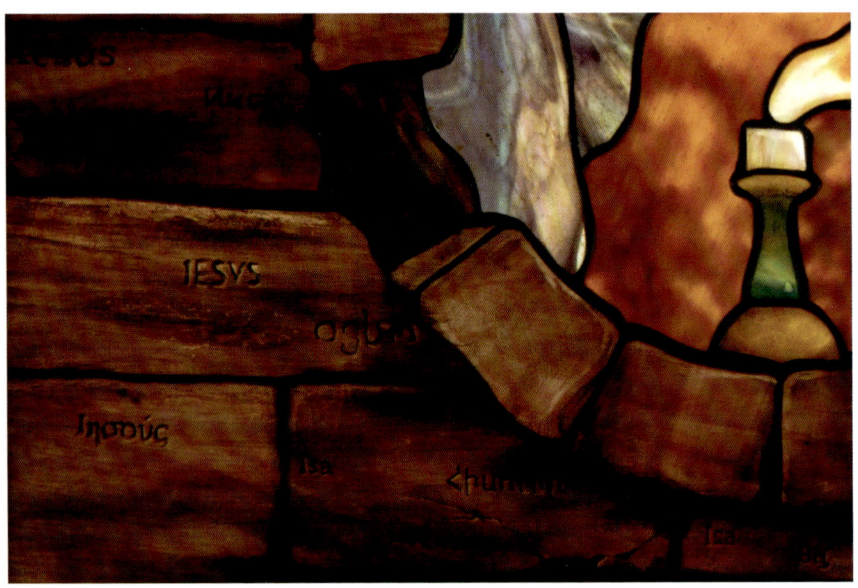

5. NAME OF JESUS IN MANY LANGUAGES

The ability to successfully communicate with another human being is a gift in and of itself. Communication brings understanding, which leads to compassion. It brings knowledge, which leads to growth. It is a blessing that edifies all involved. There is no more crucial message to be conveyed throughout the world than the good news of the gospel of Christ. With over 7,000 known human languages on the planet, it is imperative that each be able to hear the truth in a way they understand. One of the Holy Spirit's roles is to testify of Christ to God's children. "'The Spirit of truth who goes out from the Father—he will testify about me'" (John 15:26). Whatever language we may speak, we can be sure that when we hear God's truths, we can recognize them and know of their veracity through the Spirit. Symbolically surrounding the stones of the twelve apostles and the Pentecostal Spirit of God is the name of Jesus in many languages etched all around the stones on the building's wall. There's Isus (Bosnian, Bulgarian, Croatian, Serbian, Ukrainian), Ježíš (Czech and Slovak), 耶稣 (Chinese), イエス(Japanese), and Íosa (Irish), to translate a few. At first glance, the words appear to be simple cracks in the stone, but they are each a proclamation of the Savior's name, for "salvation is found in no one else, for there is no other name under heaven given to mankind by which we must be saved" (Acts 4:12). The cracks in the wall also symbolize that cultural and political and ideological obstacles and barriers that prevent the spread of the gospel to different nations will in time be broken down by God, allowing all who desire to know and choose the name of Jesus to do so, "that at the name of Jesus every knee should bow, in heaven and on earth and under the earth, and every tongue acknowledge that Jesus Christ is Lord" (Philippians 2:10–11).

6. BELIEVING THOMAS

The apostle Thomas is often referred to as "doubting Thomas." Hearing others testify that they had seen the risen Lord, Thomas said, "Unless I see the nail marks in his hands and put my finger where the nails were, and put my hand into his side, I will not believe" (John 20:25). A week later as the disciples gathered, the Savior appeared to them, including Thomas. The Lord lovingly gave him a tangible witness to His Resurrection: "Then he said to Thomas, 'Put your finger here; see my hands. Reach out your hand and put it into my side. Stop doubting and believe.' Thomas said to him, 'My Lord and my God!" (John 20:27–28). Let us not forget that at a prior time when Jesus planned to return to Jerusalem where some wanted to kill Jesus, Thomas bravely said, "Let us also go, that we may die with him" (John 11:16). This brave and bold yet disbelieving and doubtful disciple is much like many of us. At times, our faith falters. We ask where God is in our sufferings, we question our convictions, and we demand signs from heaven before we will commit. After Thomas saw the Lord, Christ taught, "Because you have seen me, you have believed; blessed are those who have not seen and yet have believed" (John 20:29). The gospel spread based on conviction from the Spirit confirming the truth of the divinity of Jesus, spoken by eyewitnesses of His Resurrection like Thomas. When we choose faith, we acknowledge that there are other ways of knowing beyond our physical senses. Our choice of faith welcomes God and Christ into our lives and with Them, growth. In this scene, Thomas testifies to two listeners of the reality of the nail prints in the hands of the resurrected Christ (American Sign Language for "Jesus").

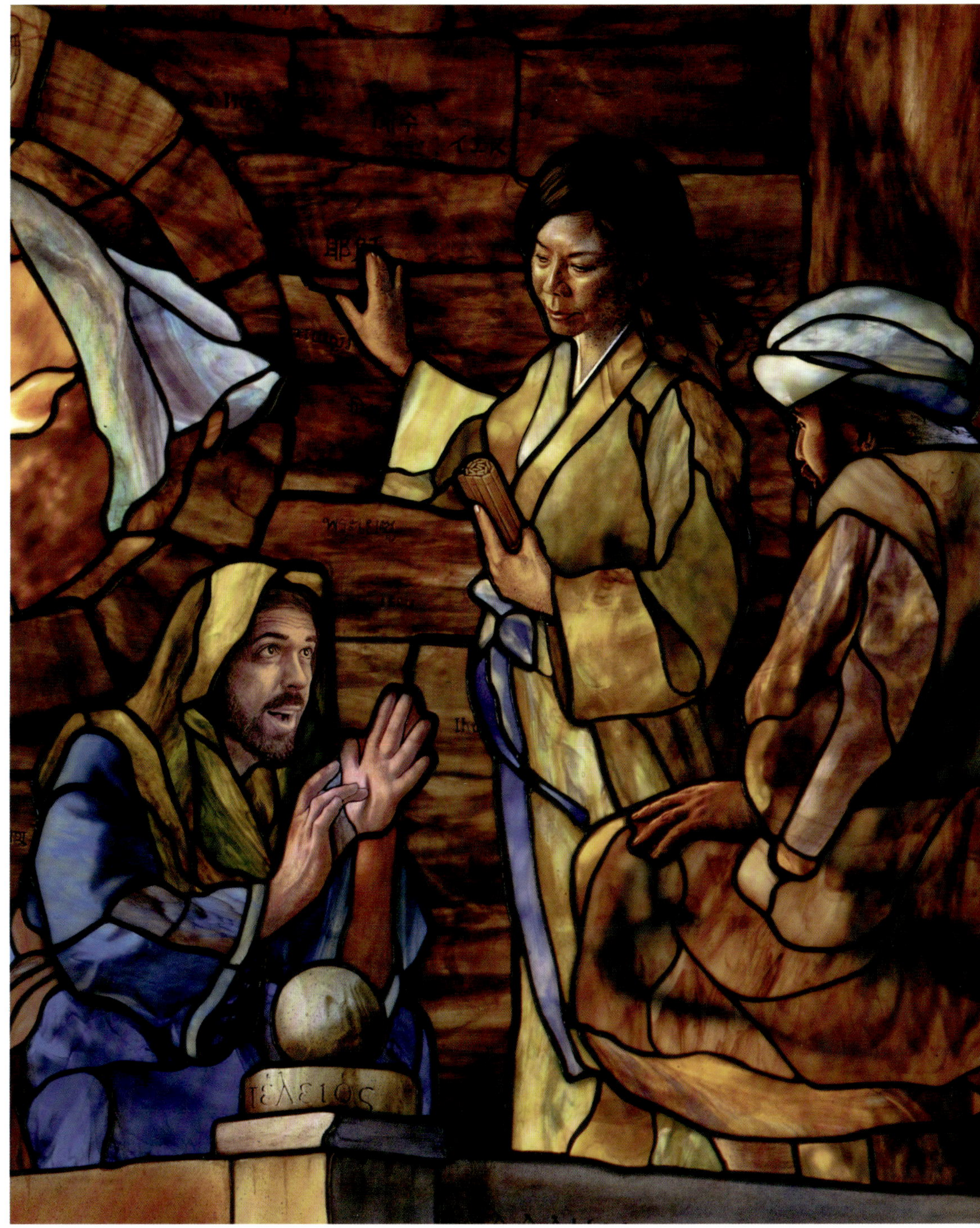

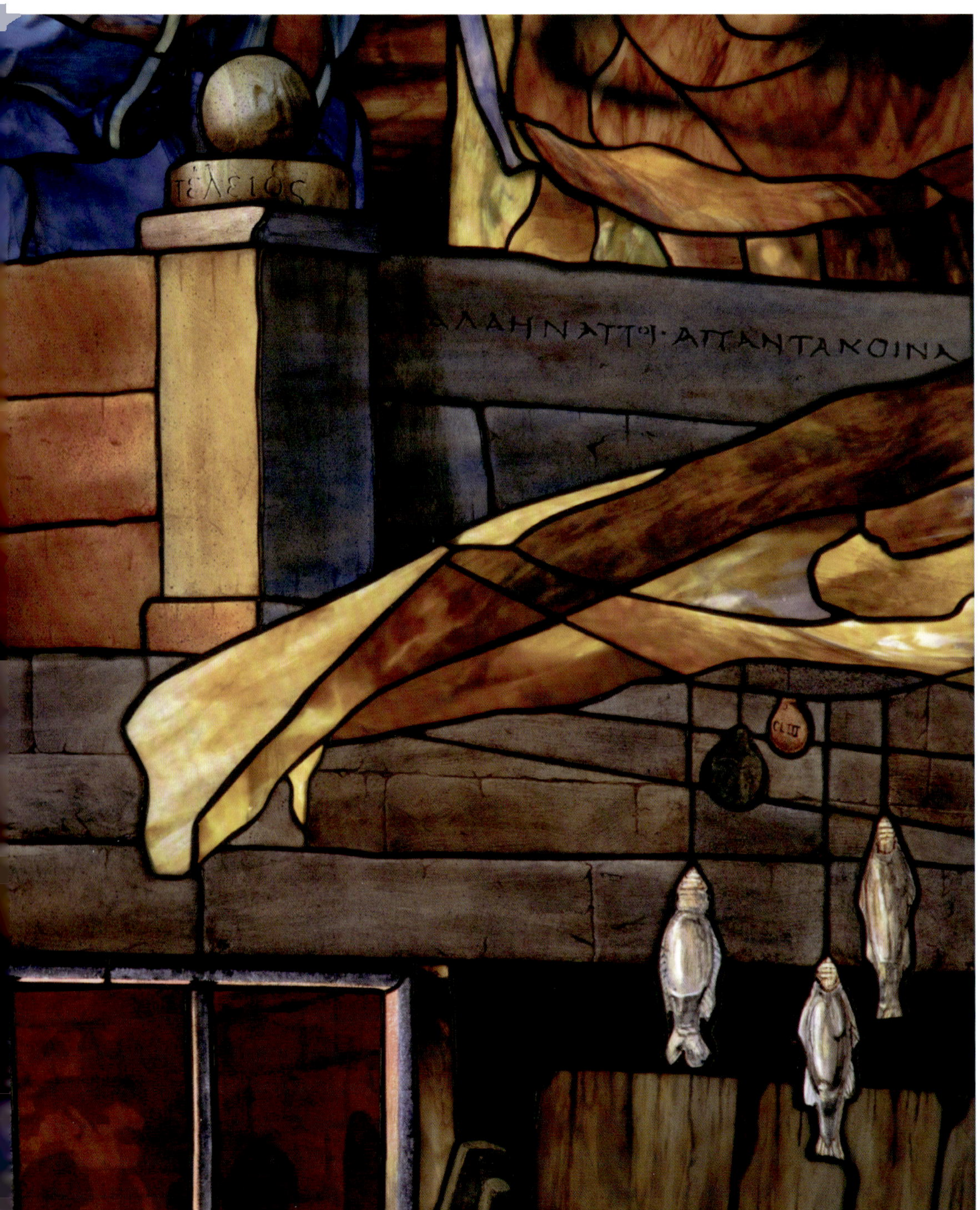

7. PERFECT SPHERE

The Beatitudes represent a progression of Christlike characteristics obtained by disciples who follow the Lord. The Sermon on the Mount (Matthew 5–7) is the Lord's instruction for living the higher law of His gospel. It doesn't encompass everything but lays out the beginning of the path. In the sermon, Jesus seeks to lift His listeners to an elevated way of living. He repeatedly taught by saying, "You have heard that it was said . . ." and then shared a law from the past. Then, He supplanted it by declaring, "But I tell you . . ." and gave a higher, holier way to live. The commandments were no longer to be measured by behaviors alone. Rather, Christ expected His followers to have righteous desires and selfless motives. The higher teachings of the Sermon on the Mount are marvelously challenging. Through them our gospel character is being tested, and through Christ our very souls are being refined. At the end of the sermon, Jesus gave His most demanding command: "Be perfect, therefore, as your heavenly Father is perfect" (Matthew 5:48). The Greek root for "perfect" is *teleios.* It seems the Lord was telling His disciples to become "complete," "fully formed," and "finished," which are some of the meanings of *teleios* or the noun *teleos.* In today's world we recognize the Greek in the prefixes of words like *telephone* and *television*—speaking or seeing at a distance. Truly, the perfection of which Christ taught is a process that will take this life and beyond. We cannot do it without His grace, His divine help, His endowment of strength. Some may think it is impossible to change and live in the way Christ taught. However, "with God all things are possible" (Matthew 19:26). In the artwork, the artists have placed a perfect sphere at the top of the stairs representing the Beatitudes. Viewers who look closely will see the word *teleios*, reminding them of Christ's command at the end of the Sermon on the Mount.

8. EVERYTHING IN COMMON

In chapter two of the Book of Acts we read these words: "All the believers were together and had everything in common. They sold property and possessions to give to anyone who had need" (Acts 2:44–45). A few chapters later, Luke recorded again: "All the believers were one in heart and mind. No one claimed that any of their possessions was their own, but they shared everything they had. . . . There were no needy persons among them. For from time to time those who owned land or houses sold them, brought the money from the sales and put it at the apostles' feet, and it was distributed to anyone who had need" (Acts 4:32, 34–35). This selfless way of living described in the New Testament is challenging for many modern believers. These words are read and interpreted in many ways, but Christians still try to give a shirt and coat to those who ask them (see Matthew 5:40–42). They seek first the kingdom of God over concerns about clothing and food (see Matthew 6:28–33). They understand that their relationship with material items often reflects what's in their hearts. They ask themselves, "Do we love God more than anything, even our income or property? Do we see the needs of others as our own?" They hope to not leave sorrowful from the Lord when He asks them to sacrifice and follow Him (see Matthew 19:22–24). The artists are encouraging viewers to wrestle with such questions as they see the words *everything in common* written in Greek on the wall.

9. "DO YOU LOVE ME MORE THAN THESE?"

Below a market tent hang three fish for sale. These fish represent a pivotal event in the life of Peter. After the resurrected Jesus had already appeared to the apostles twice, some of the apostles were fishing on the Sea of Galilee. Catching nothing all night, they saw a figure on land who told them where to cast their nets, which resulted in a miraculous catch. This reminded the apostles of when they were first called, and they knew the figure on the shore was the Lord. Later, as the group ate together, Jesus pointed to the fish and asked Peter, "Do you love me more than these?" Peter responded, "You know that I love you." The Lord then told Peter, "Feed my lambs." Shockingly, the Lord asked a second time and then a third time if Peter loved Him! "Peter was hurt because Jesus asked him the third time, 'Do you love me?' He said, 'Lord, you know all things; you know that I love you.' The Lord said, 'Feed my sheep'" (John 21:15–17). These three statements of dedicated love sit opposite to Peter's three-time denial of knowing the Lord at Caiaphas's palace (see Luke 22:54–62). Now the Lord heard a repentant Peter rededicate himself to Him. These three fish hanging in the market represent how Peter truly loved the Lord more than anything else and forsook all to feed God's lambs with his witness and ministry. Viewers who look closely will also see the number 153—the total number of fish in the miraculous catch on that occasion (see John 21:11).

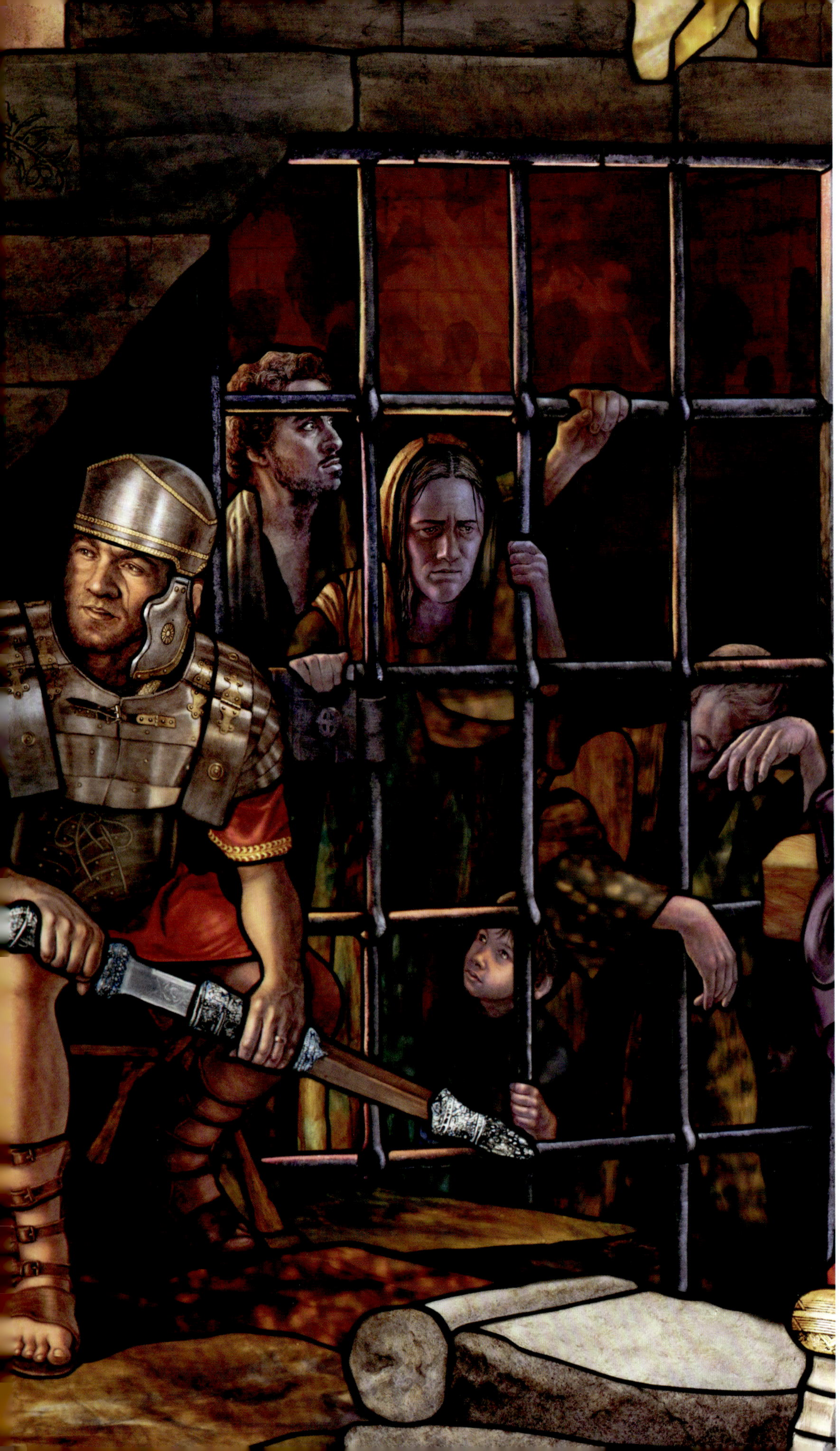

LIFE AND DEATH

10–12, 14. SPIRITUAL PRISON

The figures in the art glass represent souls imprisoned by sin, captive to their wickedness. They can find hope in Jesus: "Christ also suffered once for sins, the righteous for the unrighteous, to bring you to God" (1 Peter 3:18). The map on the wall (no. 11) signifies that this human problem of fallen sin is global. Alone, without grace, these individuals are spiritually lost. However, Isaiah wrote that the Lord is called to "free captives from prison and to release from the dungeon those who sit in darkness" (Isaiah 42:7). Paul preached, "Through him [Jesus] everyone who believes is set free from every sin" (Acts 13:39). The apostle Peter wrote that the Lord "went and made proclamation to the imprisoned spirits—to those who were disobedient long ago when God waited patiently in the days of Noah" (1 Peter 3:19–20). This salvation is made possible to all God's global children, which the map on the wall also suggests. On the upper right of the prison scene is also a door with a broken hinge (no. 12), representing Christ's sacrifice opening the way of salvation for all. The woman holds a literal and symbolic key—the cross of Christ that frees all who receive Him (no. 14).

13. ROMAN GUARD WITH SWORD

A Roman guard is depicted overseeing the keeping of the souls in prison. It is difficult to see whether he is unsheathing his sword to fight against the Lord or sheathing it to submit to the Savior. This guard is seen in contemplation, signifying the decision we all face as to where we stand. Will we join with Jesus as His servants to help Him free souls, or will we selfishly guard our pride, ego, will, and sins? Will we submit to God and join the body of Christ, or "kick against the pricks" (KJV, Acts 26:14) and fight against God?

15. BECOME AS A CHILD

Jesus taught that, if we want to be part of the kingdom of heaven, we must become like children. "Truly I tell you, unless you change and become like little children, you will never enter the kingdom of heaven. Therefore, whoever takes the lowly position of this child is the greatest in the kingdom of heaven" (Matthew 18:3–4). Children are innately submissive, full of love, forgiving, generous, and pure. How do adults become like this when surrounded by the rough realities and temptation in our society? Indeed, we must be born again (see John 3). We must be changed, justified, and sanctified by the grace of Christ through receiving the Holy Spirit. Like rocks in a river, as the Spirit of God continually washes over us, it smooths out our rough edges and polishes our souls. In the window, the child looks toward the key of Christ, symbolizing how only those who accept His divine sacrifice and come unto Him can be born again, changed in character to become as little children to inherit the kingdom of heaven.

16. ANOINTING JAR AND TEAR BOTTLE

Mary Magdalene was the first eyewitness of the resurrected Savior. But before her eyes were filled with light and life, they were filled with sorrow and tears. How could the long-promised Messiah die? Did He fail to establish the kingdom? Could the Romans and conspiring elders have won? All the believers' hopes seemed washed away in the bloodstained rocks beneath the cross. They simply didn't understand. Early on the first day of the week, Mary Magdalene and other women went to the tomb to finish anointing the body of Jesus according to custom, which had not been finished because of His rushed burial before the start of the Sabbath. When they arrived, the stone was rolled back, and the tomb was empty. Angels declared the Lord had risen. Burial linen was folded neatly as evidence. The women went to tell the disciples. Peter and John ran to confirm. The Lord was not there! Had He really risen, or had His enemies simply stolen His body? Despite angelic confirmation, Mary Magdalene wasn't sure. She lingered alone, weeping. She turned, and a man stood close. "He asked her, 'Woman, why are you crying?'" Mary thought He was the gardener, and said, "'Sir, if you have carried him away, tell me where you have put him, and I will get him.' Jesus said to her, 'Mary.' She turned toward him and cried out in Aramaic, 'Rabboni!'" (John 20:15–16). Tears of intense sorrow turned to tears of joy. Modern disciples are no different than these early ones. Sometimes, despite heavenly confirmation, we wonder and question. Like Mary, we weep. In the art glass window, down by Mary's right hand is a jar of anointing spices for Christ's burial. Attached to the jar is a smaller jar, known as a tear bottle. These bottles were used to catch and collect the tears of its owner during times of sorrow, as the Psalmist wrote, "Put thou my tears into thy bottle" (KJV, Psalm 56:8). Because of the resurrection and redemption of Jesus, however, the Lord "will wipe every tear from [our] eyes. There will be no more death or mourning or crying or pain, for the old order of things has passed away" (Revelation 21:4).

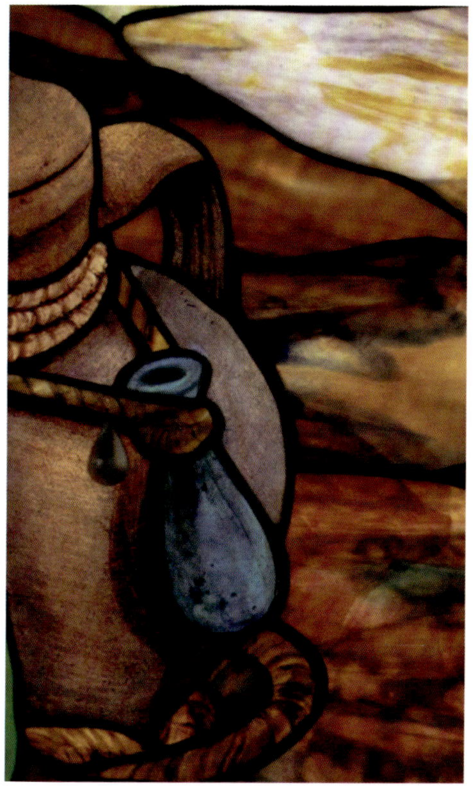

FALSE GODS AND WORLDLINESS

17. FALSE GODDESS DIANA

Ephesus (modern-day Türkiye) was one of the largest cities in the Roman empire, nearing around 250,000 people. It was a crossroads of several land routes and a center of learning. It was considered the gateway to Asia. It was also the center of pagan worship, particularly the worship of the goddess Diana (or in Greek, Artemis). Diana was the great mother-goddess of Asia Minor. She was the goddess of nature, wild animals, hunters, and childbirth. She had an entire temple built to her in Ephesus that was considered one of the wonders of the world. The worship of Diana was a major factor in the economy of Ephesus, including the selling of silver statuary of her. The apostle Paul spent about three years in Ephesus, working and preaching and building up Christianity. He was bold in condemning the worship of false gods and goddesses like Diana. Paul was so successful that a silversmith named Demetrius, who made a living selling silver statues of the goddess Diana, complained and incited a riot against Paul (see Acts 19). Demetrius declared that Paul had taught "that gods made by human hands are no gods at all" and that therefore "our trade will lose its good name, but also that the temple of the great goddess Artemis will be discredited; and the goddess herself, who is worshiped throughout the province of Asia and the world, will be robbed of her divine majesty." Upon hearing this, the crowd was furious and shouted, "Great is Artemis of the Ephesians!" (Acts 19:26–28). The silver statue on the table in the artwork represents the worship of false gods and philosophies of men, and the conflict and uproar that speaking the truth inevitably brings. In the end, like the temple of Diana in Ephesus, all false worship will crumble and be broken down, and the kingdom of God will prevail (see Daniel 2).

18. LAUREL WREATH OF VICTORY

Behind the statue of Diana is a golden laurel wreath, a symbol of victory for the Greeks and Romans. This wreath is still used in some contexts today, such as for the Olympians in the 2004 games in Athens. In the art glass window, the wreath doesn't just represent feats of physical strength and victory in the world, but the reward for the righteous as spiritual victors through Christ. The apostle Paul wrote: "I have fought the good fight, I have finished the race, I have kept the faith. Now there is in store for me the crown of righteousness, which the Lord, the righteous Judge, will award to me on that day—and not only to me, but also to all who have longed for his appearing" (2 Timothy 4:7–8).

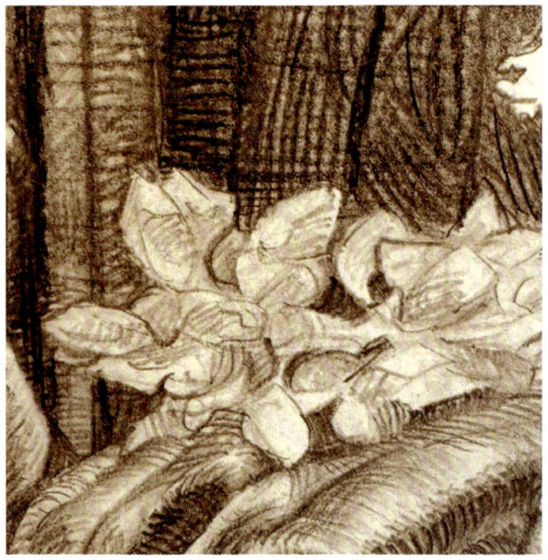

19. GOLDEN CALF

This golden calf, positioned next to the false goddess Diana, represents the worship of false idols, particularly the children of Israel worshipping the golden calf in the wilderness. While Moses summited Mount Sinai to commune with God, the impatient Israelites who tarried asked Aaron (Moses's brother) to make them an idol to worship. "Come, make us gods who will go before us. As for this fellow Moses who brought us up out of Egypt, we don't know what has happened to him" (Exodus 32:1). Aaron, in a terrible lapse of spiritual judgment, not only conceded, but *made* the false god for them, fashioning their donated gold jewelry into the shape of a calf and building an altar to worship it. The people betrayed Jehovah, claiming of the calf, "These are your gods, Israel, who brought you up out of Egypt" (Exodus 32:4). Moses descended the mount and, upon seeing what had happened, destroyed the tablets of the covenant law given to him by God and destroyed the golden calf, grinding it to powder. Are we quick to forget, quick to do iniquity, quick to turn to false gods, quick to blame, and quick to run wild? Or are we quick to remember the Lord?

20. THE *OMPHALOS* OF DELPHI

In the window is a jar representing the *Omphalo*s of Delphi. The *omphalos* (Greek for "navel," or "center point") was found in Delphi, Greece, and is a stone that represented the center of the earth. According to Greek mythology, Zeus found the earth's center by launching two eagles in opposite directions who circumnavigated the world, crossing in Delphi. On this jar are relief carvings of stones wrapped in swaddling clothes, from the Greek myth of Zeus's mother protecting her children from being eaten by swaddling stones rather than her children. This stone is symbolic of myths about, communication with, and worship of false gods.

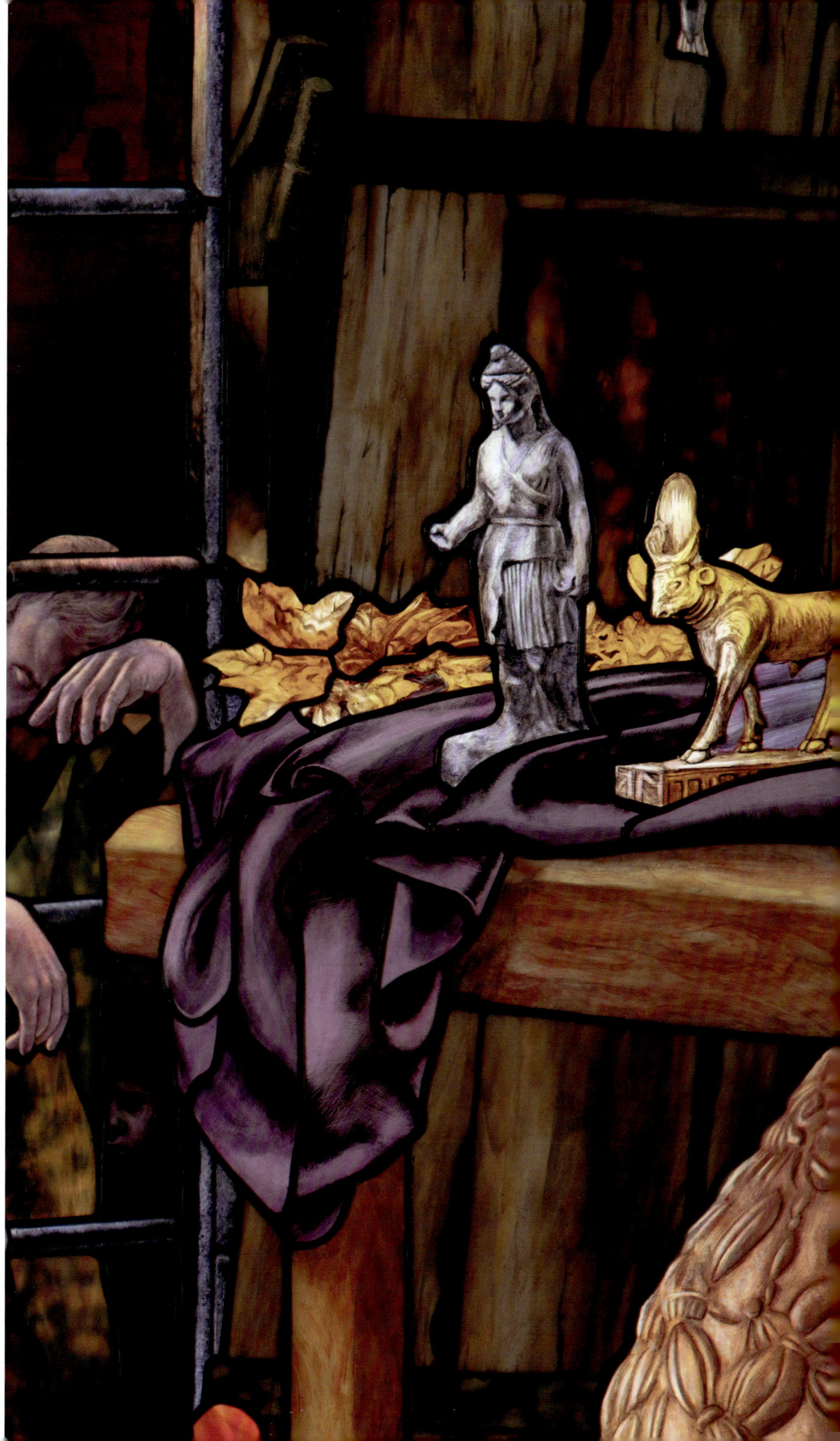

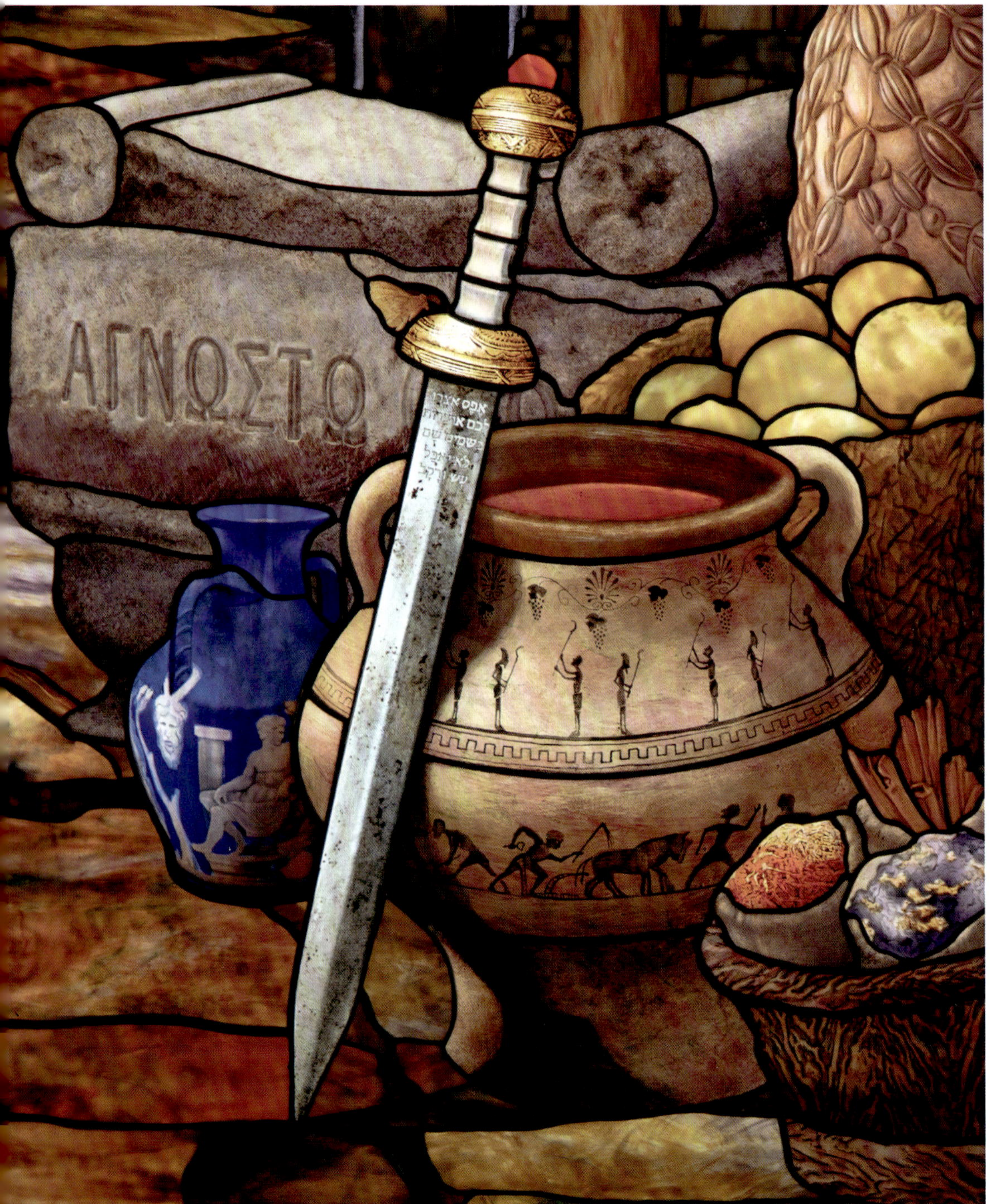

21. ALTAR TO THE UNKNOWN GOD

It was said that during Paul's time in Athens there were more gods than men. Paul came to Athens after preaching in Thessalonica and Berea. While there, Paul "was greatly distressed to see that the city was full of idols" (Acts 17:16). Paul would have seen the Acropolis, the rocky outcropping jutting up from the city where the modern famed temples of wonder stood—including the Parthenon, dedicated to the goddess Athena. Surrounded by false gods, Paul preached the true and living God to the people of Athens, teaching them "the good news about Jesus and the resurrection" (Acts 17:18). The people called him a "babbler" and a preacher of "strange ideas," and took him to the city council or judicial leaders on the Areopagus (meaning the "hill of Ares" or the Roman equivalent, "Mars Hill"), a high spot just below the Acropolis. There, Paul preached to them about the "unknown god." In a city full of statues and temples and worship of many gods, Paul had seen a stone altar with the inscription, "To an unknown god" (Acts 17:23). Were they so afraid of offending that they would even offer sacrifices to any god that the Greeks may have not known or yet identified? Paul used this opportunity to teach them about the true and living God, the creator of heaven and earth. "As some of your own poets have said, 'We are his offspring.' Therefore since we are God's offspring, we should not think that the divine being is like gold or silver or stone—an image made by human design and skill. In the past God overlooked such ignorance, but now he commands all people everywhere to repent" (Acts 17:28–31). Although some "sneered" at Paul's preaching, others "believed," such as "Dionysius, a member of the Areopagus, also a woman named Damaris, and a number of others" (Acts 17:32, 34), beginning the conversion of the Greeks.

22. RUSTING SWORD AND SYMBOLIC POT

This sword, a symbol of war, represents two teachings in the Bible. First, it represents the Lord's teaching in the Sermon on the Mount to not "store up for yourselves treasures on earth, where moths and vermin destroy, and where thieves break in and steal. But store up for yourselves treasures in heaven" (Matthew 6:19–20). Looking closely at this sword, you will see a hilt of ivory, gold, and jewels, but a rusting blade and a nearby moth ready to destroy the worldly treasure. Second, as taught by Isaiah and Micah, the sword represents that after the Lord returns, His people "will beat their swords into plowshares and their spears into pruning hooks. Nation will not take up sword against nation, nor will they train for war anymore" (Isaiah 2:4). Look closely at the pot the sword is resting on, and you will see depictions of peaceful people using pruning hooks and plowshares. Also, in the vase you will see red wine. This symbolizes the "blood of the covenant . . . for the forgiveness of sins" and the promise that one day Jesus will return to drink of the "fruit of the vine" with us (Matthew 26:28–29).

23. LEMONS OF LUXURY

Notice the basket of lemons, a luxury item for the wealthy in the time of Jesus. Research indicates that citrus lemons were an import for Romans around the time of Christ, and although able to be grown today in the Mediterranean, they were not native to the area. Lemons, beautiful but sour, represent the ultimate bitter aftertaste of worldly pursuits in this life at the expense of seeking eternal life.

24. ROMAN VASE

This beautiful blue vase of cameo glass is known as the Portland vase. The original vase dates to the time of Christ. It is considered a pinnacle of Roman art and culture from that period. The images on the vase are unclear in their official interpretation, but represent Roman mythology and history. This vase in the artwork represents Rome's influence as a world power during the time of the New Testament, and their art and culture (and worldliness) that spread throughout their empire, including the world of the New Testament.

25. BASKET OF SPICES

This basket of spices is full of cinnamon, saffron, and blue lotus petals. It represents the expensive flavors, dyes, perfumes, and derivative drugs available to the wealthy who could afford to obtain them. Those who turn from the world and choose Jesus Christ will find an endless supply of flavor, change, and healing.

AUTHORS

Due to a lifelong speech impediment, TOM HOLDMAN expresses his light best through art. He started "speaking" through glass at the age of fourteen by creating stained glass windows out of his parents' garage. Forty years later, he leads a team of more than 150 artists with his wife, Gayle. He has collaborated with thousands of artists in all fifty states and more than one hundred countries. He is building the visionary Sphere of Light to show the light within humanity.

GAYLE HOLDMAN is an award-winning author and designer, an international public speaker, and devoted mother to four children. She is co-owner of Holdman Studios with her husband, Tom, where they illuminate messages of God's love and light through stained glass. Gayle has a bachelor's degree in family science and human development and is certified in applied positive psychology.

COMMENTARY AND FOREWORD

TYLER GRIFFIN is an associate dean of Religious Education at Brigham Young University in the Department of Ancient Scripture. He received his bachelor's degree in electrical engineering and his master's and doctorate degrees in instructional technology from Utah State University. He is also a co-founder of BYU's VirtualScriptures.org, which helps to create digital models of Jerusalem at the time of Christ.

ANTHONY SWEAT is a professor of Church History and Doctrine at Brigham Young University. He received his PhD in education from Utah State University. Dr. Sweat is the author of numerous religious books and articles. He also has a bachelor's degree in painting and drawing, and as a practicing artist specializes in underrepresented scriptural scenes. Additionally, he researches the use of art in religious learning.

REVEREND DR. ANDREW TEAL is fellow, chaplain, and full member of the Faculty of Theology and Religion at Oxford University. He has been an Anglican priest for thirty-four years and has worked in multicultural parishes in the English Midlands and in the academy, having been chaplain of Pembroke College for more than seventeen years. His academic interests include early Church history and society, systematic theology, and interfaith dialogue. He is committed to building fruitful and trusting friendships between people of different faith traditions and an Interfaith Centre with The Church of Jesus Christ of Latter-day Saints in Oxford.

BRAD R. WILCOX is a professor in the Department of Ancient Scripture at Brigham Young University. He received his bachelor's and master's degrees from Brigham Young University and his PhD from the University of Wyoming in education with a focus on literacy.

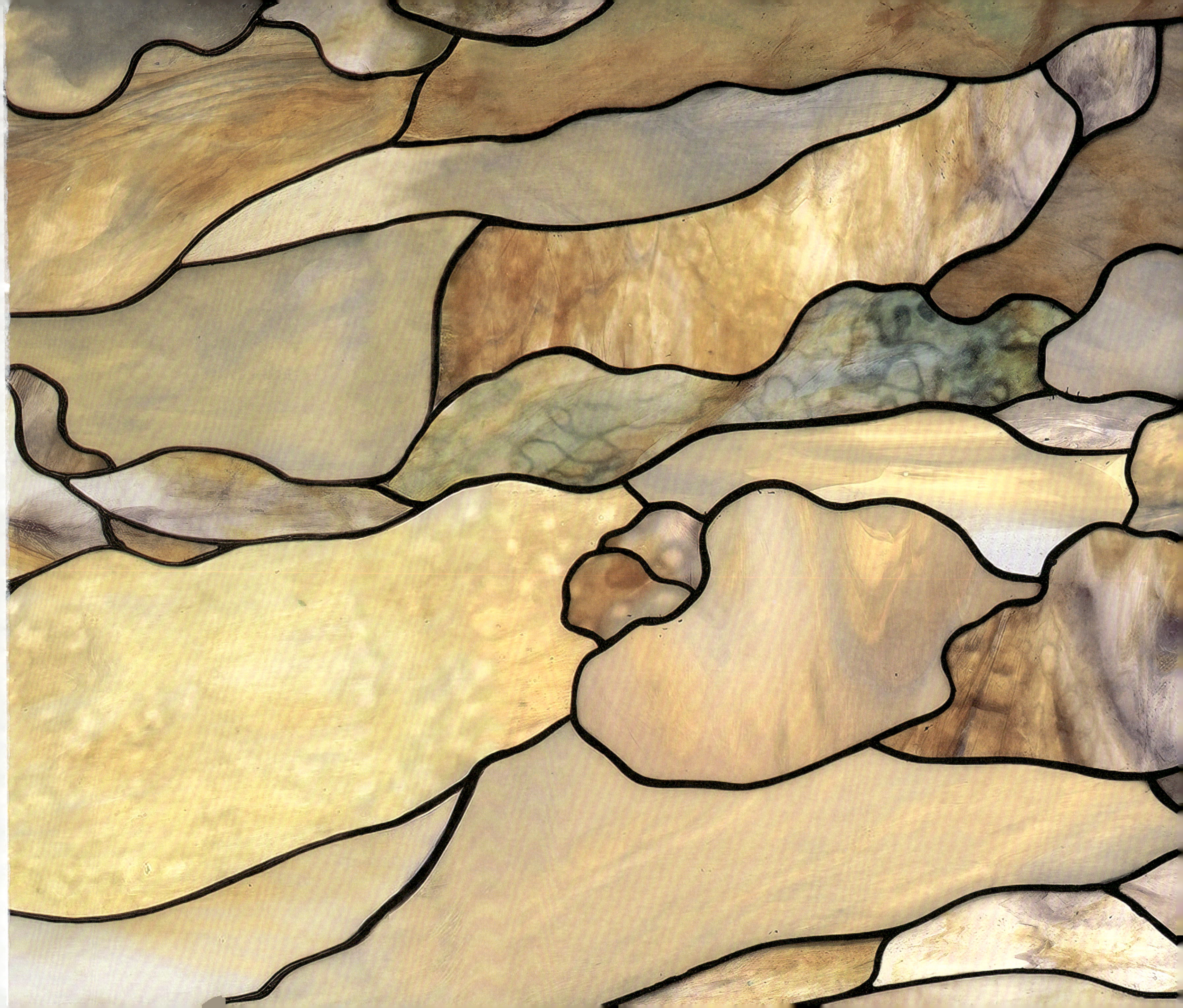

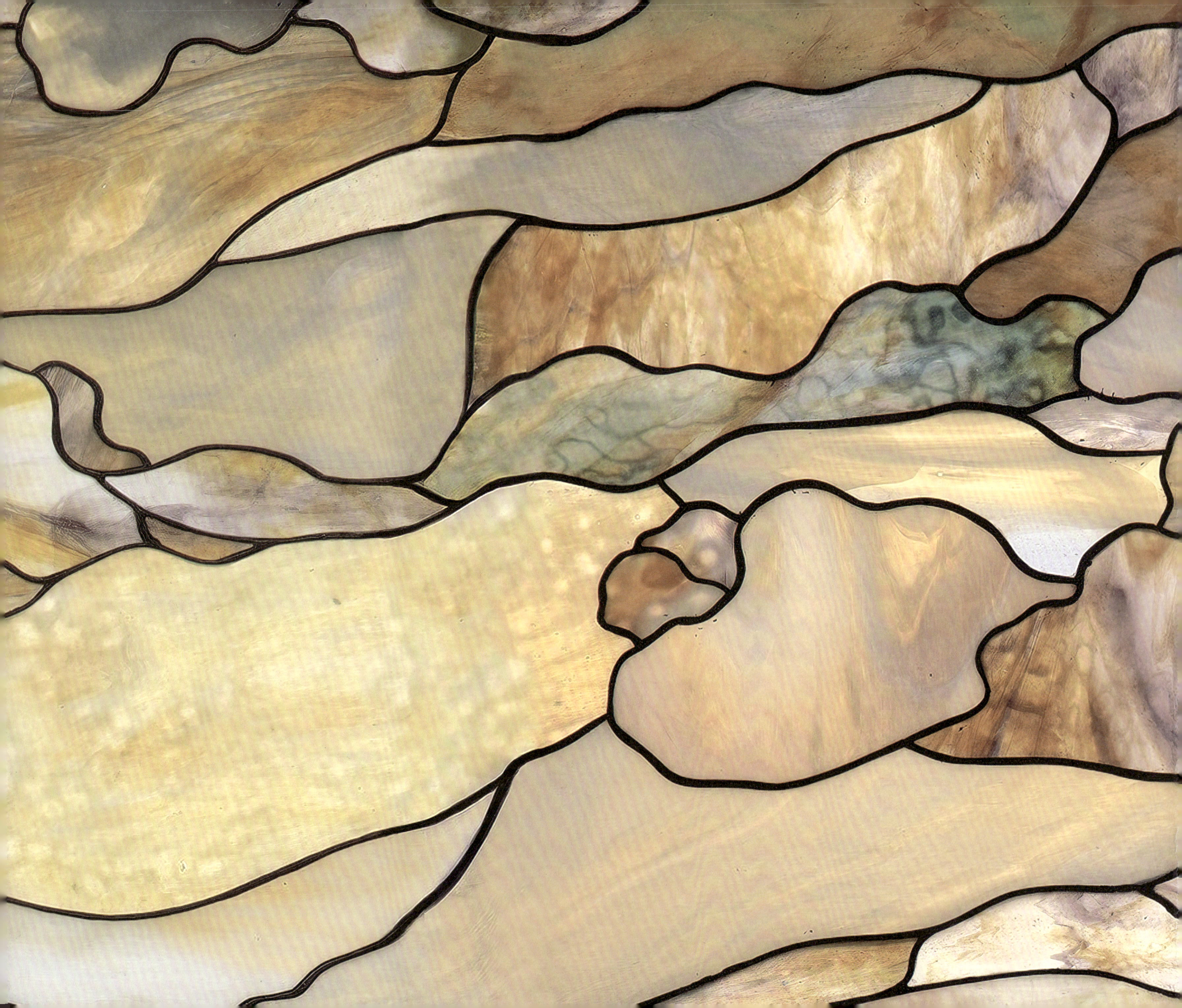